Mobile Asia:

Capitalisms, Value Chains and Mobile Telecommunication in Asia

SNUAC SERIES in Asian Studies ❻

Mobile Asia:

Capitalisms, Value Chains and
Mobile Telecommunication in Asia

Printed in Seoul, Republic of Korea

Seoul National University Press
1 Gwanak-ro, Gwanak-gu, Seoul 08826, Republic of Korea

E-mail: snubook@snu.ac.kr
Home-page: http://www.snupress.com

Second Printing: November 20, 2019
ISBN 978-89-521-1986-5 94330
978-89-521-1125-8 (set)

Mobile Asia:

Capitalisms, Value Chains and Mobile Telecommunication in Asia

Joonkoo Lee &
Hyun-Chin Lim

Seoul National University Press

CONTENTS

Section II: Mobile Transformation: Global and Regional Landscape

Section III: Convergence and Divergence in Mobile Asia

Tables

Chapter 5

Chapter 6

Chapter 7

Appendix

Figures

Chapter 6

Chapter 7

Appendix

Preface

This book reflects our collective effort to explore and understand the structure and functioning of a New Asia emerging with mobile transformation, i.e., political, social and economic changes spurred by mobile telecommunication technology. The fast growing use of mobile telecom significantly has changed Asia over the last several decades, reshaping the way Asian countries, firms and people connect one another within the region and beyond. Specifically focusing on the mobile phone industry, the book investigates how global and regional value chains have changed and restructured the patterns of production, trade, and investment inter- and intra-regionally, and how the role and position of Asian economies has shifted within an increasingly sophisticated division of labor. By doing so, we aim to advance our understanding of the changing structure of Asian capitalism, development paths, and inter- and intra-regional linkages. Also, we strive to advance our understanding of converging and diverging patterns in development paths and evolving regional connections and interaction in Asian capitalism.

We initially started a project on mobile transformation out of interest in its impact on politics, specifically the use of mobile communication on the public sphere and political participation. The paper, originally published in 2010 at *Media Asia* and reprinted in the Appendix of this book, was the first outcome of the project. Then, our attention has shifted towards the economic and industrial dimensions of mobile transformation and its implications to the convergence and divergence of capitalist development in

Asia. Earlier work on the topic was presented at various academic conferences, includeing Society for the Advancement of Socio-Economics (SASE) annual meetings at the Massachusetts Institute of Technology in 2012, and the University of Milan in 2013, as well as the 2013 Shanghai Forum at Fudan University, and the "Capitalism and Capitalisms in Asia: Origin, Commonality and Diversity" conference hosted by Seoul National University Asia Center (SNUAC) in 2015. In the meanwhile, Lee published a paper with his collaborators at the *Journal of Contemporary Asia* in 2016, which is reprinted in the book. Another author, Lim, had benefitted greatly from his experience as chairman of the board of directors at SK telecom, the largest telecommunications company in South Korea. When we proposed the project for a book-publishing grant to SNUAC, our vision was to address the political, economic and social consequences of mobile transformation. We soon realized, however, that even doing research on the economic aspects of the phenomenon was a daunting task.

We are thankful to the Samsung Economic Research Institute (SERI) for its financial support, which became a valuable seed for the project. SNUAC provided a critical financial support for research and writing. Our deep thanks go to Jongseok Yoon at Seoul National University, Jinho Lim at Seoul National University, and Jongyoon Hong at Hanyang University for their research assistance. Finally, we appreciate Director Soo-Jin Park and Dr. Suk-Ki Kong both at SNUAC for their moral support and encouragement.

July 2018

Joonkoo Lee & Hyun-Chin Lim

Glossary

APEC: Asia-Pacific Economic Cooperation
ASEAN: Association of Southeast Asian Nations
CDMA: Code Division Multiple Access
CM: contract manufacturer
CME: coordinated market economies
CSO: civil society organization
DMB: Digital Multimedia Broadcasting
EMS: electronic manufacturing service
EOI: export-oriented industrialization
EU: European Union
FDI: foreign direct investment
GCC: global commodity chain
GDP: gross domestic product
GPN: global production network
GSM: Global System for Mobile Communications
GVC: global value chain
HS: Harmonized System
ICT: information and communication technology
IMF: International Monetary Fund
INGO: international non-governmental organization
ISI: import-substituting industrialization
IT: information technology
LME: liberal market economies
MENA: Middle East and North Africa
MNE: multinational enterprise
MNO: mobile network operator

NGO: non-governmental organization
OBM: original brand manufacturing
ODM: original design manufacturer
OEM: original equipment manufacturing
OECD: Organisation for Economic Co-operation and Development
PDC: Personal Digital Cellular
RVC: regional value chain
SEC: Samsung Electronics Co.
SME: state-led market economies
SMEs: small and medium-sized enterprises
SMS: short message service
SNS: social network service
SSA: Sub-Saharan Africa
UGC: user-generated content
UK: United Kingdom
US: United States
WTO: World Trade Organization

Chapter 1

Introduction

Over the last decades or so, Asia has experienced the growth of transnational flows within the region and beyond in terms of people, money, information and technology. More nations and cities in the region are now connected to one another through dense networks of trade, investment, transportation, migration as well as advanced information technology (IT) and telecommunication. The growing interconnection has led to a heightened level of interactions and mutual awareness among countries, cities, firms and people. These emerging intra-regional connections and interactions are transforming not only the region and its internal dynamics but also its relationship with the other parts of the world. They are neither entirely influenced by one or two powerful nations nor simply explained by the sum of individual countries, cities or firms. They represent emergent political, economic and social structures that transcend nationalities and localities and generate new ideas and identities to shape and support such trans-local structures (Katzenstein and Shiraishi 2006; Pempel 2005).

In order to understand the emergent structures across Asia, this study pays attention to mobile transformation in Asia and the way it shapes a rising transnational Asia and its organizational and institutional forms of interconnection and interaction. The world where we are living has been significantly transformed by mobile technologies and services. In less than two decades or so, the mobile phone has dramatically changed our society and the way we relate with one another (Steinbock 2005). In a 'smart' world, people are instantly connected to the Internet and each other for 24/7 regardless where they are. The explosion of mobile broadband and Internet-ready smartphones has transformed not only how we shop, learn, travel, but also facilitated large-scale political and social changes, as shown in recent elections and protests across the world (Anduiza *et al.* 2009; Lim and Lee 2010). Moreover, mobile transformation is a global phenomenon. No longer the mobile phone is a luxury; now more mobile phone users are living in the developing world (World Bank 2009). Despite persisting digital divide, mobile phones provide a new tool for social change in the developing world to those who lack resources, from Indian smallholders to Chinese migrant workers (Aker and Mbiti 2010; Law and Peng 2008; Narayana 2011).

In the global mobile transformation, Asian countries have played a central role as both producers and consumers. Today, the majority of the world's mobile phones are produced in Asia (Lee and Gereffi 2013). In 2013, China and Korea, two leading mobile phone exporters, accounted for 68% of the world's mobile exports. Leading global brands like Samsung and LG are based in Asia, so are emerging brands like Huawei, Xiaomi and Micromax. Asia is also a home to major contract manufacturers in electronics like Foxconn and many high-end component suppliers that play a key role in the supply chains of global brands like Apple. Asia is also one of the most dynamic markets for mobile telecom. As of

2015, more than a half of 7.2 million active mobile subscribers in the world are living in Asia and the Pacific.[1] China and India are leading the world in mobile subscriptions. The growth of mobile subscribership was more astonishing in some of the less developed Asian countries. In 2006-2014, the number of mobile subscribers skyrocketed in Vietnam, from 22 to 147 per 100 people, indicating some people now own more than one mobile phone. Mobile subscription substantially grew even in Bangladesh, one of the region's poorest nations, from 13 to 80 per 100 people.[2] And, many Asian firms play an important role in catering to this growing population of first-time mobile phone users in developing Asia (see Chapter 7).

Despite the magnitude of these changes, the central role of Asia in the global mobile transformation and how it is intertwined with the growth of regional connections and interactions are poorly understood. Much of research has focused on a specific country or firm case, lacking a broader, intra- and trans-regional, perspective (e.g., Fan 2011; Ono and Tang 2010; Park 2013; Xia 2012). The shortage of the transnational scope is particularly striking in Korea. Despite the strong pan-Asian presence of Korean firms such as Samsung and LG in mobile telecom, little has been examined about the economic and social impacts of Korean mobile telecom firms and their products on consumers and workers at home and across Asia, with a few exceptions (e.g., Lee and Jung 2015). In spite of the growing awareness of corporate social responsibility, Korean mobile telecom firms have still much to do in mitigating negative impacts on suppliers, workers and the environment in their supply chains (Wilde and de Hann 2006). Furthermore, at a time when South Korea (Korea hereafter) is stepping up its effort to increase its international development aids and assistance, a transnational perspective is more needed than ever with emphasis on cross-national and regional connections and interactions.

How has Asia become so central in the global mobile telecom industry? How has mobile telecom changed national economies and the way they are connected with each other and to a broader global economy? How do the ways they are integrated to mobile telecom global value chains (GVCs) and international trade networks converge and diverge? How has the rise of mobile usage affected societies in Asia? More broadly, what do all these speak to the present and the future of Asian capitalism(s)? All these questions call for an examination of mobile transformation within a broader context of socio-economic changes across Asia and beyond through a lens of intra- and inter-regional connection and interaction.

Mobile Asia: Weaving Connection and Interaction in Asia and Beyond

In an era of globalization, scholars witness the increasing significance of world-regions and the rise of regional integration (Katzenstein and Shiraishi 2006; Murray and Rees 2010; Pempel 2005). Regional integration entails distinctive processes driven by different types of actor: regionalism, regionalization, and region-making. 'Regionalism' refers to the process of forming supranational institutions, mainly led by nation-states, at a regional level, such as Asia-Pacific Economic Cooperation (APEC) and the Association of Southeast Asian Nations (ASEAN). Meanwhile, 'regionalization' involves the bottom-up process of cross-border cooperation at the regional level, primarily driven by private actors, such as multinational enterprises (MNEs) and non-governmental organizations (NGOs). Furthermore, regional integration is grounded on ideas, identities and imaginations (Fligstein 2008). While regions are generally associated to natural and static geographic entities, the boundary and mixture of regions is fluid and complex, subject to the process of social construction (Katzenstein 2006).

A few key features of regional integration have been identified in the literature with respect to Asia. First, Asia lags in an institutionalized form of regional integration, or the 'regionalism' aspect, compared to other parts of the world (Pempel 2005). Despite the rise of regional institutions such as APEC and ASEAN, the region generally lacks well-structured institutional frameworks similar to what is found in, for example, the European Union (EU). Rather, a more dynamic aspect of regional integration in Asia is the rise of 'regionalization,' driven by dense webs of trade, investment, production, and ad-hoc, problem-oriented regional bodies (Pempel 2005). Regional production networks, in particular, play a key role in integrating Asian economies as a major producer and supplier of manufacturing goods to the world economy, such as automobiles and consumer electronics (WTO and IDE-JETRO 2011). Third, regional integration in Asia takes a hybrid form. It is not an extension of any single, dominant national model, such as *Japanization* or *Sinicization,* but rather driven by "variegated processes well beyond the regional extension of specific national models" (Katzenstein 2006, 28).

While these findings offer valuable insights, the existing literature has significant gaps in fully understanding regional integration in Asia. First, the literature largely focuses on *intra-regional* process, with only scant attention to the role of global or trans-regional forces in shaping regional integration. Regional integration tends to be considered as the outcome of interaction between national actors and institutions within Asia, or a process whereby national actors extend their influence into the region. The region is portrayed as self-contained, with little linkage to the rest of the world and external actors. Even when the fact that regional integration can be "porous" and fused by global processes is acknowledged (Katzenstein 2006, 31), the literature offers little specifics on how trans-regional processes play a part. For example, the expansion of regional production networks is considered as evidence to the presence of strong regionalization in East Asia (Hamilton-Hart 2005; Tachiki 2005). However, Asian production networks are not the sole product of either Japanese, Korean or Chinese firms, but rather have been *coproduced* by extra-regional, mainly Western, firms through collaboration and competition with Asian firms (Borrus *et al.* 2000). In this regard, regional connections and interactions need to be examined from the perspective of how the global, the regional, and the local are intertwined in the making and integration of a region.

Second, regional integration and connection does not necessarily lead to the convergence of organizational and institutional forms across Asia. The expectation that globalization would lead to homogenization and convergence is not materialized; nations and firms have responded differently to globalization challenges. Their responses are affected not only by difference in various organizational and institutional configurations at home (Djelic and Ainamo 1999; Fligstein 2001; Weiss 2003; Woo 2007), but also reflect complex interactions between the local and the global, or different ways in which existing national systems and actors interact with new developments in the global economy (Guillén 2001). Similarly, nations and firms may respond differently to the rise of transnational relationships, leading to more variegated and hybridized outcomes. In this regard, we need to pay more attention to such complexity and diversity that the regionalization process generates.

To address this concern, we use the concept of global value chains (GVCs) to highlight the changing structure of the mobile telecom industry. GVCs refer to "the full range of activities that firms and workers perform to bring a specific product from its conception to its end use and beyond" (Gereffi and Fernandez-Stark 2011). A GVC approach views the global economy as a complex network linking a series of suppliers and buyers together, supported by various institutions (see Chapter 3). It is particularly relevant to a cross-national production system fragmented and decentralized through offshoring and outsourcing, such as mobile telecom (see Chapter 4).

Asia's ascendance as the major producer and consumer of mobile telecommunication has been facilitated by the strong presence of mobile telecom value chains in the region (see Chapter 5). As in the apparel and electronics of the past decades, countries, firms and workers across Asia are tightly linked to one another through regional production and service networks in mobile telcommunication. Japan, Korea and Taiwan provide cutting-edge technology and sophisticated parts and components; countries like Vietnam and the Philippines supply the labor and skills critical to manufacture mass-market components; and all these parts are eventually assembled in countries like China and India and exported to the world (Wilde and de Hann 2006). Regional production networks, along with foreign direct investment (FDI), increase the intra-regional flow of mobile phones and components as well as technology and skills. This regional integration is not confined to hardware but now extending to software, service and content, like music, videos and online games, providing a state-of-the-art mobile platform for expanding intra-Asian cultural exchange (Chua and Iwabuchi 2008; Keane *et al.* 2007).

Research Questions and Findings

Building upon the literatures of convergence and divergence in Asian capitalisms and global and regional value chains, this book is distinctive in that it aims to present a fuller picture of the global and regional mobile phone value chains, and show how inter- and intra-regional value chains shape the way regional connection and interaction emerges and persists. Specifically, it addresses the following research questions: (a) what are the key trends and dynamics in the global mobile telecom value chains and how they affect the positions and roles of Asian countries and firms in the fast growing sector; (b) how have international trade networks evolved in the mobile telecom industry and how has inter- and intra-regional division of labor changed in the rise of Asia as the center of mobile phone production and consumption; (c) whether, and how, have Asian countries' paths to GVC integration converged or diverged and what are the implications of such paths to the future of Asian capitalisms; (d) what roles are regional and extra-regional firms playing in shaping regional connection and interaction in Asia?

The book highlights a dynamic nature of the mobile telecom GVC. Growing vertical fragmentation through outsourcing and geographic dispersion of value chain activities significantly changed the chains, including the rise of the developing world as the center of production and the emergence of new value chain actors like contract manufacturers at the mid-stream of the chain. Asia has emerged as the center of the mobile phone industry in the midst of geographic and organizational concentration of a post-crisis mobile phone GVC. The dual concentration is mutually enforcing as consolidated OEMs facilitate the geographic concentration of production, specifically, to East Asia.

We argue that the rise of Asia is significantly attributed to internal and external connections that the region has developed through global and regional production networks. A dense web of inter-firm networks plays a key role in deepening regional integration but also in advancing the region's position in the mobile phone GVC. The agglomeration of capable suppliers in the region and the co-evolution between geographic and organization concentration facilitated regionally-based MNEs to consolidate their positions in the highly competitive industry plagued with frequent market and technological disruption. Furthermore, our inter-regional trade analysis presents that mobile phone trade within Europe and Latin America became less significant as these regions strengthened a cross-regional trade linkage with East Asia, indicating a replacement effect of intra-regional by inter-regional trade.

At the same time, our trade pattern analysis illustrates the dynamic change of countries' position in the mobile phone GVC. China and Korea have consolidated their generalist position. So has Vietnam as an assembly specialist as the country rose to the world's second largest mobile phone exporter. Vietnam's rise depends on its embeddedness in Asian mobile phone production networks. The positional shift of Japan, Malaysia, and Singapore to be come a parts specialist indicates persisting specialization and differentiation within the regional division of labor. Our analysis of inter- and intra-regional trade network also shows that China is leading in the Asian trade networks of final products and parts but also expanding its role as a parts exporter to major emerging production hubs like Vietnam and India (see Chapter 5). This intra-regional divergence reverberates in our four-country case study, which found a significant divergence among China, Japan, Korea and Taiwan with regard to both the position in the global mobile phone value chain and market orientation. We also find the concurrent development of multiple trajectories as a unique characteristic of China's mobile phone industry, which can have a significant impact on neighboring countries (see Chapter 6)

Finally, we highlight the interaction of firm strategies and regional value chains. Asian and non-Asian MNEs play a key role in shaping the structure of regional value chain(RVCs) and, at the same time, RVCs facilitate the rise of new forms of firm actors and market strategies. Samsung Electronics vertically integrative regional value chains have significantly affected an Asian country's GVC integration and economic upgrading, as best illustrated by the case of Vietnam. Meanwhile, Apple's value chains have facilitated the growth of specialized suppliers like Foxconn and regional value chains in East Asia. The cases of Shanzhai phones in China and emerging new brands in developing Asia illuminate that RVCs play a key role in the rise of new breeds of value chain actors and business strategies (see Chapter 7)

Overall, this study provides a valuable assessment of how Asia *as a whole* has emerged as a key player in the global mobile telecom industry, how Asian countries are integrated to global and regional value chains similarly and differently, and how the convergent and divergent development paths and firms' business strategies have affected the growth and upgrading trajectories of Asian economies and firms in the global mobile telecom industry.

This book aims to contribute to the existing literature, including Asian studies, for several aspects. First, it will provide a better understanding of the mobile telecom industry in Asia within a broader context of global value chains. The existing research has its limitation in showing how inter- and intra-regional linkages are positioned within wider global networks. Our research identifies the structure of the mobile telecom industry from a regional perspective in conjunction with global/local dynamics, partly utilizing international trade data analysis based on a GVC-oriented framework.

Moreover, this book provides a compelling case for a continuing divergence among countries and firms within Asia in the midst of the region's rise as a whole in the global economy. With qualitative and quantitative analysis, it shows the changing positions of Asian economies as well as their diverging industrial upgrading paths in the mobile phone GVC through constant interactions with other countries inside and outside the region, both competition and cooperation.

Finally, our research highlights 'Asia-making' as an interactive and co-evolving process of global, regional and local dynamics and a project involving global, regional and local actors all together.

Also, it illuminates the role played by firm actors, both regional and extra-regional, and their strategies and inter-firm networks in shaping the dynamics of regional connections and interactions. Globalization has prompted a question of what Asia is: "are they any new Asias?" (Lim *et al.* 2010) The (re-)emergence of Asia(s) in an era of globalization questions the very nature of Asia(s) as a social construct that goes beyond a geographical and physical boundary (Katzenstein and Shiraishi 2006; Lim *et al.* 2010). This perspective reverberates Nederveen Pieterse's (2010) argument that regions and world economies emerge through the interactions of different forms of socio-economic systems, or "interaction of capitalisms" (p. 138). From our perspective, Mobile Asia is a product of complex interactions between intra-, inter- and trans-regional socio-economic processes, although a further research is warranted for a fuller understanding of political and social dimensions.

Methodological Note

Comparative capitalism studies have undergone three stages of development over the last three decades. The first stage initiated the so-called "Variety of Capitalism" debates in advanced capitalist economies; the second stage was concerned with the interconnectedness between economic actors across national boundaries, such as MNEs and international institutions like ASEAN, EU and the World Trade Organization (WTO); and the third stage focuses on the non-Western capitalist economies in Asia, South America, and Africa. BRICS countries, Brazil, Russia, India, China, and South Africa, would be good examples (Kristensen and Morgan 2012, 12-13).

In a contemporary world of globalization, capitalism has integrated all the nation-states through free flows of goods, labor, and capital. It goes beyond national boundary of political organization and territorial control that key institutions governing economic activities develop strong complementarities at home and abroad. The different combination of organizing competition, innovation, and collective capabilities with distinctive ways of dominant political-economic coalitions and institutions governing the behavior of economic actors have led to different types of capitalism (Whitley and Morgan 2014, 1).

Comparative capitalism studies have contributed to identifying the diversity of capitalism, as shown by Hall and Soskice (2001), Nederveen Pieterse (2015), and Amable (2003). In analyzing capitalism in Asia, we would like to move from "classification" to "comparison". In Kalleberg's observation, "classification is a matter of 'either-or'; comparison is a matter of 'more or less'" (Kallerberg 1966, 81). Methodologically, classification is one of the ways to control suspected sources of variations by converting them into parameters. When it comes to Asian capitalism, comparison could be more confident since Asia as a world region has more parameters in terms of historical and cultural contexts (Smelser 1976, 170. 169). Even if Asian countries are different from each other in terms of political systems, economic institutions, social structures and cultural patterns, they have been interconnected through constant contact, exchange, trade and warfare. They have converged on regional commonness despite intra-regional disparities. More parameteric control is allowed to control independent and dependent variables in establishing causal relationship concerning the origin, development, and consequences of capitalism in Asian countries.

A one-shot case study usually suffers from limitations in establishing causal relationships among the phenomenon to be studied, though it proves to be useful in generating new assumptions and refining existing observations. We need rich case studies of capitalist development in Asian countries. In the cross-sectional observation of a single case, however, there is no variation in either independent or dependent variables. A single, cross-sectional case study ceases to be a fixed pattern of relationship due to the lack of variation in possible causes and effects (Smelser 1976, 199).

Smelser (1976, 217) has recommended us two ways to increase the possibility of establishing such causal relationship even in a single case. One is expanding observations by introducing time dimension to provide additional within-case, and the other is by subdividing national society to increase the number of within-case. These two ways of within-nation analysis can overcome the chronic problem inherent in the limited number of cases.

A lot of works have been produced on Asian capitalism in terms of case study (cf. Kim 2017a, b, c). We believe that these works have been conducive to leading a deeper and more thorough analysis of capitalist development, respectively, in Japan, China, and Korea. In studying the underlying nature of capitalism in Asia, however, we think comparative analysis could have more advantages than a single case study in finding out similarities and differences in the processes of capitalist development across Asian countries. Within-region analysis can be combined with between-region analysis. To this end, qualitative, quantitative, or mixed methods can be implemented according to the nature of the subjects. Particularly in the case of the comparative analysis, the availability of cases determines the type of research. Variable-oriented research is possible if there are plenty of cases, whereas case-oriented research is usually applied when the cases are scarce (Prezeworski and Teune 1970).

That being said, the key analytical themes that run through the study are: *interconnectedness* and *co-evolution* between different levels and domains of analysis. First of all, mobile transformation and its social consequences are interrogated from the interactive perspective that what is happening on the local is always linked to regional and global dynamics through various mechanisms, such as cross-national production network and the flow of people, capital and ideas, and *vice versa*. Regional and global dynamics have consequences on the local without necessarily determining local repercussions. Convergence or divergence is not simply based on the individual traits of each unit, as often presumed in cross-national comparison, but on their different relationship with one another as well as with a bigger structure (McMichael 1990; Tilly 1984).

Methodologically, this study uses multiple methods with both quantitative and qualitative data. It combines an extensive review of scholarly work and other primary and secondary documents from various sources, e.g., industry and firm-level publications from private and public sector, articles from newspapers, magazines, and trade journals. It also uses quantitative data from national governments and international organizations, most notably United Nations Comtrade dataset, a compiled database of annual international trade statistics from 1962 (http://comtrade.un.org/) (see Chapter 5 for more methodological details).

According to the United Nations,[3] Asia refers to a vast geographic area in the world, encompassing from Japan to the east to many Middle East countries to the west. Asia is diverse politically, economically, socially and culturally. It consists of four sub-regional geographic groups that include Eastern, Southern, Southeastern and Western Asia. The primary focus of our book lies in East Asia, including China, Japan, Korea and Taiwan, which was the center of Asian economic development in the post-World War II era as well as the hub of Asian regional production networks. Two other Asia sub-regions are also considered given its increasingly closer ties to East Asia: Southeast Asia, which includes Vietnam, Singapore and Malaysia, and South Asia, including India and Bangladesh. Therefore, when we refers to Asia without specifically indicating any of the sub-regions, it means East Asia in a narrow sense and in a broad sense the three sub-regions except for West Asia, which corresponds to most of the Middle East. For our quantitative analysis in Chapter 5, we use the World Bank country classification because of the availability of income-based grouping. In this scheme, 'East Asia' includes Pacific countries and territories, including Australia, as well as Southeast Asian countries, whereas 'South Asia' is a separate category (see Chapter 5 for more details).

Organization of the Book

The first section, provides a theoretical and conceptual background for our analysis of the mobile telecom industry in Asia in the context of the commonalities and diversities of capitalisms in Asia and evolving global and regional value chains.

Chapter 2 discusses the historical rise of Asia in the context of globalization and regionalization and economic, social and cultural commonalities and diversities. It highlights capitalism as *plural* forms, where several families of capitalism coexist with Asian capitalism one of them. At the same time, Asian capitalism itself is not homogenous as state-interventionist economies like Japan, Korea and Taiwan coexist with free market-oriented ones like Singapore and Hong Kong. The chapter discusses the history of capitalist development and the role of the developmental state in East Asia and the current state of four East Asian economies – Japan, Korea, Taiwan and China – in the global economy and some of the major manufacturing industries.

Chapter 3 brings these topics to a more meso-level of dynamics in the global economy, that is, global value chains (GVCs) as a web of cross-national, inter-firm relationship in trade, investment and production. One of the defining changes in the global economy over the last several decades was the increasing fragmentation and decentralization of production, and the ensuing rise of GVCs, which are increasingly governed by multinational enterprises (MNEs). The chapter overviews the key conceptual building blocks of the GVC perspective and propose analytical frameworks to understand countries' converging and diverging paths of GVC integration and changing trade patterns and positions in GVCs. Finally, the chapter addresses deepening regional integration and the rise of regional value chains (RVCs) in East Asia and highlights the role of corporate actors, both Asian and extra-regional, in shaping regional connection and interaction.

Section II examines the global and regional landscape of mobile transformation, focusing on key trends and patterns of production, trade and investment in the global mobile phone industry. Chapter 4 provides a map of the mobile telecom GVC with key segments and major actors identified. It also discusses key dynamics in the mobile telecom GVC, focusing on geographic and organizational concentration of mobile phone production, the co-evolution of value chain actors, and changing governance structure between major firm actors. Finally, it presents the findings of our trade position analysis using international trade data, illustrating how countries move up and down in the global value chains of mobile phones and components.

Chapter 5 presents a more detailed view of international trade networks in the mobile phone GVC. By linking the proposed framework in Chapter 3 with UN Comtrade dataset, the chapter analyzes the differentiation of regions' and countries' roles in *inter-* and *intra-regional* trade networks in the mobile phone GVCs, and, specifically, the role of East Asia in inter- and intra-regional trade networks, and the divergent positions of East Asian countries in this high-tech sector.

Section III addresses convergence and divergence and regional connections in Asia through a lens of mobile telecommunication. Chapter 6 address the topic of convergence and divergence in East Asian industrial development by examining the paths of GVC integration and upgrading of China, Japan, Korea and Taiwan in mobile phone manufacturing. Based on a framework proposed in Chapter 3, it examines how the four countries and firms in these countries responded to the challenges from the rise of global value chains and intensified competition, focusing on how their positions in the mobile phone GVC and their orientation toward global markets changed.

Chapter 7 examines how the evolving strategies of MNEs are intertwined with regional production networks, highlighting the important role of MNEs, including extra-regional firms, in shaping the structure of regional trade networks and value chains in Asia. It also illuminates how the rise of emerging economies as the center of production and consumption in the mobile phone GVC can disrupt the existing market structure and destabilize the competitive landscape. These two points are illustrated with three cases from the mobile phone industry: a) Samsung Electronics (SEC) as the leading regional and global mobile phone brand; b) Apple and Foxconn, a trans-regional relationship that has dramatically changed how the mobile phone GVC works; and c) the case of *unbranded* mobile phones in China, known as 'Shanzhai', and the quick surge of local brands in emerging economies.

Notes

1. International Telecommunication Union, "Key ICT indicators for developed and developing countries and the world" (http://www.itu.int/en/ITU-D/Statistics/Documents/statistics/2016/ITU_Key_2005-2016_ICT_data.xls, Accessed on July 25, 2017).

2. World Bank Databank (http://databank.worldbank.org/data/home.aspx).

3. United Nations Statistics Division (UNSD), "Composition of macro geographical (continental) regions, geographical sub-regions, and selected economic and other groupings" (http://unstats.un.org/unsd/methods/m49/m49regin.htm).

Section I

Capitalisms, Global Value Chains, and Integration and Divergence in East Asia: Conceptual Framework

Chapter 2

Capitalism in Globalizing Asia

Asia on the Rise

Emerging Asia

Asia is on the rise. It has shown remarkable developmental dynamism compared to Europe and North America. Despite being one of the late- or late-late-developers in terms of industrialization and democratization, Asia now spearheads the world's most rapid transformation into the 21st capitalism.

More than forty years ago, Norman Macrae, who was then a deputy editor of the *Economist*, talked about the coming of the "Pacific Century." According to him, the world had gone through the "British Century" (1775-1875), the "American Century" (1875-1975), and was entering the "Pacific Century" (1975-2075?). Asia was seen as a newly rising leader in the international political and economic realms. Its extraordinary vitality has forced development scholars and practitioners to "Re-Orient" the history of capitalist development in the region (Abu-Lughod 1989; McNeill 1963).

With the coming of the 21st century, Asia has undoubtedly solidified its global stance in wealth and power, as well as in knowledge and culture. Nevertheless, the rise of Asia does not mean collapse of the West. We should be cautious about Occidentalism implying a counteraction to "Orientalism." Exclusive Asianism under the guise of "De-Eurocentrism" merely represents "Reverse Orientalism." Historically, Asia has largely stayed ahead of Europe. As every civilization has its downfall, Asia took precedence over Europe during the first five centuries of the second millennium A.D. (1000-1500 A.D.), but Europe surpassed Asia during the next five centuries (1500-2000 A.D.). As historian Geoffrey Barraclough (1955, 205) puts it, "every age needs its own view of history." In this regard, the so-called "reversal of civilization" does not indicate the end of one history but the beginning of another.

Europe was able to gain ascendancy over Asia only because it benefited from advanced Eastern heritage making a revolutionary breakthrough in science and technology. Around 1000 A.D., China and the Middle East became highly urbanized, while the entire population of Rome declined dramatically from 450,000 persons to 35,000. The Spanish area of Córdova, under Islamic rule, had 500,000 residents. Baghdad was the world's largest city, with about 1,000,000 inhabitants. For the period from the 9th century to the 13th century, the House of Wisdom in Baghdad undertook the collection, translation, and synthesization of works of "foreign sciences," containing the essence of Greek, Persian and Indian political, medical and scientific treatises (Schäfer and Lim 2010, xv). Europe's precedence over Asia was witnessed during Europe's Scientific Revolution combined with "geographical discovery."

Today, Asia is creating new history as the most dynamic region in the world.[1] Together with Europe and North America, Asia is highly acclaimed as one of the three central pillars of the modern industrialized world. Japan became the first non-Western state to achieve modernization, accompanied by the phenomenal economic success of "The Four Dragons of Asia" (Korea, Taiwan, Hong Kong, and Singapore). It was then followed by the emergence of "The Five Tigers" (Thailand, Indonesia, Malaysia, the Philippines, and Vietnam) as industrial nations. CHINDIA, referring to China and India together, is rising as a global political and economic powerhouse. These changes usher in the advent of the Asian Century, initially mentioned in the mid-1970s, during the encounter between Deng Xiaoping and Rajiv Gandhi.

Over the last decades, Asia has demonstrated its unparalleled dynamism throughout the world. Its population and geographical size are larger than North America, South America, Europe or even Africa. Despite later attainment of industrialization, Asia now spearheads the world's most rapid transformation into the 21st knowledge-based society through prompt responses to informatization.

It would be tempting to say that the global center has moved from the Atlantic, between Europe and the United States (US), to the Pacific, linking the US and China. Simply put, the world is witnessing a hegemonic shift from Europe to Asia. In particular, China's rise and Europe's downfall provides a vivid portrayal of a hegemonic shift. China has supplanted the place of Europe within G2 to stand abreast with the US The size of Chinese economy has already surpassed Japan and Germany and is closing into the US. Its economic volume is projected to surpass that of the US in 2020. The records of other Asian countries, such as Japan, Korea, Taiwan, Singapore, India, Malaysia, Vietnam and Indonesia are also remarkable. Some of the Asian countries have overtaken other regional economies in computer and internet access, progress of the digital industry, mobile phone penetration, and the use of social network service (SNS).

Asia bears the hallmark of commonality within diversity and this is clearly embodied in the following concepts: the "Asian Way," "Asian Values," the "Asian View" or "Neo-Asianism." However, we do not know yet of whether Asia could be really nicknamed "the second modernity," an alternative to Western modernity. Even if Asia has shown remarkable development dynamism, it has been plagued by problems on economic equality, social conflict, political instability, environmental degradation and more.

Asia accounts for more than half of the world production and marked to be the most promising regional bloc to surpass the US and Europe. In particular, Korea, China, Taiwan and Japan play crucial roles in the global economy and international relations. Accounting for more than 75% of the regional gross output, these nations have become a global hub of production, investment, trade and consumption. Following the Japanese precedent of industrial success, China has aspired to become an economic powerhouse, with Taiwan maintaining its economic cooperation with mainland China. Squeezed between China and Japan, world's second and third economies, Korea is doing its best to join the advanced countries. Asia's aggressive dynamism is causing lasting reverberations across the five oceans and six continents.

Globalization and regionalization

There are generally two distinct types of globalization: one occurring from the top and one occurring from the bottom. In response to "globalization from above," dominated by transnational actors such as international economic institutions and MNEs, "globalization from below" has emerged to reclaim its power. Figuratively speaking, globalization from above is becoming "a brakeless train wreaking havoc" that should be checked by a new set of rules. Changes occurring from above can be labeled "neoliberal/ capitalist globalization" and globalization from the bottom can be branded "emancipatory/ civil society globalization." The latter mobilizes cross-border social movements and targets the global civil society, fueled by growing activities of international non-governmental organizations (INGOs) (Boli and Thomas 1999; Folk 1993; Keck and Sikkink 1998).

Asia is now undergoing a rapid and drastic globalization unprecedented in history that is by nature neo-liberal. Almost every Asian country has been integrated into the global economy. Globalization has permeated to every corner of the Asian continent. While globalization has provided opportunities for some countries, it has also posed as threats for other countries. It would not be an exaggeration to say that although Asia has tried to use globalization as a stimulus for industrial advancement, each Asian country has experienced different successes and failures in the process of national development. The future of national development in the end then depends significantly on the country's ability to make use of globalization.

In terms of democratic achievement and industrial progress, globalization has accounted for mixed results in Asian countries. It is widely recognized that globalization generates both international and domestic disparities where there is a minority of winners and a majority of losers. Among the Asian countries, there have not been many, which have benefited from the process of globalization. Except for a few countries, democratic consolidation has not been able to complete the transition from authoritarianism in the midst of growing disparities and inequalities. Globalization has brought about the expansion of democratic ideals, without the institutionalization of democratic practices. What globalization really promotes is a type of democracy that allows for the free flow of capital, goods and services across borders to generate accumulation on a worldwide scale. It also replaces class politics with identity politics, resulting in diverse possibilities for political conflict. In Asia, democracy has functioned only in a procedural manner, without enlarging social and economic citizenship. Often times, even economic development has been emasculated due to increasing social cleavages and political struggles. In the long run, these social cleavages and political struggles can be detrimental to the sustainability of democracy.

In the throes of deepening globalization, Asia has undergone intra-regional integration. Today Asia has a number of intra-regional cooperative bodies such as APEC, ASEAN, ASEAN+3 and ASEAN+6 (see Figure 1). With the involvement of 21 members, the APEC is short of being a powerful economic cooperative body. Even though the 1994 Bogor Summit generated regional consensus about the timeline of intra-regional trade liberalization (2010 for advanced countries and 2020 for developing countries), enormous obstacles still lie ahead of the APEC in pursuit of a viable economic bloc in Asia. APEC's institutionalization is being delayed by the US and China's striving for economic supremacy across Asia.

With a total of ten members, ASEAN focuses its primary attention on economic cooperation but it falls short of yielding expected tangible outcomes. It tries to keep good relations with the US for security concerns, but at the same time, take advantage

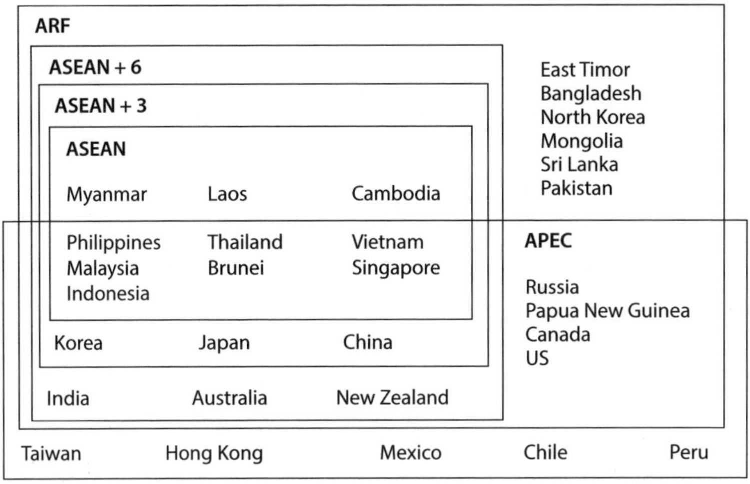

Figure 1. Varieties of regional community in Asia

Source: Authors.

of China for economic stakes. It also maintains a reserved stance towards APEC under the US influence in fear of weakening its position as an alliance of emerging economies. With the involvement of Korea, China and Japan in ASEAN, the ASEAN+3 was founded to handle the Asian financial crisis, represented only as a forum for exchange of views and ideas without having a decision-making authority. In addition, the ASEAN+6 (including India, Australia and New Zealand) was established as the biggest free-trade market on the globe.[2] Nevertheless, there is a high likelihood of coexistence of ASEAN+3, ASEAN+6 and APEC in the future.

The formation of a regional community is crucial for China, Japan and Korea in Northeast Asia to turn tension and conflict into cooperation and coexistence but this is hampered by an excessive hegemonic competition under the banner of nationalism. Thus, Korea, China, and Japan should take not only economic but also cultural approaches toward the creation of a regional community. Instead of being hard-pressed to build an economic community like the APEC, they should foster reconciliation and cooperation according to bilateral principles. It is hoped that regional community will play an important role in the cooperation and harmony of the region.

Commonality among diversity

There is not a single Asia but rather a presence of multiple entities. Asia is really a vast continent comprised northern, eastern, western and southerneastern sections. It does not stand for a single zone of civilization but is a mixture of various languages, races and religions. Most Asian countries have their own native languages against a backdrop of unique ethnicities. Asia has been the birthplace of the world's major religions, such as Confucianism, Buddhism, Hinduism and Islam. It is marked by a coexistence of following religions: Confucianism in Korea, North Korea, China, Japan, Vietnam, Taiwan and Singapore; Hinduism in India; Buddhism in Thailand and Myanmar; Islam in Indonesia and Malaysia and Catholicism in the Philippines.

Asia reveals a considerable disparity in political systems, economic institutions, social structures and cultural patterns. As most countries follow the capitalist model, there are few socialist states like North Korea as well as states in transition from socialism to capitalism such as China and Vietnam. Under the capitalist model, there are various types of economic systems ranging from government-interventionist economies (Japan, Korea, Taiwan and Malaysia) to laissez-faire economies (Singapore and Hong Kong) and mixed economies (Indonesia, Thailand and the Philippines).

Such diversity is also manifested in democracy, civil society and economic development. Asian countries are largely classified into developed, semi-developed and developing economies depending on their economic statuses. In other words, they can be categorized into wealthy developed countries, poor underdeveloped countries or developing countries from the latter group to the former group. Recently, China, India, Indonesia, Malaysia and Vietnam have earned the title of emerging market economies.

Notwithstanding the aforesaid diversity, Asian countries have maintained cultural and institutional connections within the region through constant contact, exchange, trade and warfare. This cultural and institutional linkage serves as a cohesive factor for Asian countries to converge on regional commonness despite intra-regional disparities. For instance, Buddhism was propagated to Korea and Japan after its origination in India. With its fundamental roots in China, Confucianism became widespread in Korea, Japan and Taiwan as well as Vietnam. Based upon Japan's government-led industrialization model, Asian countries have proceeded with their own economic development processes while transmitting the development experiences of predecessors.[3]

There has recently been increasing interactions among Korea, Japan and China in terms of economic and cultural exchange. Not only capital and commodities but also labor power and information have moved from country to country in an unprecedented way. Table 1 reveals the increasing volume of exports and imports among Korea, Japan and China. In particular, trade between Korea and China has boosted almost sevenfold from 2002 to 2015, compared with a small rise in trade between Korea and Japan. Increasing number of tourists and students studying abroad are good signs

Table 1. Trade relation among Korea, China and Japan (unit: 100 million dollars)

Year	Korea - Japan		Korea - China		Japan - China	
	Export to Japan	Import from Japan	Export to China	Import from China	Export to China	Import from China
2002	151	299	238	174	399	617
2003	173	363	351	219	572	752
2004	217	461	498	296	738	942
2005	240	484	619	386	803	1,091
2006	265	519	695	486	1,080	1,377
2007	264	563	820	630	1,284	1,504
2008	283	610	914	769	1,296	1,483
2009	218	494	867	542	1,024	1,143
2010	282	643	1,168	716	1,309	1,341
2011	397	683	1,342	864	1,290	1,463
2012	388	644	1,343	808	1,447	1,890
2013	347	600	1,459	831	1,299	1,822
2014	322	538	1,453	901	1,271	1,821
2015	256	459	1,371	903	1,093	1,607

Sources: Korea International Trade Association (http://www.kita.net/) & Japan External Trade Organization (www.jetro.co.jp).

of personal exchange among Korea, China and Japan. For example, since the early 2000s, Korean students studying in China has more than tripled. As of now, they occupy half of the total foreign students' population in China.

It can be assumed that information and communication technology (ICT) has contributed significantly to widening mutual understanding among people in Korea, China and Japan. The three countries learn about one another through songs, drama, films and other cultural products. As shown in Table 2, telephone, broadband and cellular subscribers have increased to an enormous degree during the last three decades in China, Korea and Japan. In 2013, households with computers account for 35.4% of the population

Table 2. Media & communications indicators

	Fixed telephone subscriptions (per 1,000 people)			Fixed broadband subscriptions (per 1,000 people)			Mobile cellular subscriptions (per 1,000 people)			Households with computer[1)] (%)	Individuals using internet[2)] (%)
	'90	'14	%	'00	'14	%	'93	'14	%	'13	'13
China	6	179	2,883.3	0.01	144	1,439,900	0.5	923	184,600	35.4	38.3
Japan	446	501	12.3	6.80	293	4,208.8	17.1	1,202	7,029	82.4	89.7
Korea	309	595	93.6	84.10	388	361.4	10.7	1,157	10,813	78.2	84.3

Notes: 1), 2) For China, year of data is from 2011.
Sources: Helmut Anheier & H. Katz. Global Civil Society Yearbook 2005/6.
ITU World Telecommunication/ICT Indicators.

in China, 82.4% in Japan and 78.2% in Korea, while individuals using internets are reported to be 38.3% of the population in China, 89.7% in Japan and 84.3% in Korea.

Dynamics of Capitalism in Asia

Capitalism as plural forms

Capitalism has become the encompassing economic system worldwide for countries in the process of globalization. Every country is integrated deeply into a global capitalist system. As an economic system, capitalism can be characterized by traits such as private ownership, profit maximization, capital accumulation, wage labor, voluntary exchange and competitive markets. We believe that there may be an ideal type of capitalism but have to admit that there is a variety of capitalism existing in different national forms (Morgan and Whitley 2012, 38-39). Capitalism can take dissimilar forms nationally, depending on development strategy, state-society relations, class coalition, business-government nexus, labor market structure, industrial relations, corporate governance system and innovative system. We fully agree with the idea of plural forms of capitalism. Nederveen Pieterse (2015, 11) is right in saying that "capitalism survives thanks to the diversity of capitalisms." The diversity of capitalism has given itself adaptability, flexibility, changeability, and durability, as compared with short-lived, actually existing socialism.

There are several families of capitalism, such as Anglo-American capitalism, Rhinish capitalism, Nordic capitalism, Mediterranean capitalism, East Asian capitalism amongst others. Comparative capitalism perspective following varieties of capitalism literature has differentiated three basic types of capitalism that are analytically very useful: liberal market economies (LME), coordinated market economies (CME) and state-led market economies (SME) (Amable 2003; Hall and Soskice 2001; Morgan and Whitley 2012; Storz *et al.* 2013). Table 3 presents a schematic overview of three basic types of capitalism by country (Nederveen Pieterse 2015, 2). It can be argued from the overview that most of Asian countries are dominated by SME, even though some are categorized with CME.

Capitalism as a whole has recently revealed contradictions rather than dynamics, marked by a couple of financial crises. In the throes of globalization, internationalization of finance, global network of production, trade openness across borders, international labor migration and free and speculative movement of capital have increased to a degree, weakening the national platform of industrial and financial policymaking. In addition, market-oriented globalization has undermined the state capacity in implementing regulations to protect national economy. Slowing economic growth has led to a rise in unemployment, dualization of labor markets and increased concentration of wealth and incomes—all signs of contra-

Table 3. Varieties of capitalism by country

Capitalism	Country
LME	US, Australia, New Zealand, UK, Ireland
CME	Germany, France, Austria, Switzerland, Belgium, Denmark, the Netherlands, Finland, Sweden, Norway, Canada, Japan, Brazil, Argentina, Chile, Mexico
SME	Singapore, Korea, Taiwan, China, Vietnam, Indonesia, Malaysia, Thailand, Laos, Russia, Cuba, Venezuela, Iran, Saudi Arabia, United Arab Emirates

Source: Reconstructed based on Nederveen Pieterse (2015, 2).

dictions. The breakdown of political representation fuels popular dissatisfaction and cynicism with democracy and partisan competition, an erosion of public trust and civic-mindedness, as well as a decline in political participation (Beramendi *et al.* 2015, 15).

It is interesting to point out, however, that East Asian capitalism is relatively immune from severe contradictions, when compared with those of Anglo-American, Mediterranean and even Rhinish capitalism. In Asia, capitalism has been mostly figured as a category in the singular with variations in the margins—market economies with variations in degrees and styles of state guidance, in historical trajectories and institutional makeup.

There are some distinct features of capitalism in Asia (see Lim *et al.* Forthcoming). First, historical perspectives do not tally with the idea of Asian capitalism as being extensions of Western or American dynamics. Oriental prosperity and globalization has long preceded occidental globalization. Departing from a Eurocentric view, Frank (1998) pointed out that European ascendency did not really emerge until the 19th century. Until then, the global economy was centered around China and Europe was yet to become a major player. The main economic players at that time were China, India, Persia and the Ottoman Empire. Europe was able to enter into the existing global economy, thanks to the windfalls of American silver and the Atlantic slave trade after the "geographical discovery."

Second, the category "Western capitalism" glosses over glaring differences in the West—Nordic Europe is quite different from American capitalism; Mediterranean Europe and Eastern Europe are also very dissimilar. There are indeed marked differences between coordinated market economies (Germany, Japan, Switzerland, the Netherlands, Belgium, Sweden, Norway, Denmark, Finland and Austria) and the liberal market economies (the US, Britain, Australia, Canada, New Zealand and Ireland). Between those two different economies, exist "Mediterranean" economies, represented by France, Italy, Spain, Portugal, Greece, and Turkey.

Third, by world standards, American capitalism is an anomaly, an outlier that achieved model status because of its hegemony, (under the heading of "free market and democracy") which is structurally different from the majority of world economies.

Fourth, Asian capitalism is not homogeneous in that state-interventionist Japan, Korea, Taiwan and Malaysia are dissimilar with free market-oriented Singapore and Hong Kong. In particular, East Asian political economies have more in common with Nordic European capitalism than with Anglo-American capitalism.

Fifth, the rise of China opens a different chapter that cannot be comprehended in terms of existing scripts. Regionally, it reshapes dynamics, while globally it yields "globalization with Chinese characteristics."

Explaining capitalist development

Asia exhibits the possibilities and limitations of capitalist development for other parts of the world. It is worthwhile to start by placing the Asian development experience into the broader context of development theories.

Three lines of analysis have been used to explain the dynamics and contradictions of capitalist development in Asia. First, the *market approach* emphasizes the rules of the game made by government. Such institutional rules contribute to the enhancement of markets in a way to promote competition and efficiency (World Bank 1993). Government's intervention is limited, however, to sponsoring the manufacture of exportable goods. Second, the *state approach* focuses on government's careful development strategy, which is instrumental to economic development (Amsden 1989; Johnson 1982; Wade 1990). According to this perspective, government designs industrial and financial policies in order to lead markets toward the goal of effective capital accumulation. Third, the *culture approach* stresses the role of traditional Confucian ethics, which emphasize achievement, self-discipline, education, strong family ties, and loyalty to the organization and communitarian values (Morishima 1982; Tu 1984). These Confucian principles act as institutionalized cultural arrangements for economic development.

Each of these approaches has merits and demerits. While the market approach gives priority to the increasing importance of the market mechanism in the overall development process, it does not take into account the government's central role in the process of capital accumulation. The state approach touches on the significance of discretionary policies in promoting economic development but fails to consider the negative outcomes that can be produced by state intervention into economic activities. By solely focusing on Confucian ethics as the functional requisite of economic development, the culture approach leaves the workings of institutions, such as the state or the market, unexplained in the accumulation process.

The Asian economic crisis in the late 1990s has provided a valuable opportunity to test the validity and reliability of these three approaches. Some mistakes in Asian development are manifested by the Asian crisis: excessive government intervention, the lack of a market mechanism, collusion between government and business, a precarious financial system, moral hazards, pervasive corruption and more. These problems point to weaknesses inherent in each approach. The market approach overlooks the foundation of the financial system as a basis for corporate transparency, efficiency and accountability. The state approach neglects the requirement of free and competitive markets that prevent the rent-seeking behavior that results from government-business collusion. The culture approach does not take seriously the importance of a development strategy that provides industrial and financial policies geared toward spurring economic growth.

Before the 1997 crisis, Paul Krugman (1994) had already pointed out the illusory nature of economic success in Asia. According to him, rapid economic growth in Asia can be attributed mostly to high rates of capital formation and labor mobilization in the accumulation process. It was not high rates of technology innovation that led to economic growth in the region. Japan is the only exception among Asian countries where skill has multiplied the output produced by capital and labor.

Krugman's criticism of Asian economic success is not entirely appropriate. History has shown that every country experiencing economic development has moved from extensive growth to intensive growth in the process. For instance, not only Japan as an early developer but Taiwan, Korea, Singapore and Hong Kong as latecomers have undergone continuous economic growth by way of labor-intensive industrialization followed by technology-intensive industrialization. China, India, Malaysia, Indonesia, and Vietnam as the latest developers are also recognized to be in transition from extensive to intensive growth.

The global economic crisis in 2008 has given another important opportunity to prove the possibility of capitalist development in Asia. Some Asian countries including China, Taiwan, Korea and Japan bounced back from the recession within a relatively short period of time, while the US and most of European countries continued to suffer.[4] The crisis has definitely invigorated the discussion on the basic mechanism of capitalist development in Asia.[5] No region has been more dynamic than Asia. Even though there have been ups and downs in economic performances, Asia has not ceased to evade challenges to overcome crisis.

In fact, Asia is an ideal case demonstrating the dynamics and contradictions of capitalist development. Even though it has undergone rapid industrialization and steady democratization, considerable ruptures and tensions have developed these two ideals. In a sense, Asia's economic development has taken place under the guidance of authoritarian leadership and in the context of an illiberal democracy. The state has dominated civil society, as well as the market. For these reasons, the states in Asia have been described as merely "developmental." The developmental state usually creates "growth coalitions" between the state and the capital, excluding labor. Asia now stands at the critical juncture in changing this pattern and establishing a new partnership that incorporates state, capital and labor in order to survive in an era of globalization.

The developmental state in action

It will be interesting to argue that since the 1997 financial crisis hit Asia, the role of the state has been questioned. Paradoxically enough, however, the global economic crisis of 2008 has renewed the importance of government role in the context of developmental state model. The developmental state has continued to survive in Asian countries, at least in old form in strong states or still elements of it have remained intact, especially after 2008 (Lim 2010; Park 2011; Stubbs 2011).

This developmental state theory has opposed the prevailing neoclassical explanation of the free-market mechanism of development in Asia. The founding work in this new paradigm was Chalmers Johnson's study of the Japanese economic bureaucracy, MITI (the Ministry of International Trade and Industry) and industrial policy formulated and executed by the ministry, focusing on its role in Japan's rise as an economic giant during the post-1945 era (Johnson 1982). Johnson attempts to explain the state bureaucracy's active and strategic role in Japan's economic development, dating back to the pre-war period when similar bureaucratic activities were used to mobilize industrial resources efficiently for the purpose of wars in the 1930-40s. He constructs the Japanese case as a different economic model from both the American-style capitalist system and the Soviet-style communist one. According to him, Japan's model is "plan-rational," (*developmental state*) while the US's is "market-rational" (*regulatory state*) and the Soviet's is "plan-ideological." He focuses his discussion mainly on the differences between the market-rational and the plan-rational economic models (Johnson 1982, 18-26). In the current post-Cold War context, his early construction of the ideal types of different capitalist systems seem to be a precedent for the typology of different capitalisms, which was considered to be heretical in the early 1980s but is more popular now.

Since Johnson's work on the Japanese case was out, there have been several additional works focusing on East Asian cases, especially on Korea and Taiwan. Amsden (1989, 14) highlights the efficient state-bureaucracy's role in Korea's technological learning and industrial transformation from its war-torn condition of the 1950s. She attributes this transformation to the state's "deliberately getting relative prices wrong" mechanism in the economy for the purpose of achieving long-term development goals as a late industrializing country. Differing from the political science perspective presented by Johnson, Amsden's work, based on "institutionalist" economics, seems to be directly opposing the neoclassical explanation of growth in Asian NIEs (the newly industrialized economies). Soon after her work was published, Wade (1990) suggested the "governed-market theory" (GMT) in the analysis of Taiwan's (and Korea's) industrialization, which was also intended to refute the neoclassical "free-market theory" (FMT) or "simulated-market theory" (SMT) of economic development. Again, regarding the case of Korea, Woo-Cumings (1991) examined historically the important role of "state-guided financing through banks" in economic development while Chang (1994) investigated on "industrial policy". Constructing the ideal-types of the different states in terms of developmental functioning under labels of "developmental", "predatory" or "intermediate," sociologist Evans (1995) emphasized in his comparative study on the development of the information technology (IT) industries of Korea, Brazil and India, that the state bureaucracy should not only be "embedded" in the private sectors but also "autonomous" of their particularistic interests in order to achieve domestically-based industrial transformation while also furthering economic development. Kim (1997) traced the "relationship between state and big business" changing from state-dominance to symbiosis in Korea's recent history. Defining state power as "infrastructural" rather than "coercive," based on Michael Mann's terminology, Weiss (1998) argues that even under the strong pressure of globalization popularly assumed and argued to have severely weakened the nation-state's autonomy and capacity to intervene in the economy, the state capacity as an institutional complex is still important for competitiveness. She uses not only Asian states but also Germany as examples of developmental states, even emphasizing strengths of Japan and Germany as "dualist states" which are "distributive" as well as "developmental." Chibber (2002) develops a detailed explanation of "intra-bureaucracy dynamics" in a comparative study of India and Korea suggesting the ironic case where bureaucratic mechanisms based on the logic of rationality can weaken the state capacity of cohesiveness as the Indian case shows in his study. After all, the developmental state in Japan, Korea, Taiwan and China can be said to have been "based on a close collaboration between the state, banks, and (the business), with the state as the dominant player" (Shin and Chang 2003, 1).

While the developmental state theory suggests condition of economic development with specific institutional arrangements and state's activities which have been adopted in some countries with further adaptation potential, it needs to be critically assessed. A careful look at the world-system especially at the "geopolitical" context of developments in history can prevent an ahistorical model in generalizing some cases as something that can be replicated everywhere (Cumings 1999, 64, 91-92; Evans 1995, 232, 245; Johnson 1999, 55; Lee 2013, 367-368; Pempel 1999, 174-180; Wade 1990, 346; Woo-Cumings 1999, 21). This critique is legitimate insofar as it emphasizes that the developmental state is a historically-conditioned outcome, and pays attention to the possible transformation tied to the changes in historical conditions.

After the Second World War, Korea, Taiwan, China and Japan underwent their own development processes. Amid the state-led economic and social overhaul, Japan implemented an outward-oriented development strategy favoring the business sector. Korea and Taiwan embraced Japan's developmental state model to undergo a rapid economic growth. After its adoption of reform and open-door policies, the Chinese economy followed the same track of ongoing growth typical of the developmental state model of Japan, Korea and Taiwan. Developmental state model is characterized by the following features: state interference and guidance, long-term economic development planning, rapid and continuous economic growth, a quality education system, an abundant pool of cheap and skilled manpower, strategic industrial and financial policies and more. The developmental state model stimulated Japan's economic recovery in the 1950s after the Second World War, played a key role in both Korea and Taiwan's rapid economic development from the 1970s to the 1990s and spurred China's ongoing sustained economic growth driven by industrialization from the 1990s up to now. Today, the reduction of state role and the expansion of market functions are gathering considerable momentum amid the prevalence of neo-liberalism empowered by globalization. But this situation raises the necessity of appropriate state intervention in the provision of social welfare, the settlement of conflicting interests and the construction of a stable infrastructure. In sum, a developmental state does not completely fade away but is being reborn into a new type of "post-developmental state" in some countries.

Japan, Korea, Taiwan and China

Asia accounts for more than half of the world production and marked to be the most promising regional bloc to surpass the US and Europe. In particular, Korea, Taiwan, China, and Japan play a crucial role in the global economy and international relations. Accounting for more than 75% of the regional gross output, these nations have become a global hub of production, investment, trade and consumption. Japan has already become an economic powerhouse and China has economically beaten Japan and has tried to surpass the US as a global superpower. Taiwan attempts to collaborate, not politically but economically, with China and Korea strategically wishes to remain a middle power. The aggressive dynamism of these countries is causing enormous reverberations across the five oceans and six continents.

China, Japan, Korea and Taiwan now have a firm and solid economic presence worldwide. As of 2016, China, Japan, Taiwan and Korea hold foreign exchange reserves of more than $ 5.2 trillion (see Table 4). Eight Asian countries take the place of the world's top 10 holders of foreign exchange reserves, which include China, Japan, Russia, Taiwan, India, Korea, Hong Kong and Singapore. Brazil and Switzerland are the remaining two holders.

Historically, industrial success or failure relies on the usage of iron, called the rice of industries and late industrial starters tend to

Table 4. Foreign exchange reserve of top 10 countries (As of the end of March, 2016)
(unit: 100 million dollars)

Rank	Country	Foreign exchange reserve	Rank	Country	Foreign exchange reserve
1	China	32,126(103)	6	Russia	3,870(65)
2	Japan	12,621(80)	7	Korea	3,698(41)
3	Switzerland	6,492(305)	8	Hong Kong	3,620(20)
4	Saudi Arabia	5,871(-56)	9	India	3,602(118)
5	Taiwan	4,316(28)	10	Brazil	3,577(-17)

Notes: Foreign Exchange Reserve means the amount of stock.
Number in parentheses shows preceding monthly change.
Source: The Bank of Korea, Press Release, 2016.5.3.

catch up with early starters through upgraded crude steel production. Germany and the US tried to overtake the United Kingdom (UK) and Europe respectively through strides in the steel industry. Japan endeavored to expand crude steel output with the aim of outdoing Europe and the US In 1968, Korea embarked on national industrialization with the launch of POSCO. As shown in Table 5, China is the world's largest crude steel producer, followed by Japan, the US, India, Russia and Korea.

Asian countries show their strength not only in traditional chimney industry but also in the leading edge technology industries. The rice of industries of 21st century, semiconductor production is also noticeable among Asian companies. Five Korean and Japanese firms take the place of top ten sales leaders listed in this industry, as Table 6 demonstrates.

China no longer remains a sleeping lion. Since its entry into the WTO and successful launch of the manned spacecraft "Shenzhou" in 2001, China has cemented its global presence through the hosting of the 2008 Beijing Olympics and the 2010 Shanghai EXPO. China has ambitious plans to nurture over 50 Chinese

Table 5. Top 10 steel-producing countries (as of 2015) (unit: Megaton (Mt))

Rank	Country	Crude steel output	Rank	Country	Crude steel output
1	China	803.8	6	South Korea	69.7
2	Japan	105.2	7	Germany	42.7
3	India	89.6	8	Brazil	33.2
4	U.S.	78.9	9	Turkey	31.5
5	Russia	71.1	10	Ukraine	22.9

Source: World Steel Association, *Crude Steel Statistics Total 2015*. (http://www.worldsteel.org/media-centre/press-releases/2016/--World-crude-steel-output-decreases-by--2.8--in-2015.html).

Table 6. Top 10 semiconductor sales leaders

Rank			Company	Country	Total sales (billion USD)	2014/2013 change rate (%)	Market share (%)
2014	2013	2012					
1	1	1	Intel Corporation	US	49,964	+6.3	14.1
2	2	2	Samsung Electronics	Korea	38,273	+15.6	10.8
3	3	3	Qualcomm	US	19,266	+11.9	5.5
4	4	10	Micron Technology	US	16,389	+16.1	4.6
5	5	7	SK Hynix	Korea	15,737	+22.9	4.5
6	6	4	Texas Instruments	US	11,420	+6.8	3.5
7	7	5	Toshiba Semiconductor	Japan	8,496	-9.6	2.4
8	8	9	Broadcom	US	8,387	+2.5	2.4
9	9	8	STMicroelectronics	France, Italy	7,395	-8.5	2.1
10	15	18	MediaTek	Taiwan	7,194	+57.5	2.0

Source: Wikipedia (Total Sales, Market Share as of 2014).

firms for entry into the world's top 500 enterprises in the foreseeable future. It recently built an aircraft carrier as part of an effort to make inroads in the Indian Ocean as well as the Pacific Ocean. Furthermore, China is striving to climb its way to a position of unchallenged supremacy over not only Asia but the rest of the world. It has offered a massive amount of development assistance and financial investment to African and Latin American countries.

In 2010, China overtook Japan to rank second globally in terms of gross domestic product (GDP). Five years ago, the Chinese GDP amounted to only half of the Japanese GDP. If current trends continue, the International Monetary Fund (IMF) predicts that Chinese GDP might catch up with the US GDP within a minimum of five years.

Japan is undoubtedly an economic giant, but on a political front, it resembles a dwarf in the political sense. In addition to economic strength, Japan seeks ways to consolidate diplomatic and military capabilities through the revision of self-defense laws for rearmament. However, Japan is no longer a rising sun. Political leadership has become fragile, as proved by the recent inauguration of five Prime Ministers in less than five years. As interested parties still dominate the National Diet, the Democratic Party has difficulty in executing national reform in the face of the Liberal Democratic Party. The Democratic Party proposed a coalition cabinet for efficient crisis management of the Fukushima nuclear reactors but it obtained cold responses from the Liberal Democratic Party and the New Komeito Party. It will take several years for Japan to bounce back from the 2011 tsunami setbacks but Japan undoubtedly wants to reemerge as a global economic power backed by strong technological edges and abundant capital stocks.

As of 2015, Korea stands as the world's 7th exporter as well as the world's 9th trading country and ranks 11th in GDP. It has reinforced its global presence through concurrent execution of industrialization and democratization but retains serious limitations as a divided nation. Although Korea is in the league of middle powers, it stands at a disadvantageous position compared to China and Japan due to its inherent limitations as a divided nation, preventing

Korea from serving as a Northeast Asian balancer for coexistence and harmony. Nevertheless, Korea upholds a strong presence in international relations and the global economy as evidenced by its efforts to build a bridge between advanced and developing worlds through the hosting of the G20 Summit in 2010.

Notes

1. Frank explains Asia's global reemergence following the 1400-1800s as "The Re-orientation of the Orient." Refer to Frank (1998).

2. To facilitate the cooperation among the ASEAN+3, the East Asia Forum (EAF) was established for governmental, academic and business circles. In the same vein, the East Asia Summit (EAS) is held for the leaders from the ASEAN+6, US and Russia after annual ASEAN leaders' meeting.

3. In Asia, many countries have followed one another in a development trajectory in which the latecomers try to replicate the success of the early developers (Cumings 1984). Akamatsu (1962) has described this interrelationship between the different latecomer countries as the "flying-geese pattern."

4. Stubbs (2011, 159-162) summarizes how the great recession changed the perception of the two economic models, neoliberalism and developmental statism represented by the US and China respectively.

5. New discussions on the state in the 21st century such as "state capitalism" (Bremmer 2010) or "capitalism 4.0" (Kaletsky 2010) address the repercussions of the great economic recession in 2008.

Chapter 3

Global Value Chains, Divergence, and Regionalization

Introduction

The global economy has been transformed significantly over the last few decades or so. One of the defining changes is the increasing fragmentation and decentralization of production, and the ensuing rise of GVCs. From a GVC lens, the global economy is considered as a web of complex trade and transaction networks, increasingly governed by MNEs. The rise of GVCs has changed the way countries and firms pursue economic and industrial development; upgrading, or moving from lower to higher value-added activities, is important in advancing their positions in a fragmented global industry.

GVCs play a key role in East Asia's economic development. In the face of expanding economic globalization, the region has built sophisticated trade and supply chain linkages inside and outside the region. Embedded in this complex network of production, and cooperating and competing with each other, East Asian countries have tried to respond to various challenges from the global economy, including the rising fragmentation of production, and the emergence of developing economies as end markets. While whether their development trajectories are converging or diverging is still under debate, the frameworks we propose in this chapter provide a useful analytical tool to understand the integration of East Asian economies into the global economy as well as the convergence and divergence of their development paths in the GVC.

Furthermore, the expansion of RVCs has facilitated the progress of regional integration in East Asia. In the midst of geographic and organizational concentration in GVCs, East Asian RVCs have emerged as the center of global production in many manufacturing sectors. This chapter highlights the role of firms, both Asian MNEs and ones from outside the region, in shaping RVCs and regional connection and interaction.

Transformations of the Global Economy from a GVC Lens

The GVC approach has changed the way we understand the global economy. Focusing on the growing organizational fragmentation and geographic dispersion of production process, it provides a new perspective on how the global economy works and changes. Through extensive offshoring and outsourcing, the global economy has become increasingly a web of cross-national trade and inter-firm transactions, where MNEs play a key role in governing an international economic relationship (De Marchi *et al.* 2014; Gereffi and Fernandez-Stark 2011; Gereffi and Lee 2012; OECD 2013). In the following, the key concepts of the GVC approach are introduced and the key transformations in the global economy are discussed to highlight the need to view the global economy from a

GVC lens.

Global value chains: Key dimensions and a brief history

GVCs refer to "the full range of activities that firms and workers perform to bring a specific product or service from its conception to its end use and beyond" (Gereffi and Fernandez-Stark 2011). Each stage of the GVC – e.g., research and development (R&D), production, sales and marketing – adds a varying amount of value to the final product or service. The GVC approach pays a particular attention to the increasing phenomenon that production process is *organizationally* fragmented into a narrower range of tasks and *spatially* dispersed beyond a single country, or what Krugman called "slicing up the value chains"(Krugman 1995). The perspective understands the global economy as complex inter-firm networks linking a series of value-adding stages and the relationship between buyers and suppliers engaged in such value-adding activities (Gereffi 2005). The term "global" has two different meanings: the first is geographic, referring to the fact that value chains are now extended globally, not limited to a national, or regional boundary. The second is that, in order to better understand the dynamic of one segment of the chains, we need to look at the entire value chains and the interaction of different actors at the different nodes of the chains because each node is interdependent.

The expansion of GVCs in the global economy over the past few decades was driven by multiple factors, notably declining trade costs facilitated by rapid advances in telecommunications and logistics, and a series of liberalization and deregulation in international trade and investment. The expansion has also been enabled by corporate strategies to focus on core competencies while outsourcing non-core activities and extending supply chains abroad through offshore outsourcing in pursuit of efficiency, market access and new resources. Local suppliers' growing participation in foreign buyers' supply chains, has also contributed to the diffusion of GVCs (OECD 2013, 19-20).

A GVC consists of four key dimensions, as illustrated in Figure 1 (Gereffi and Fernandez-Stark 2011):

Input-output structure: the way key value-adding activities are linked with each other;

Geography: the distribution of locations where those activities are conducted;

Governance: the way the flow and allocation of financial, material, and human resources are coordinated among supply chain actors, including ownership structure and the decision to conduct certain activities in-house or outsource to a third-party supplier ('make-or-buy'); and

Institutions: institutional arrangements — local, regional, national, and international — that affect the operation of GVCs (e.g., government regulations; trade agreements).

GVCs are socially contested terrains, where multiple — private, public and social — actors interact with one another with distinctive goals and interests through competition and cooperation (Bair and Palpacuer 2015; Neilson and Pritchard 2009). The principal actors in GVCs are MNEs, particularly global buyers, and their suppliers (De Marchi *et al.* 2014). MNEs play a key role in shaping GVCs through cross-national trade and investment (UNCTAD 2013, 134-137). In many economies, exports are driven by a relatively small number of large, often multinational,

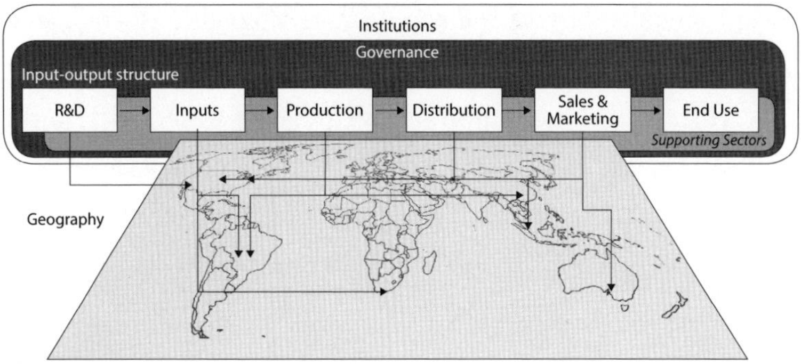

Figure 1. Illustration of key dimensions of global value chains
Source: Authors.

companies. The large firms are supplied by many smaller-sized firms as well as large transnational suppliers (OECD 2013, 21). A typical US MNE, for example, buys a total of more than $3 billion in inputs from over 6,000 small and medium-sized enterprises (SMEs), which does not include its purchase from foreign small and medium-sized enterprises SMEs (Slaughter 2013, 48).

The supplier-buyer transactions in GVCs are facilitated by a variety of supporting sectors, such as transportation and logistics, ICT, finance and other business service sectors, which also form their own supply chains (Coe 2014; Hesse and Rodrigue 2006; Newman 2009), highlighting the importance of services for the operation of supply chains (Low 2013). In addition, public institutional actors, such as governments at all levels, from local to international, affect the institutional conditions under which GVCs operate. Finally, civil society organizations (CSOs), including workers' organizations and NGOs, have raised their voices over how GVCs should be governed, particularly in social and environmental aspects, leading to a multi-stakeholder governance that includes public, private and social actors altogether (Gereffi *et al.* 2001a; Gereffi and Lee 2016; O'Rourke 2006).

Historically, the notion of GVCs can be traced back to the mid-1980s, and multiple concepts have since been developed to understand the increasing organizational fragmentation and geographic decentralization of production process in the global economy (see Bair 2005; Lee 2010 for a review). At the beginning, world-system scholars proposed in the mid-1980s the idea of 'commodity chains' to comprehend the expansion and contraction of world-capitalist system (Hopkins and Wallerstein 1986; Hopkins and Wallerstein 1994). A commodity chain were defined as "a network of labor and production processes whose end result is a finished commodity" (Hopkins and Wallerstein 1986, 159).[1]

Later, the commodity chain concept was appropriated by development scholars who were grappling with the emerging paradox that Third World countries were struggling in achieving economic development despite the rise of their industrial outputs (Gereffi and Korzeniewicz 1990; Martin 1990). With the concept of 'global commodity chains' (GCCs), the scholars began to explain the paradox; Third World countries failed to reap the benefit from industrialization because they mostly engaged in low value-added activities like simple assembly for exports, while core countries in the world economy, or Western industrialized economies, tended to engage in higher value-added nodes of the chains, like branding, marketing and R&D. They also argued that the core country sets the conditions for developing countries to enter the commodity chains and how value is distributed among participating firms and countries. Economic development through industrialization, thus, would be limited and unsustainable without upgrading to higher value-added parts in the hierarchy of value chains. In a sense, economic development was reformulated in terms of industrial upgrading. The upgrading dynamics were illustrated by a series of empirical research on apparel GCCs in the mid-1990s (Appelbaum and Gereffi 1994; Gereffi 1999).

New dynamics emerged in the early 2000s as different streams of research converged and diverged around the GCC concept. First, two groups of development scholars converged to propose the 'GVC' concept. Those who worked on industrial and agro-food clusters in the developing world were increasingly drawn to the GCC approach as they took notice of the effects of global buyers on the developing country suppliers. At the same time, GCC scholars found the term of "commodity," which generally refers to undifferentiated products, was too restrictive to be applied into a variety of sectors, from agriculture to manufacturing and services, and a wide range of differentiated products. Therefore, the scholars began to use the concept of 'value chain', focusing on the creation, capture and distribution of value across chain actors regardless of product types (Gereffi *et al.* 2001b; Humphrey and Schmitz 2001).

Second, economic geographers, who are interested in the spatial expansion of existing economic geographies as a result of globalization, began to formulate the concept of 'global production networks' (GPNs) (Coe and Yeung 2015; Dicken *et al.* 2001), defined as "the nexus of interconnected functions and operations through which goods and services are produced, distributed and consumed" (Henderson *et al.* 2002, 445). While GPN scholars acknowledge the importance of the growing fragmentation and dispersion of production process in understanding contemporary economic geography, two additional points were highlighted in the

GPN formulation: first, the 'production network' concept was introduced since a linear concept like 'chains' was no longer adequate to analyze a complicated 'network' of firms and actors. Secondly, unlike GVCs highlighting inter-firm governance (see below), the GPN approach pays more attention to institutions at different scales — global, regional, national and local, and how different institutions affect firms' locational and supply chain strategies.[2]

Despite the differences among GCC, GVC, GPN approaches and their emphasis, the entire literature encompassing the three concepts is common in that it pays attention to the fragmented, dispersed, and networked nature of the global economy, and emphasizes that contemporary industrial production cannot be understood without comprehending cross-national, intra- and inter-regional dynamics of networked production, and power and authority relations embedded in inter-firm production relations and institutional factors cutting across them.

Fragmented and dispersed production and trade of intermediate goods

The rise of GVCs is attributed to the fragmentation and decentralization of production that occurred over the past few decades (Arndt and Kierzkowski 2001; Milberg and Winkler 2013). Vertically integrated production, where a considerable part of the production process is conducted within a single firm or in-house, has increasingly given way to a variety of flexible modes of production (Piore and Sabel 1984). The decentralization takes place both organizationally and spatially, as illustrated in Figure 2.

Organizationally, a firm decentralizes its production by outsourcing 'non-core' activities to third-party suppliers while focus-

<table>
<tr><td colspan="2" rowspan="2"></td><td colspan="2">Organizational dimension</td></tr>
<tr><td>Direct (in-house) production</td><td>Outsourced production</td></tr>
<tr><td rowspan="2">Spatial dimension</td><td>Domestic production</td><td>In-house production</td><td>Outsourcing</td></tr>
<tr><td>Foreign production</td><td>Offshoring</td><td>Offshore outsourcing</td></tr>
</table>

Figure 2. Organizational and spatial dimension of production
Source: Adapted from WTO and IDE-JETRO (2011, 20).

ing on 'core' activities where it has a greater deal of core competence and competitive advantage. As a result, the production process is fragmented and sliced into multiple phases of value-adding activities, each of which is conducted by specialized firms (Arndt and Kierzkowski 2001; Krugman 1995). At the same time, production is geographically decentralized through offshoring as firms move some part of it to offshore locations through FDI in an effort to lower costs and access new resources or markets. The increase of offshoring extends the geography of the production process, where now different tasks are conducted across national borders. For example, raw materials from *Country A* are imported by *Country B* to produce a part or component, which is then exported to *Country C* to be assembled with other, domestic or imported, intermediate goods to become a final product consumed in *Country D*. This indicates that materials and intermediate goods often travel more than once across national borders to undergo multiple different stages of processing, resulting in the growth of intermediate goods trade in the global economy. Finally, offshore outsourcing combines organizational and geographic decentralization. Firms try to take advantage of both outsourcing and offshoring by farming out part of production to a third-party supplier located abroad. In this way, production goes through multiple different firms and countries, and it articulates different organizational and institutional modes of production and form a complex network of production, trade, and investment, leading to the emergence of GVCs.

One of the consequences of the rise of GVCs is, therefore, the growth of intermediate goods trade. International trade has increased at the level of intermediate goods and value-adding tasks ('trade in tasks') through coordinated transactions between suppliers and buyers in the form of offshoring and outsourcing (OECD 2013; Sturgeon and Gereffi 2009; WTO and IDE-JETRO 2011). The world economy is no longer characterized by the international trade of final goods, like producing and exporting wine in exchange of clothing. Many goods and services are produced through the participation of multiple different countries in different parts of GVCs, and international trade involves not only final goods but also a variety of intermediate goods.

This changing nature of international trade is exemplified by Apple's iPhone and iPod products (Kraemer *et al.* 2011; Linden *et al.* 2009; Xing and Detert 2010). While those high-tech gadgets are designed by and branded with Apple, headquartered in California, US, most of the parts and components for those products, nowadays several hundred or a thousand, are manufactured by third-party specialized part suppliers, big or small, and many of their factories are clustered in East Asia. Apple also outsources the assembly part of its chains to specialized contract manufacturers, called 'electronic manufacturing service' (EMS) providers, prominently Foxconn, a Taiwanese firm. The EMS firms take a responsibility for sourcing inputs and components and assembling them to the final product in accordance to the specifications provided by branded buyers like Apple. Most of Apple products are produced outside the US, mostly in China, to take advantage of lower production costs and a well-established supply base in Asia. Meanwhile, Apple focuses on higher value-added activities like R&D, product design, branding, and marketing as well as coordination of its GVCs. That allows Apple, one of the most profitable companies in the world, to claim the majority of the value created by their products. According to an estimate in 2010, Apple's profits from the iPhone accounted for 58% of the sales price of the iPhone 4 (Kraemer *et al.* 2011).

The emergence of GVCs like Apple's supply chains prompts us to rethink the relationship between international trade and value capture in the global economy (Gereffi and Lee 2012; OECD 2011). For the iPhone 4, when a traditional measure is used that assigns the gross export value of the product to the exporting country, China is charged the total factory gate price ($194.04) in its entirety for exporting one unit of the product. However, most of the value for the iPhone 4 is actually created in Korea ($80.05), US($24.6), Germany($16.1), and other developed countries that supply high-end components (Keller 2010). China only contributed $6.54 to the value of the product by assuming the assembly of the final product. Therefore, the biggest portion of the US trade deficit from its iPhone 4 imports is not with China, which only represents a small fraction of the total value of the product, but incurred via indirect exports from Korea and other component-supplying countries (Xing and Detert 2010). This example highlights the complexity of international trade and value capture at the level of firms and countries in GVCs.[3]

Lead firms, governance and upgrading: How firms matter in GVCs

One of the key insights in the GVC literature is that MNEs play an important role as lead firms in the integration and upgrading of developing countries and firms in GVCs, highlighting the relevance of firm-level analysis in understanding economic development in the contemporary global economy. According to an UNCTAD (2013, 135) estimate, nearly 80% of global trade is nowadays associated with the global value chains of MNEs. It includes *intra-firm* trade between the MNE's parent company and its affiliates or among the affiliates, or *inter-firm* trade between the MNE and its unrelated suppliers.

In many sectors, MNEs are the orchestrators of GVCs and international trade networks. They, as lead firms, govern the chains in a sense that their strategies and decisions play a key role in shaping the structure and dynamics of GVCs. Yet, the way they govern GVCs varies by sector and firm. Initially, two different forms of governance were identified: *producer-driven* and *buyer-driven* (Gereffi 1994). Producer-driven chains, mostly found in capital- and technology-intensive sectors, such as automobiles and aircraft manufacturing, are characterized by the key role played by large capital-intensive firms that control the production process almost entirely through direct ownership or production partnership. Buyer-driven chains, in contrast, are driven by lead firms as buyers (e.g., retailers, marketers, and brand manufacturers) that rely on external sourcing networks that consist of a wide range of independent suppliers for production while focusing on their competence in non-production activities, such as design, sales, and marketing. This form of governance is typical in labor-intensive, consumer goods industries, such as garments, footwear, or consumer electronics.

This dichotomous typology of GVC governance was later expanded by a more elaborated distinctions that include a variety of network forms of inter-firm governance (Humphrey and Schmitz 2001). Gereffi *et al.* (2005)'s typology is an exemplar. It specifies five distinctive forms of GVC governance. In addition to the widely known distinction of *market* (arms-length transactions) and *hierarchy* (vertical integration) (Williamson 1975; Williamson 1985), three intermediate forms of governance are additionally specified: *captive, relational,* and *modular*. These governance types are different in terms of the complexity and codifiability of inter-firm transactions, and suppliers' capability to meet buyers' requirements.

This typology illuminates that a firm's decision-making options regarding managing supply chains are not limited to a simple dichotomy of 'make' (in-house production) or 'buy' (vertical disintegration) but more diversified forms of GVC governance can be implemented. Furthermore, different governance forms have different implications to the level of entry barrier and the degree of market access on the supplier side as well as how much value is created and who captures the value at different nodes of the value chain, which has a consequence on the supplier's upgrading outcomes. Finally, the typology also highlights that suppliers are not all the same. They are varied in terms of their capabilities as well as their relationship with buyers depending on governance forms. Turn-key suppliers at modular governance are much capable of independently dealing with a variety of supply chain activities and demands from multiple different buyers at the same time, and the presence of such capable suppliers facilitates the decision of buyers to outsource more complicated tasks (Sturgeon and Lee 2005). In contrast, the captive supplier is highly dependent on the buyer's inputs and market channels. And, the increasing outsourcing throughout the GVCs has led to the rise of multi-tier supply chains, where suppliers with different capabilities are located at different layers of the hierarchy in the supply chain (Dicken 2011), and a different part of the chains may be characterized by a different form of chain governance (Ponte and Sturgeon 2014).

Meanwhile, economic upgrading is defined as "a process of improving the ability of a firm or an economy to move to a more profitable and/or technologically sophisticated capital- and skill-intensive economic niche" (Gereffi 1999, 51-52). One of the central arguments of the GVC approach is that the type of governance structure driven by lead firms significantly affects the outcome of upgrading. Depending on the 'niche' where upgrading takes place, upgrading takes a different form (Humphrey and Schmitz 2002): (1) *process upgrading*: making production processes more efficient by reorganizing the production system and using advanced technology; (2) *product upgrading*: moving into more sophisticated, or higher-value, product lines; (3) *functional upgrading*: occupying more profitable functional nodes within a chain; and (4) *chain upgrading*: diversifying into more profitable value chains.

A supplier's product and process upgrading are generally facilitated by learning from global buyers (Schmitz 2004), whereas global buyers do not necessarily support their suppliers to upgrade functionally out of concern that it might bring greater competition

(Bazan and Navas-Alemán 2004). In Brazil's Sinos Valley shoe cluster, for instance, tight coordination by foreign buyers created favorable conditions for local suppliers to achieve product and process upgrading. However, functional upgrading to higher-value activities like branding and design was constrained by a captive mode of governance between the two (Navas-Alemán 2011).

In sum, the contemporary global economy is characterized by the organizational and geographic decentralization of production, leading to the rise of GVCs. The decentralization takes place through offshoring, outsourcing, and both. As a result, the production of any good or service involves the participation of multiple different firms and countries that exchange raw materials, intermediate and final goods through a complex network at a different stage of production. MNEs play a key role in governing the GVC through trade, investment and sourcing. The way GVCs are governed varies, from market to hierarchy and different network modes of inter-firm coordination and control. Economic upgrading, or moving up to higher value-added activities, is significantly affected by how the chain is governed by lead firms.

Integration, Convergence and Divergence in GVCs: East Asia Context

GVCs have been playing an important role in industrial development in East Asia. Yet, their roles have been less paid attention to compared to two contrasting perspective on East Asian economic development, i.e., market-oriented and state-centered explanations. In the following, we briefly discuss the two perspectives and present a GVC approach on East Asian economic development. To advance the debate of convergence and divergence in East Asian capitalism in the era of economic globalization, we present frameworks to better understand a country's changing positions in a global value chain, which reflect new developments in the global economy, notably, the presence of multiple entry points to GVCs, the rise of developing economies as an end market, and the growth of intermediate trade.

Global and regional linkages in East Asian economic growth

In the post-war global economy, East Asia emerged as a late developer, following the trajectories of industrial development taken by advanced industrialized economies like the US and Western European nations. Export-driven economic growth and industrial upgrading to compete in advanced markets played a key role in the East Asian economic success. Yet, what brought the success to the region has been extensively debated (Chibber 2003; Cumings 1984; Evans 1995; Evans 1997; Johnson 1982; Lane 2008; Woo-Cumings 1999; World Bank 1993). A market-based explanation highlights the role of market incentives to drive local producers to compete in global markets with minimal intervention by the state, or at most market-minded, "careful policy interventions" by governments (World Bank 1993, 24). In contrast, a state-centered, institutional perspective emphasizes the critical role played by development-minded states and government bureaucracy that effectively used 'carrots and sticks' to prod local producers to advance their positions in global markets, often bending rules and 'getting the price wrong' (Chang 2006; Evans 1995; Woo-Cumings 1999).

These two different perspectives provide compelling yet contrasting explanations of the East Asia economic development, and their differences linger on in a more recent debate over the effect of economic globalization on the future of development in East Asia (see below). However, in order to fully understand the historical and contemporary developments of Asian economies, the role of GVCs has to be taken seriously as well (Feenstra and Hamilton 2006; Hamilton and Gereffi 2009; Lee *et al.* forthcoming).[4] From the early years of export-driven growth, East Asia was engaged in the production networks of large MNEs in advanced industrialized economies, and the GVC integration played a significant role in export growth by facilitating East Asian exporters to find the buyer who could link them to major consumer markets in North America and Western Europe. For instance, revisiting East Asian industrial development, Feenstra and Hamilton (2006) highlights the significant role played by the rise of large Western retail buyers in Korea's and Taiwan's export growth. The foreign buyers developed new forms of offshore manufacturing, organizationally supporting the emergence of "demand-responsive" suppliers in East Asia. These suppliers organized and developed their production system and capabilities to respond to the demand from the global buyers in a timely and effective manner.[5]

The importance of organizational linkages like GVCs also applies to the cross-national division of labor within East Asia. Sequential upgrading and organizational succession between East Asian firms within GVCs played a key part in the emergence of the so-called 'flying-geese' pattern of regional industrial development (Akamatsu 1962; Edgington and Hayter 2000). As the leader like Japan moved to a higher value-added node of the chains, the node vacated by the move was relegated to or occupied by the follower. Or, the follower's participation in the node of the chains put the pressure for the leader to upgrade to improve its position in value distribution. This pattern of 'catching-up' and 'upgrading' has not only linked East Asia to advanced markets in the global economy in North America and Western Europe, but also generated the intra-regional linkages and division of labor among East Asian countries and firms, or 'regional value chains,' as discussed further below.

An well-known exemplar is the evolution of textile and apparel value chains in Asia (Appelbaum and Gereffi 1994; Gereffi 1999). Historically, the sector worked as a key stepping stone for industrialization as many developing countries with a pool of unskilled workforce entered the labor-intensive, export-oriented parts of the chains. In East Asia, Japan led the post-war growth of textile and apparel exports. However, as the costs of domestic production began to rise in the 1960s and 1970s, lower value-added parts of the chains, such as cut-make-trim (CMT), were moved to then newly industrializing countries, such as Korea, Taiwan and Hong Kong through Japanese firms' FDI and offshore outsourcing. Instead, Japanese firms focused on high-end garment production as well as an intermediary role linking other East Asian producers to Western buyers. Later in the 1990s, a similar shift occurred in the face of rising production costs in Korea, Taiwan and Hong Kong as garment production shifted to late-late industrializing countries like China, Vietnam, Bangladesh and Cambodia. At the same time, the former attempted to move up the value chains into higher value-added nodes like textile production, and began to assume a mediating role just as Japanese firms had done in the previous decades. In the meanwhile, Japanese firms further shifted to more capital-intensive parts of the chains, such as manufacturing equipment for apparel and textile production.

This development indicates that GVCs play an important role in industrial development in East Asia. Firms and countries cooperate with each other by participating and playing a different or complementary role in GVCs. At the same time, they compete to occupy a more profitable position to in the chains capture higher value. As the speed of late developers' upgrading and catching-up accelerates as exemplified by China's compressed, multi-path development (Lee *et al.* 2016; Whittaker *et al.* 2010; see also Chapter 6), firms and countries within the region increasingly find themselves in direct competition with each other. This implies that an orderly sequential or "flying geese" pattern of industrial development may no longer valid, raising a new question of convergence and divergence in the path of industrial development, as discussed next.

Convergence and divergence in post-crisis East Asia[6]

Economic globalization over the last few decades has revived a long-standing debate on industrial development in the global economy (Guillen 2001; Held *et al.* 1999). An earlier debate centered on whether lowered cross-national barriers in trade and investment and the rise of neo-liberal economic norms and regulations would lead to a similar pattern of industrial development across countries. The convergence perspective held that nation-states would follow a common path, notably neo-liberal prescriptions like the Washington Consensus, as a "best practice" influenced by powerful nations and international organizations (Petras 2006). The divergence view, in contrast, highlighted the persisting influence of distinctive national institutions, contending that countries respond differently to globalization, generating divergent development paths across countries (Fourcade-Gourinchas and Babb 2002; Weiss 2005).

Despite these differences, both convergence and divergence perspectives have a common limitation in that they largely regard global and national economies as separate, paying little attention to the interaction and linkage between the two. The former views national economies as subject to a common set of challenges and choices presented by globalization regardless of the differences in their positions in global industries as well as domestic capabilities. The latter emphasizes the enduring impact of national institutional and organizational patterns on development paths, although globalization reshapes the manner in which local industries are linked to a global economy. Both approaches fail to pay sufficient attention to the changes in the world economic contexts in which industrial development occurs as a result of economic globalization and the global recession of 2008-2009 and how those changes have reshaped opportunities and constraints for industrial development.

A recent debate is, therefore, centered more on how increasingly fragmented and decentralized production affects development paths and outcomes (Cattaneo *et al.* 2010a; Neilson *et al.* 2014). The rise of the GVC has significantly transformed the context and manner of industrial development in a global economy (Gereffi *et al.* 2001b; UNCTAD 2013). Production activities, once contained in a single company or country, have become fragmented and sliced up into multiple value-adding stages located in different countries (Krugman 1995). Facilitated by the rise of offshoring and outsourcing, production tasks are conducted in different countries as intermediate goods travel across borders multiple times for further processing (Arndt and Kierzkowski 2001; Milberg and Winkler 2013). A series of geographically dispersed value-adding tasks is integrated and governed by MNEs through various governance mechanisms to regulate buyer-supplier relations (Gereffi *et al.* 2005; Humphrey and Schmitz 2001). Countries or firms specialize in specific value chain functions (for example, design, production, marketing, branding) although gains from each activity may not be equal, with some activities more value-added than others and having a more positive impact on economic growth and employment. The way global lead firms govern supply chains significantly affects where value is created, how it is distributed, and who capture it in the chain (Gereffi *et al.* 2005; Pietrobelli and Saliola 2008).

One of the key implications of this new form of production system is that industrial development can be pursued through multiple entry points. Industrial development involves less selection of a sector or end product or nurturing vertically integrated firms as a national champion, and the linkage to the global economy is not simply reduced to the degree of export-orientedness. Rather, industrial development is more associated with which segment of the GVCs to engage in and how much value to capture from it(Kaplinsky 2000; Lee 2010). Different GVC nodes provide countries and firms with distinctive opportunities and constraints for participation and value capture in the global economy. For example, while almost all of Apple's iPod and iPhone products are manufactured and exported in China, contract manufacturers and suppliers in China, whose roles are limited to assembly and production of low-end components, account for only a small fraction of the total value generated by the products. The majority of the value is captured by Apple for its R&D, marketing and branding and other high-end component suppliers in countries like Japan, Korea or Germany (Linden *et al.* 2009; Xing and Detert 2010).

Post-recession dynamics have complicated the debate on industrial development as GVCs underwent significant changes (Cattaneo *et al.* 2010a; Gereffi 2014). First, development prospects have diverged across countries as key segments in many GVCs became more concentrated to a handful of large emerging economies with robust supply bases and are now controlled by fewer global lead firms. While the geographic concentration created 'manufacturing hotspots' in countries like China, India and Brazil, where exports and jobs exploded, many other – both developing and developed – countries suffered from a series of deindustrialization and job losses (Lee and Gereffi 2013). Also, global lead firms now have greater power in shaping development paths as fewer MNEs control a larger share of the market through mergers, acquisitions and the exit of many rivals.[7] These lead firms are increasingly served by a smaller number of more capable mega-suppliers and transnational intermediaries, such as Foxconn in electronics and Li & Fung in apparel, through streamlined supply chains located in major emerging economies like China, Brazil and India (Gereffi 2014).

Second, the rise of developing economies as a new end market presents a new pathway for industrial development (Kaplinsky *et al.* 2011; Morris *et al.* 2011). The export-oriented industrialization (EOI) model was essentially based on advanced economies as final markets, implying that developing countries would be better off by producing for advanced industrial markets than for their home markets (Hamilton and Gereffi 2009). While advanced-economy markets remain important for developing country exporters, the rise of emerging economies as a new end market has become prominent as a result of a decade of urbanization, rising income and the growing middle class, particularly in countries with large domestic markets like Brazil, Russia, India and China (Nederveen Pieterse 2012). These countries have fared better than many advanced economies in the recent global recession, emerging as alternative end markets of many GVCs (Cattaneo *et al.* 2010a). The resulting growth of trade and value chain linkages among developing countries presents new opportunities for industrial development that may not be available in the trade with advanced economies (Kaplinsky *et al.* 2011). Lower entry barriers in many developing country markets can increase the opportunity for SMEs to participate in exports to those markets, which also provides more favorable conditions for upgrading into more value-added functions such as design and branding.

Some of these changes raise the question of whether they have made it more difficult for countries to achieve industrial development. Large mobile phone assembly factories, for instance, may generate a great number of new jobs but the value captured by those jobs is likely much limited and fragile nowadays given the uneven distribution of value in GVCs and frequent factory relocation and closure (Lee and Gereffi 2013). But, at the same time, the new developments demand researchers pay closer attention to new opportunities and constraints for industrial development and the way countries and firms respond. While it is not new for development to entail inequality and unevenness (McMichael 2012), what drives the processes constantly changes, with the rise of GVCs being the latest driving force. In this sense, the changes in the global economy highlight the need for a new framework to understand a country's industrial development path, particularly in conjunction with its position in and linkage to GVCs.

GVC integration, development path and trade patterns: Analytical frameworks

We propose an analytical framework to distinguish the development paths of countries in the mobile phone industry. As shown in Figure 3, the framework is based on two dimensions: value chain positioning and global market orientation. The four boxes in the figure represent primary niches for industrial development, although the actual development path is likely more complex.

The first dimension (the vertical axis in Figure 3) is a country's position in the value chain. There are multiple different nodes in the mobile phone value chain: pre-production (such as R&D), main production (parts and component manufacturing and final assembly) and post-production (sales, branding and so on). Each node requires different skills and capabilities, and the amount of value captured varies; it is generally higher in pre- and post-production than in main production (Mudambi 2008). The most important division in the value chain is between producing parts and components and/or conducting assembly as a supplier for branded producers, also known as original equipment manufacturing (OEM), and producing and selling final products with proprietary brands, or original brand manufacturing (OBM). A current mobile phone consists of hundreds of parts and components manufactured by as many different suppliers. While some of the suppliers are quite large and technology-intensive, a great number of suppliers are much smaller, with lesser-known brand names (if any),

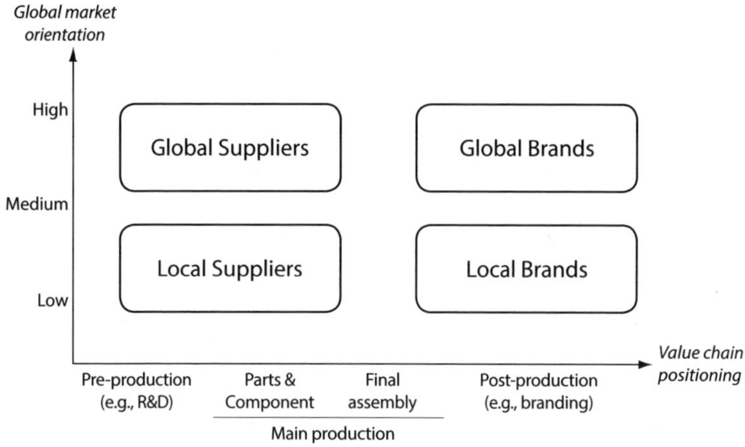

Figure 3. A framework of GVC integration and industrial development

Source: Authors.

compared to brand manufacturers such as Apple and Samsung that sell products with their own design and brands to the end consumer. Branded manufacturers tend to capture much more value than their suppliers (Ali-Yrkkö *et al.* 2011; Dedrick *et al.* 2011).

The second dimension in the framework is global market orientation, that is, the extent to which a country's firms are oriented toward competing in global markets relative to its domestic market. Engaging in foreign markets enables firms to take advantage of larger market demand and economies of scale, as well as providing opportunities for learning and upgrading (Baldwin and Gu 2004; Schmitz and Knorringa 2000). Nowadays, the notion of market orientation is less simple than is suggested by the distinction of EOI and import-substituting industrialization (ISI). Most notably, export markets are no longer unitary, as developing countries have emerged as alternative markets for developing country exporters. For many mobile phone firms, emerging markets have increasingly become an important growth engine thanks to the rapid expansion of mobile phone users in these markets (Grundberg and Gryta 2014). Furthermore, developing country markets have different dynamics than advanced economy markets, challenging the existing business models of MNEs mostly based in the latter (Sinkovics *et al.* 2014). For example, the presence of a large population of low-income consumers, or the so-called "bottom of the pyramid," has generated a strong demand for low-end, more affordable mobile phones with relatively basic functions. The supply of such phones, such as unbranded "Shanzhai" product from China, has fueled the explosion of mobile users in many developing countries in Asia and Africa.

The proposed framework thus highlights distinctive GVC niches in which a country can be positioned. It is not straightforward to identify and interpret a country's development path. There are likely more variations in actual development paths than the four primary niches. A country can occupy multiple niches simultaneously, with firms in the country located in different niches. However, the framework provides an analytical lens through which to understand the path of industrial development in a more sophisticated, yet concise manner compared to the dichotomy of EOI and ISI, as well as in the context of a global economy with fragmented production systems.

Building upon this GVC-minded framework of convergence and divergence, we further extend to generate a framework to allow comparing a much greater number of countries and their GVC roles with internationally comparable quantitative data, i.e., international trade statistics. Along with FDI, international trade is one of the major ways for countries to engage in the global economy,

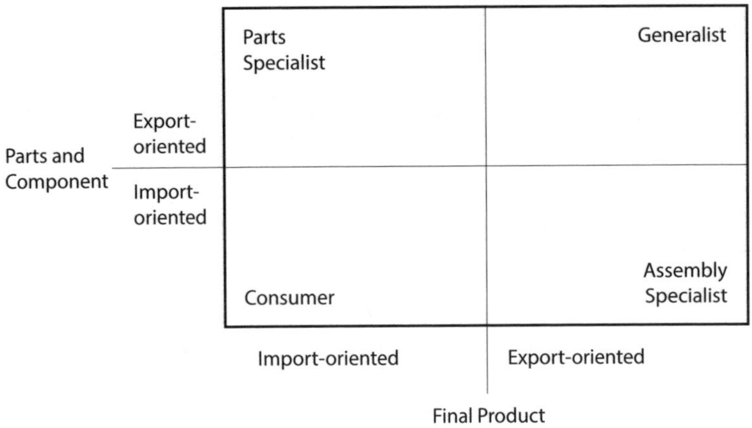

Figure 4. Trade patterns and roles in GVCs: A framework
Source: Authors.

and the rise of GVCs highlights that not only final goods but also increasingly raw materials and intermediate goods are traded internationally to be assembled together in another country (Sturgeon and Memedovic 2011; WTO and IDE-JETRO 2011). Thus, to understand a country's mode of integration in GVCs, it is critical to analyze the country's position and role in the trade network and their change.

An extended framework is illustrated in Figure 4 to linking the trade pattern of a country with the country's role in a GVC. The two most distinctive roles in the GVC are, first, producing and exporting intermediate goods such as parts and component that are used for final assembly; and, second, producing and exporting end products. By juxtaposing trade patterns in these two roles, the four distinctive role-positions are identified. First, when a country is strong in exporting both parts and the product, it can be considered as a *GENERALIST* (upper-right). Second, a country can excel in one of the activities, either exporting parts, or be a *PARTS SPECIALIST* (upper-left), or putting parts together into a final product, or be an *ASSEMBLY SPECIALIST* (lower-right). If a country is in a position to import both final products and the parts, it is likely to rely on imported phones at the same time importing parts necessary for repair and we call it a *CONSUMER* (lower-left). With this framework, we examine how countries are positioned in different parts of the GVC and which role they play, as presented in Chapter 5.

In short, the GVC approach provides a useful insight to understand the integration of East Asia into the global economy as well as the convergence and divergence of their development paths in the face of economic globalization. Countries and firms are embedded in the complex networks of trade, investment and supply chains within and across regions. The proposed frameworks highlight their roles in the intra- and inter-regional value chains and trade networks.

Regionalization and Regional Value Chains: Linking the Global and the Local

Regional integration has significantly risen in East Asia, mainly driven by a dense web of trade, investment, and production. The expansion of RVCs plays a key role in facilitating regionalization in East Asia. In the midst of geographic and organizational concentration in GVCs, East Asian RVCs have emerged as the center of global manufacturing in many industries. Regional countries and firms cooperate but also compete one another to advance their positions in regional, and global, value chains. The agglomeration of capable suppliers in Asia has prompted MNEs bring more production to the region. In the rise of RVCs, more MNEs have emerged from the region, increasingly from developing Asia, and they influence the dynamic of RVCs through trade and investment and establish their own supply chains, shaping the opportunities and constraints of countries and firms' economic and social upgrading. Not only Asian MNEs but also extra-regional, or non-Asian, firms play a significant role in shaping regional integration.

GVC concentration and regional value chains in East Asian Context

The expansion of regional value chains or production networks is considered as key evidence to the presence of a strong regionalization process in East Asia (Hamilton-Hart 2005; Tachiki 2005). As illuminated in this book, they play an important role in integrating East Asian economies as a key supplier of high-value manufacturing goods to the world economy (WTO and IDE-JETRO 2011). The sophisticated form of regional division of labor has been facilitated by the growth of FDI flows between East Asian countries, which complements rather than substituting trade flows (Lee and Lee 2012). The patterns of Japanese, Korea and Taiwan FDI to other Asian economies show that the level of FDIs corresponds to these countries' exports of intermediate goods to host countries (Baldwin and Toshihiro 2014; Thorbecke and Salike 2011). In this way, a regional flow of capital, goods, and technology and knowledge advances regional integration in East Asia, despite a slow progress in formally institutionalizing regional integration (Pempel 2005).

In recent years and particularly since the global economic crisis, production has significantly shifted to a few large emerging economies that offer a dense network of capable suppliers as well as a fast growing domestic market. These include China, India, and Brazil, but also new manufacturing centers like Vietnam. For instance, 64% of the world apparel export value was accounted for by China and five other leading exporters, including Bangladesh, Turkey, Italy, India, and Vietnam, in 2010 (Bernhardt 2013). In mobile phones, three East Asian economies, i.e., China, Korea and Hong Kong, exported 61% of the world total exports in 2011 (Lee and Gereffi 2013). Also, organizationally, the key nodes of GVCs in many industries are controlled by a handful of MNEs. Nowadays, just a handful of MNEs control the manufacture of many products in the global market, from large commercial aircraft and heavy-duty trucks to digital cameras and smartphones (Nolan 2012). The downstream segments of GVCs like marketing and sales are also consolidated to bigger and more powerful retailers and brand buyers (Hamilton *et al.* 2011; Humphrey 2007). Furthermore, lead firms are increasingly working with a fewer number of trans-national first-tier suppliers, notably Li & Fung (apparel), Yue Yuen (footwear), and, as shown in this book, large transnational EMS providers like Foxconn and Flex (formerly Flextronics), leading to the ensuing consolidation in the mid-stream of GVCs (Appelbaum 2008; Sturgeon and Lee 2005).

It is well known that historically East Asia played a key role in world manufacturing in a post-war economy, and it helped countries in the region achieve relatively faster economic development than those in other regions. The forerunners, such as Taiwan and Korea, were plugged into the mid-stream of GVCs with abundant low-cost workforce and successfully upgraded to higher value-added nodes of GVCs to diversify their exports and capture more value (Hamilton and Gereffi 2009). The latecomers, such as China and many Southeast Asian economies, have emulated such success with an export-oriented, GVC-based development strategy. The experience of integration and upgrading in GVCs on the regional scale is notable, as shown in the aforementioned case of textile and apparel.

As a result, the regional division of labor in East Asia have become more sophisticated, and production networks has evolved into a dense and matured form of RVCs, where countries and firms cooperate but also compete one another (WTO and IDE-JETRO 2011). As industrial capabilities become matured on the regional level, Asian RVCs are supported by strong supplier bases within the region. It increases the regional sourcing of raw materials and intermediate goods, facilitated by an increasing flow of FDIs within the region (Lee and Lee 2012).

This rising level of within-region specialization and the development of sophisticated intra-regional division of labor generates an agglomeration effect on the global level. The agglomeration of capable suppliers and manufacturers in East Asia further affects the decision-making of MNEs to bring more production to the region and move production *within* the region instead of relocating to other regions. Therefore, when the cost of production increased in the coastal region of mainland China with a shortage of workforce, many MNEs have decided to relocate production to inland provinces in China where they find a new pool of low-cost workers (Zhu and Pickles 2014). Others have shifted production locations to other parts of Asia, notably Southeast and South Asian countries like Vietnam, Indonesia and Bangladesh, and newly opening Myanmar (*The Economist* 2015).

While there is a growing discussion in recent years — especially under the Trump administration — about the possibility of 'back-shoring' of manufacturing activities, or bringing manufacturing jobs back to advanced economies where they used to be located (Bailey and De Propris 2014; Kinkel 2012), the advantage of regional agglomeration is likely to make many firms reluctant to move production out from Asia. It is now famous that when Steve Jobs, the late founder of Apple, Inc., was asked about a possibility of bringing manufacturing jobs back to the US, his response was negative mainly because even Apple would not be able to replicate well-established supply chains in East Asia back in the US (Duhigg and Bradsher 2012).

As the profile of East Asia rose as the center of manufacturing production, more MNEs have emerged from the region. It is related to a broader phenomenon that more MNEs come from emerging economies, which are called 'emerging market MNEs' (EMNEs) (Bonaglia *et al.* 2007; Giuliani *et al.* 2014; Ramamurti and Singh 2009). Although many largest MNEs still come from advanced economies like the US, Japan, France and Germany, the number of EMNEs in *Fortune Global 500* increased from 21 to 131 companies in 2000-2014, shown in Table 1. Not surprisingly, many Chinese firms joined this group of global elite companies over the last decade or so; 95 companies headquartered in China in 2014, compared to 10 in 2000 (Carroll *et al.* 2014). Three East Asian countries, China, Japan and Korea are also the major sources of MNEs, 169 companies on the list.

The growing prominence of EMNEs is also driven by the

Table 1. Headquarters location of Fortune Global 500 companies, 2000 and 2014

Location	2000		2014		% Change
	Number	Share(%)	Number	Share(%)	
US	179	36	128	26	-10.2
China	10	2	95	19	17.0
Japan	107	21	57	11	-10.0
France	37	7	31	6	-1.2
Germany	37	7	28	6	-1.8
UK	38	8	28	6	-2.0
Korea	12	2	17	3	1.0
Switzerland	11	2	13	3	0.4
Netherlands	10	2	12	2	0.4
Canada	12	2	10	2	-0.4
Other	47	9	81	16	6.8
Advanced economies	479	96	368	74	-22.2
Emerging economies	21	4	131	26	22.2

Source: Carroll *et al.* (2014).

rising importance of domestic markets in emerging economies. A decade of economic expansion fueled by rising exports and the growth of urban middle class spurred the fast growth of domestic markets in the global South. As a result, a traditional division of labor between advanced industrializing nations and developing countries that characterized the post-war global economy has changed. Nowadays, more and more products from developing countries are produced and exported to be exported to other developing countries, leading to the rise of South-to-South flows in international trade. As a result, more GVCs are heading for the South as the end market (Kaplinsky and Farooki 2010; Morris *et al.* 2011). In 1995-2012, the share of South-South trade in world trade more than doubled, from 12 to 26% while North-North trade declined from 51% to 34% (Horner 2016), despite the recent slowdown of the Southern shift and sectoral variations in the pace of the shift (Lee 2016).

The emergence of the global South is reshaping the relationship between developing countries. On the one hand, they are competing for a better position in GVCs to capture more value from GVC integration. The countries try to attract foreign investment and invite MNEs' supply chains to boost exports and employment. For example, Mexico was in intense competition with China and other emerging countries to play a bigger role in many manufacturing GVCs (Gereffi 2009). At the same time, countries and regions become specialized in a cross-national, cross-regional production networks. For example, as more manufacturing goods are manufactured in Asia, other regions like Central and Latin America and Africa, not only being an end market for the goods imported from Asia, also play a role in supplying raw materials and intermediate goods to Asia (Kaplinsky *et al.* 2011). In this way, inter-regional trade flows reflect not only competition but also a new form of specialization and cooperation between regions, as shown in our analysis of inter-regional trade networks in the mobile phone GVC in Chapter 5.

Firms as region-making actors and the role of external actors in RVCs

MNEs affect the structure and dynamic of regional value chains through their decisions on trade, investment and sourcing and supply chains, thereby shaping the opportunities and constraints of countries and firms' economic and social upgrading (Gereffi and Lee 2012; Yamin and Sinkovics 2009). Through their decision for offshoring, outsourcing and FDI (see Figure 3 above), they can play a role as a facilitator of regional connection and interaction. For instance, MNEs' 'make-or-buy' decision determines the boundary of the organization and which value chain activities are vertically integrated and conducted in-house or outsourced to third-party suppliers (Williamson 1985). Such a decision affects the types of tasks avaiable to external supplier firms as well as jobs available to workers in those firms. What tasks to be outsourced is contingent on a plethora of factors, including the complexity and codifiability of transactions as well as how capable the supplier is (Gereffi *et al.* 2005). Yet, what is 'supposed to be outsourced' is not always 'actually outsourced' (OECD 2013), indicating the importance of the buyer's strategic decision-making and socio-economic and institutional settings such decision is embedded in. In addition, the level of supply chain consolidation can affect the structure and dynamic of regional value chains. Consolidation in many GVC segments can lead to the rise of large and capable suppliers, limiting the opportunity for smaller suppliers with limited capabilities to participate and upgrade in the value chains, as shown in the post-crisis GVCs (Appelbaum 2008; Cattaneo *et al.* 2010b; Lee and Gereffi 2013).

Also, MNEs' location decision influences regional value chains. It involves the location of their investment, such as setting up a new factory or acquiring an existing facility, as well as where they source key inputs and intermediate goods from. The decision is also affected by a variety of endowment elements as well as other factors, such as exchange rates, transportation costs, trade agreements, and government incentives (Taplin 2014). Countries and firms can mostly rely on far-shoring by investing in or sourcing from far distant locations, e.g., East Asia for US firms, or near-shoring from neighboring countries or within the same region, e.g., East Asia for Japanese firms or East Europe for Western European firms. Historically, US firms played a significant role in creating a regional value chain in East Asia by establishing their subsidiaries and contracting out to local suppliers (Borrus *et al.* 2000), indicating the role of extra-regional actors in regional value chains (see below). Since the mid-1980s, Japanese firms actively invested in Asia in the face of rising Japanese yen against US dollars and production costs at home, forming another sets of supply chains, which were later emulated by Korean and Taiwanese firms in the 1990s (Ernst 2000).

At the same time, extra-regional, or non-Asian, actors and processes and their interactions with regional ones can also play a significant role in shaping regional integration although the regional integration literature mainly focuses on *intra-regional* processes and actors. Regional integration often tends to be considered as the outcome of interactions among national actors and institutions within East Asia, or a process whereby national actors extend their influence into the region. The region is portrayed as self-contained, with little linkage to the rest of the world and outside actors. However, regional integration can be porous, and fused by global processes (Katzenstein 2006, 31). For instance, East Asian production networks have been the creation of American and European firms as much as that of Japanese, Korean or Taiwan firms (Borrus *et al.* 2000). Since the 1960s, Western firms used East Asia as an export platform for their own markets, and a sophisticated division of labor emerged intra- and inter-regionally as East Asian firms moved up the value chain (Feenstra and Hamilton 2006; Gereffi 1996).

It highlights the role of external actors, particularly foreign buyers, and their relationships with regional and local partners in advancing regional integration. Therefore, we need to put RVCs in a larger context they are embedded in, i.e., global value chains by analyzing how the global, the regional, and the local are intertwined in the creation and change of RVCs.

Notes

1. The concept of commodity chains was not particularly singular or original. A similar concept emerged almost around the same period to in agri-food research as an industrial organization approach (Friedland 1994) or filière approach (Raikes *et al.* 2000).

2. At the same time, some scholars have chosen to maintain the commodity chain concept, arguing that uneven power relations among countries and firms were not adequately stressed in the GVC concept (Bair 2009).

3. The Apple case is revisited in detail at Chapter 7 in the context of its role in Asian regional value chains.

4. This part is drawn from Lee *et al.* (forthcoming), which revisits the role of GVCs in Korea's industrial development, focusing on three sectors: apparel, automobile and animation.

5. This also highlights the role of extra-regional actors in shaping supplier bases and value chain in East Asia. See below in this chapter and Chapter 7 for more discussion on this topic.

6. This and the following sections are drawn from the theory section of Lee *et al.* (2016) and expanded in the next section. The empirical findings and discussion of the paper are presented in Chapter 6 of this book.

7. For example, in smartphones, Apple and Samsung accounted for nearly half of global sales and nearly all of the industry's operating profits (Dediu 2012). Two smartphone operating systems (OS), Google's Android and Apple's iOS, accounted for over 90% of the mobile phones sold in 2013 (Gartner 2014b).

Section II

Mobile Transformation: Global and Regional Landscape

Chapter 4

Mobile Telecom Global Value Chains: Key Actors, Trends and Dynamics

Introduction

Mobile telecom provides telephone and data services in mobility. It is one of the fast growing subsectors in the telecom industry, increasingly substituting fixed service. Over the last few decades, the mobile telecom industry transformed from a nationally monopoly system providing a simple voice service to a vibrant global industry serving over seven billion subscribers and sophisticated multimedia and Internet service.

At the same time, the geography of production and consumption in the industry has dramatically changed. Developing countries play an increasing role in the industry both as a producer and as a consumer. Until the early 1990s, mobile telecom was a privilege of developed nations and most of the users were clustered in the US, Europe and the affluent part of Asia. But now the majority of mobile phones are produced in China, India and other emerging economies and mobile subscribers in least developed countries are growing faster than in any part of the world.

In this chapter, we outline the major trends in the mobile telecom industry and key actors and governance structure in the mobile telecom GVCs. The chapter also examines the different paths or modes of GVC integration and upgrading at regional and country levels.

Mapping the Mobile Telecom GVC

The mobile telecom GVC is complex, consisting of multiple sub-chains, which are put together to offer the consumer various mobile telecom services.[1] Figure 1 provides an overall structure of the mobile telecom chain, which generally entails five key domains: 1) hardware manufacturing, 2) software development, 3) sales and marketing, 4) mobile service and use, 5) after-use. Each domain has its own key actors, as discussed.

Hardware manufacturing: Two essential kinds of equipment need to be in place to make mobile telecommunication possible: mobile phones and mobile network equipment. Any mobile call and data transfer involves communication between the mobile phone and the mobile network (mobile-to-mobile) and between the mobile network and the public telephone network (mobile-to-land). Mobile phone manufacturers and mobile equipment manufacturers are the key actors in this upstream stage of the mobile telecom GVC, and they rely on a wide range of specialized parts and component suppliers. As discussed below, as a result of growing outsourcing of production, contract manufacturers (CMs) have emerged as specialized suppliers of mobile phones for branded producers, facilitating the fragmentation of the value chains.

Software development: Mobile phone software used to be preinstalled prior to the sale of the phone, but as phones get a higher

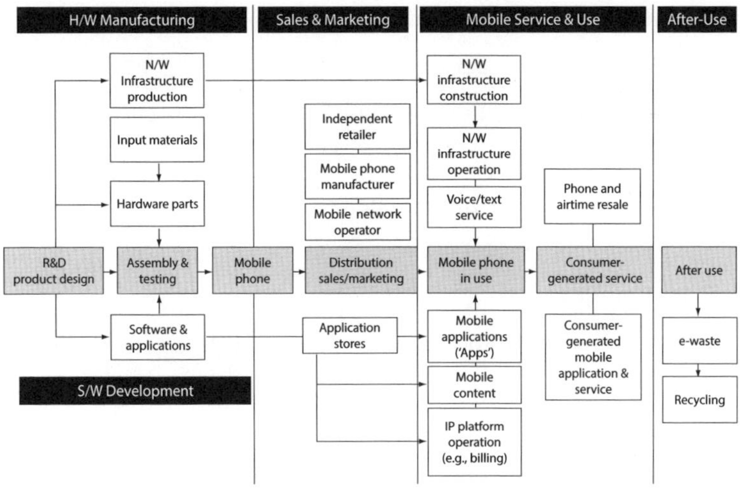

Figure 1. Mobile telecom value chains

Source: Authors.

capacity of processing and storage with the example of smartphones, a growing number of mobile software and applications (or "apps") are now sold independently and can be downloaded from app stores and installed when needed. This emergence of third-party mobile software and apps has given rise to specialized new actors: software/application developers and distributors.

Sales and marketing: Once produced, mobile handsets and network equipment are sold to the end user. Network equipment is generally sold directly to mobile network operators (MNOs) that provide mobile telecom service to the consumer. Meanwhile, mobile phones are generally sold to the consumer via three sales channels: MNOs, branded manufacturers and independent retailers. MNOs (e.g., SK Telecom, China Mobile and Verizon Mobile) source mobile phones from manufacturers and usually sell it to the consumer as a package to their calling plan or service contract (often involved a discount for the phone). Branded manufacturers (e.g., Samsung Electronics, Apple and Huawei) can sell phones through their own retail channels. In this case, the customer has to separately subscribe to a calling plan or purchase a SIM card from a MNO to make the phone operational. Finally, there are general and specialized independent retailers (e.g., Wal-Mart, Carphone Warehouse), which also include small street vendors populated in many developing countries (Datamonitor 2009).

Mobile service provision: Mobile network operators offer mobile telecom service to the end user by operating mobile network and utilizing the radio frequency assigned by governments (mostly through auctions). As mobile service evolved to high-speed mobile Internet, the content plays an bigger role in mobile business than in the past, and this gives rise to content providers that specialize in the production and distribution of mobile Internet content (Funk 2009).

Mobile use: One of the most prominent phenomena in mobile telecom in recent years is the increasing role played by individual consumers in the chain. They are no longer simply a buyer and user of mobile service. They are the active reviewer of mobile gadgets and influence the design and production of the products. Further, they develop their own applications or content either to be sold online or distributed freely as open sources. Meanwhile, in many developing countries where telecom service, fixed and mobile, is still scarce, people use their mobile devices to provide telecom service by selling airtime (e.g., village mobile phones). This provides the poor who cannot afford to buy their own cellphones with a key tool to access the Internet in place of fixed networks, usually underdeveloped in many developing countries (Donner

2008; Zainudeen 2006).

After-use: Mobile phones and other equipment are discarded when they become obsolete. As with other high-tech gadgets, mobile phones contain many hazardous materials that should be properly handled to minimize impacts on the environment. As consumers replace or upgrade their phones frequently, often in less than two years, the disposal and recycling of used phones and components has become a serious environmental issue at home as well as abroad as electronic waste ("e-waste") is flowed from developed countries into developing countries, where regulations are often less strict (Laha 2014).

In short, the mobile telecom value chain entails multiple activities encompassing production and consumption. It combines hardware manufacturing and software development. As advanced and sophisticated mobile service has become a key to market competition, innovation in service becomes as significant as in hardware. While an integrative nature as such is not totally unique to mobile telecom and observed also in other IT sectors (e.g., personal computers, video games) (Hess and Coe 2006), the resulting complexity poses significant challenges to any attempt to analyzing the mobile telecom industry in its entirety.

Key Actors in the Mobile Telecom GVC

In the mobile telecom GVC, equipment manufacturers — both mobile phones and network equipment — generally control much of the value chain from R&D through sales and distribution of devices or equipment, while MNOs play a key role in providing

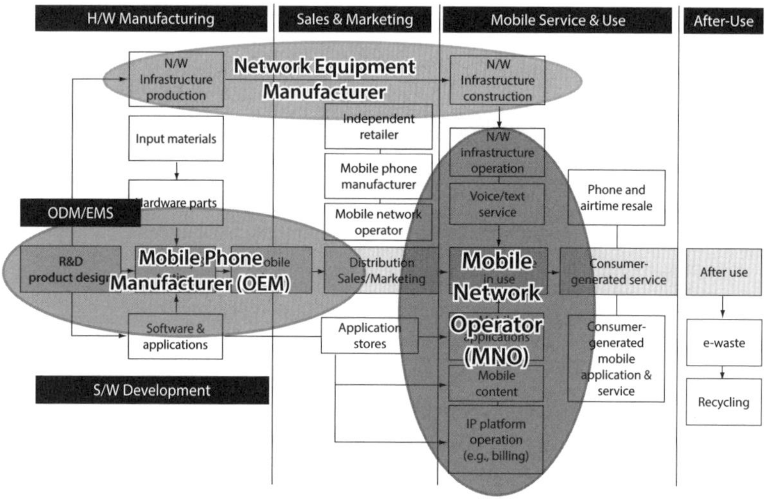

Figure 2. Key actors in mobile telecom value chains

Source: Authors.

mobile telecom service to the end user. In both domains, markets are significantly consolidated as a result of the rise of large branded manufacturers as well as the internationalization of MNOs. At the same time, increased vertical specialization, "slicing up the value chains" (Timmer *et al.* 2014), has led to the emergence of new value chain actors, such as contract manufacturers (CMs) in mobile phone manufacturing. They are located in specialized niches within the domains previously occupied by original equipment manufacturers (OEMs) or MNOs. Figure 2 illustrates these key chain actors in the mobile telecom value chain.

Mobile phone manufacturers

The mobile phone manufacturer produces its own branded mobile phone. Usually it designs a product and sources raw material and components from various specialized suppliers. Then it assembles them and installs necessary software before getting a final product ready for sale. While much of the phones are sold directly to MNOs, their main buyers, depending on markets it operates its own retail channels and provides its own after-sale services, such as repairing.

While a significant number of mobile phones are still produced in-house by branded manufacturers and carry the manufacturer's brand, more and more mobile phones are made by third-party contract manufacturers like Foxconn and Flex. Also, there is a considerable variation among branded manufacturers in the degree of in-house production. While Samsung produces all phone in-house, other brands use extensively CMs, notably Apple, whose iPhones are produced by EMS providers like Foxconn and Pegatron (Wilde and de Hann 2006, 19-20). Even when branded producers both 'make' and 'buy', mobile phone manufacturers tend to farm out the design and production of low-end and mid-range phones while retaining production lines for high-end products.

Over the last decade or so, the competitive landscape of mobile phone manufacturing changed dramatically (see Table 1). In 2005, Nokia, Motorola, Samsung, LG and Sony Ericsson accounted for more than 70% of the world mobile phone sale. In 2014, only Samsung and LG managed to stay on the top 5 leaderboard, and the other disappeared from it by being acquired (e.g., Nokia and Motorola) or due to disappointing sales performance. At the same time, Apple has emerged as one of the leading producers thanks to the phenomenal success of its smartphone sales, and many Chinese firms, such as Lenovo, Huawei, TCL, Xiaomi, and ZTE, have joined the leaderboard mainly thanks to their strong performance in the local Chinese market, the largest and fast grow-

Table 1. Mobile phone world market share by brands

(a) Mobile phone: 2005, 2010, 2014

2005	%	2010	%	2014	%
Nokia	32.5	Nokia	28.9	Samsung	20.9
Motorola	17.7	Samsung	17.6	Apple	10.2
Samsung	12.7	LG	7.1	Microsoft*	9.9
LG	6.7	Research In Motion	3.0	Lenovo**	4.5
Sony Ericsson***	6.3	Apple	2.9	LG	4.0
Siemens	3.5	Sony Ericsson	2.6	Huawei	3.8
Sagem	2.0	Motorola	2.4	TCL	3.4
Panasonic	1.4	ZTE	1.8	Xiaomi	3.0
BenQ	1.4	HTC	1.5	ZTE	2.9
Sanyo	1.3	Huawei	1.5	Micromax	2.0
Others	14.5	Others	30.6	Others	33.5

(b) Smartphone: 2015-2017

2015	%	2016	%	2017	%
Samsung	22.5	Samsung	20.5	Samsung	20.9
Apple	15.9	Apple	14.4	Apple	14.0
Huawei	7.3	Huawei	8.9	Huawei	9.8
Lenovo	5.1	Oppo	5.7	Oppo	7.3
Xiaomi	4.6	Vivo	4.8	Vivo	6.5
Others	44.6	Others	44.6	Others	41.5

Notes: * acquired Nokia in 2014, ** acquired Motorola Mobility in 2014, *** Sony's joint-venture with Ericsson.

Sources: Gartner (2006, 2011, 2015, 2016c, 2017, 2018).

ing one in the world. Finally, new mobile phone makers are rising in other emerging economies like India over the last few years as they combine localized brands with imported phones or semi-knocked-down kits from Chinese OEMs (see Chapter 7). Micromax (India) has become the one of the ten largest mobile phone brands in 2014 in terms of world market sales.

Contract manufacturers

The rise of CMs in electronics is well documented (Sturgeon 2002). In the mobile phone chain, there are two different types of CMs. One is 'electronics manufacturing service' (EMS) providers and the other 'original design manufacturers' (ODMs). The former manufacture the mobile phones designed by branded manufacturers. They are generally responsible for sourcing components, assembly, and logistics with design and branding functions left to buyers. Hon Hai (Foxconn) and Flex are the examples. In contrast, ODMs design and manufacture phones for the buyers (including MNOs). Since they produce own-designed phones unlike EMS providers, they can own the intellectual property rights (IPRs) of the design. Arima, Compal, Quanta, and Lite-On, mostly from Taiwan, are the examples (Wilde and de Hann 2006, 24-25).[2]

As more OEMs are considering an outsourcing option to reduce costs, the role of CMs in mobile phone production has become important. Table 2 shows the status of contract manufacturing in the mobile phone sector. Most of the major mobile phone brands outsource their production to contract manufacturers, mostly Taiwanese, US and Chinese firms. Only a few companies, such as Samsung, HTC and TCL, do not rely on the third-party manufacturers.

While contract manufacturers are on the rise, they are no less free from cost-cutting pressures and market competition. They tend to operate with a slim margin (9-10% for ODM; 3-5% for EMS) (Wilde and de Hann 2006, 24). The CM market is also concentrated as a few large EMS providers dominate the market. In 2010, the top five companies – Foxconn, Flextronics (now Flex), Jabil Circuit, Celestica and Sanmina-SCI – represented 75% of the

Table 2. Contracting manufacturing in mobile phone

Mobile phone brands		Share of In-house manufacturing(%)	Major contract manufacturers
Korea	Samsung	100.0	-
	LGE	99.2	Arima (Taiwan)
Japan	Sony Mobile	69.9	Foxconn, Arima (Taiwan above)
Taiwan	HTC	100.0	-
China	Lenovo	69.8	Compal, Winstron (Taiwan above)
	Huawei	0.0	Foxconn, Flextronics (US above), BYD (China)
	ZTE	59.2	Foxconn, Flextronics
	Xiaomi	0.0	Foxconn, Invectec (Taiwan above)
	TCL	100.0	-
Non-Asia	Apple	0.0	Foxconn, Pegatron (Taiwan above)
	Nokia*	96.9	Foxconn, Compal, BYD (China)
	Motorola**	52.4	Foxconn, Arima, Compal
	BlackBerry	17.2	Flextronics, Jabil (US above)

Notes: * Nokia: acquired by Microsoft, ** Motorola: acquired by Lenovo.
Source: Fuji Kimera Research Institute.

global EMS market (NIPA 2011). The economy of scale and the concentration of buyers, i.e., OEMs, are putting pressure on CMs, to upgrade in various ways, potentially to market their own branded phones.

Parts and component suppliers

Mobile phones require as many as several hundreds of different parts and components. Semiconductor, digital signal controller, RAM/ROM/flash memory and RF controllers are produced by multinational electronics companies, such as Intel, IBM, Texas Instruments, Samsung, and Toshiba. Advanced phones require new kinds of components, such as a high-pixel camera module, a big LCD/OLED panel and a longer-hour battery. Some components

Table 3. Tear-down analysis of Apple's iPhone 6 Plus

Components	Estimated costs (US$)	Share of total BOM costs (%)
Display & touchscreen	52.50	24
Wireless section - BB/RF/PA	33.00	15
User iiterface & sensors	22.00	10
Application processor	20.00	9
NAND Flash + DRAM	15.00	7
Camera(s)	12.50	6
Power management	7.00	3
Battery	4.60	2
Bluetooth/Wireless LAN	4.50	2
Others	40.00	18
Manufacturing cost	4.50	2
Total BOM cost	215.60	100

Source: Rassweiler (2014).

are quite high-tech and requiring substantial investment in R&D to develop and produce, while others, more commodified ones, are less so and supplied by a number of firms, usually SMEs. As shown in the case of iPods and other teardown analyses (Dedrick *et al.* 2010), about a dozen of key components account for the vast majority of the costs, while a large number of low-end components represent only a small fraction of the production cost (Wilde and de Hann 2006). For example, nine most expensive components account for 79% of the total bill of material (BOM) costs of Apple's iPhone 6 Plus, as shown in Table 3.

Software and application developers

As voice-based mobile phones evolve to smartphones with advanced functions, the importance of OSs and software is increasing. This has led to the rising prominence of software developers,

Table 4. Worldwide smartphone sales to end users by operating system

Operating system	2016 1Q units ('000)	2016 1Q market share (%)	2014 units ('000)	2014 market share (%)
Android	293,771	84.1	1,004,675	80.7
iOS	51,630	14.8	191,426	15.4
Windows	2,400	0.7	35,133	2.8
BlackBerry	660	0.2	7,911	0.6
Others	791	0.2	5,745	0.5
Total	349,251	100.0	1,244,890	100

Sources: Gartner (2015; 2016a).

such as Apple, Google, and other IT firms, in mobile telecom value chains. For example, mobile OS is the operating system to controls a mobile device and various applications installed, just as what Windows does for personal computers.

Google's Android remains leading in the mobile OS market with an 84% share in the first quarter of 2016, strengthening its leading position further compared to 2014. It is trailed by Apple's iOS (14.8%). Meanwhile, Microsoft has still been in difficulty translating its success in the PC market to the mobile market, accounting for just 0.7% of the market sales in 1Q 2016, a significant drop from 2.8% of the share in 2014.

High-capacity smart devices, broadband infrastructure, and sophisticated software all facilitate a wider range of mobile Internet service offering. And, they provide a growing opportunity for independent specialized mobile app developers and content providers from both developed and developing economies.

Mobile network operators

The liberalization and privatization of mobile service worldwide and the explosion of mobile subscriptions in developing

Table 5. Top 15 mobile network operators worldwide in total subscribers

Rank	Company	Headquarters	Total subscribers (in millions)	
1	China Mobile	China	835.4	May-16
2	Vodafone	UK	464.6	Jun-16
3	Airtel	India	357.4	Mar-16
4	China Unicom	China	286.6	Dec-15
5	América Móvil	Mexico	284.0	Mar-16
6	Axiata	Malaysia	275.0	Dec-15
7	Telefónica	Spain	246.9	Mar-16
8	MTN Group	South Africa	229.3	Mar-16
9	VimpelCom	Netherlands	214.9	Mar-15
10	Telenor	Norway	208.4	Mar-16
11	China Telecom	China	205.5	May-16
12	Orange	France	191.1	Mar-16
13	Idea Cellular	India	175.1	Mar-16
14	Etisalat	United Arab Emirates	167.0	Dec-15
15	STC	Saudi Arabia	161.0	Dec-13

Source: List of mobile network operators, Wikipedia (http://en.wikipedia.org/wiki/List_of_mobile_network_operators) [Accessed July 26, 2016].

countries changed the competitive landscape of mobile service in recent decades. Table 5 presents the top 15 MNOs worldwide in terms of total subscribers.

This leading group consists of firms from each of two origins. One is Europe-based MNOs with significant footprints in developing countries as a result of their active investment overseas. These include Vodafone, Telefonica, Orange, and Telenor and TeliaSonera. The other, expanding, group is developing country MNOs. China Mobile, the largest mobile operator with 835 million subscribers (mostly in mainland China), China Unicom, India's Airtel, Mexico's America Movil, and South Africa's MTN are all ranked at the top ten list. They are now trailed by operators from Africa, the

Middle East and Russia, which have their own large national and regional market.

The rise of cross-national MNOs with multi-million subscribers across markets has increased their buying power vis-à-vis mobile phone manufacturers. For example, Vodafone has a central purchasing system of mobile phones that its affiliated local operators can use, although they can opt out for other suppliers. Furthermore, MNOs increasingly offer their own brand phones, which are designed and manufactured by ODMs. This is similar to store brand or private label products by retailers, although the degree to which much MNOs are involved in the design process varies by operator and product (Wilde and de Hann 2006, 61). This governance issue between OEMs and MNOs are discussed in detail below.

Network equipment manufacturers

Telecom network equipment vendors generally develop, manufacture, and install various network equipment mostly for MNOs, which are their main buyer. Their products include core network equipment (e.g., routers, nodes, mobile switching centers, servers, storage), radio access equipment (e.g., base stations, base transceiver stations, base station controllers), and other infrastructure (e.g., cell tower and cell site) (Sabat 2002).

After a bust of the IT bubble in the early 2000s, the equipment vendor market underwent a painful restructuring in the face of MNOs' slowed investment in migration to mobile broadband and resulting shrunken demand. A long-time incumbent such as Canada's Nortel went disbanded, while others merged compete.

One noticeable development over the last decade was the

Table 6. Key value chain actors and corporate examples in mobile telecom

Key value chain actor	Value chain activity	Major corporate player
Branded mobile phone manufacturer (a.k.a. OEM)	Developing, manufacturing, and distributing mobile phones for own brand	Samsung, Apple, Huawei, LG, Lenovo
Original design manufacturer (ODM)	Developing and manufacturing mobile phones for OEM brands	Arima, Quanta, Lite-On, Compal
Electronic manufacturing service (EMS)	Manufacturing mobile phones for OEM brands	Flextronics, Foxconn, Jabil, Elcoteq
Component suppliers	Developing, manufacturing, and supplying components for mobile phone assembly	Texas Instrument, Intel, Qualcomm, ARM, Samsung
Software/application developer	Developing and distributing mobile OS and applications	Apple, Microsoft, Google, Adobe
Mobile network equipment manufacturer	Developing, manufacturing, and distributing mobile network equipments for MNOs	Ericsson, Nokia Siemens Network, Huawei, ZTE
Mobile network operator (MNO)	Offering mobile telecom service using its own mobile network	China Mobile, Vodafone, Telefonica, America Movil, Orange
Content provider (CP)	Offering the content to mobile device	YouTube, Facebook, Twitter, Amazon

Source: Authors.

rapid surge of Chinese equipment vendors. Huawei and ZTE are now among the world's leading makers of telecom network equipment. Equipped with quick learning, cheap labor and cost-effective products, they now secure orders from leading MNOs, such as Vodafone and Telefonica, not only from expanding developing country buyers as well as their home market MNOs.

In short, Table 6 summarizes the key actors in mobile telecom value chain and their key activities as well as the examples of major corporate players for each category.

Key Trends and Dynamics in the Mobile Telecom GVC

Mobile phone production, export, and consumption

The global mobile phone market accounted for US$163 billion in 2013 (Figure 3). In terms of unit sales, 1.4 billion units of mobile phones were sold globally in 2013, 34% higher than 2009. While the market continued to grow, growth is much slower compared to 2010 when the market bounced back from the global economic recession.

The world's exports of mobile phones grew considerably over the decade. Exports almost tripled in 2001-2006, from $64 billion to $183 billion. Trade figures in the paper were compiled from UN Comtrade (http://comtrade.un.org/), unless stated otherwise. While the economic crisis of 2007-2008 reversed the expansion, world exports have recovered since 2010, reaching $165 billion in

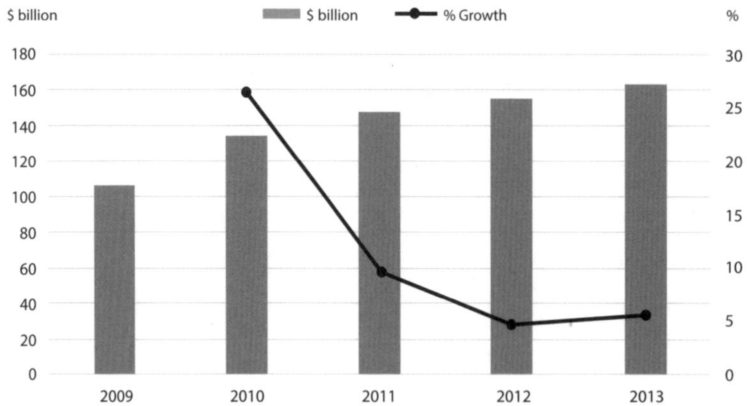

Figure 3. Global mobile phones market by value, 2009-2013
Source: MarketLine (2014).

2012. Overall, the growth was attributed to rising demand across the world and the geographic shift of production. Until the 1990s, mobile phones were mostly made and consumed in advanced industrial countries. However, the ensuring shift of production to developing economies and further geographic concentration has increased international trade substantially since most mobile phones are produced in a few emerging economies and exported worldwide.

At the same time, global mobile phone exports are highly concentrated geographically. Exports are concentrated to 'manufacturing hotspots', a handful of leading export countries and regions where value chain activities are highly clusters. Almost three-quarters of world exports come from five largest exporting nations and 90% from only a dozen countries.

Shown in Table 7, in 2001 mobile phone exports were mainly driven by developed economies such as Germany, the United Kingdom, the US and Finland. In 2013, they were dominated by emerging economies like China, Korea, and Vietnam. A small number of countries now represent the majority of the world's exports, leading to a significant geographic consolidation. China represents more than a half of the world's exports. Together with Korea and Vietnam, the three East Asian countries account for 76% of the world's exports in 2013, indicating a high regional concentration of mobile phone production and exports.

Mobile subscribers rapidly increased over the last decades. In 1990, there were only 11 million mobile subscribers in the world. In 2013, the world had 6.6 billion subscribers. China accounted for 18.5% of the world total with 1.2 billion subscriptions. India is the second largest mobile market in terms of subscription with 886

Table 7. The top exporting countries of mobile phones (unit: %)

2001		2005		2010		2013	
Germany	13.0	China	16.4	China	45.5	China	59.9
UK	12.8	Korea	13.5	Korea	11.0	Vietnam	8.9
Korea	11.7	UK	12.2	Mexico	7.0	Korea	7.2
Finland	7.5	Germany	10.5	Hungary	6.9	Netherlands	3.7
US	7.4	Finland	6.0	Taiwan	5.3	Taiwan	3.2
China	7.1	Singapore	4.8	US	2.5	Mexico	2.3
Mexico	5.4	Hungary	4.0	Finland	2.1	US	2.0
France	5.1	US	3.5	Netherlands	2.0	Germany	1.0
Malaysia	3.7	France	3.1	India	1.9	India	1.0
Sweden	3.6	Sweden	2.9	UK	1.7	Hungary	0.9
ROW	22.7	ROW	23.1	ROW	14.2	ROW	10.0

Notes: For 2001 and 2005, HS codes 8525.20 and exporter-reporting data are used; for 2010 and 2013, HS codes 8517.12 and importer-reporting data are used.
ROW: the rest of the world.
Source: UN Comtrade (Accessed on March 3, 2016).

Table 8. The world's top 10 countries in mobile subscriptions, 2013

Country	Mobile cellular subscribers (million)	% World
China	1,229.1	18.5
India	886.3	13.4
US	305.7	4.6
Indonesia	303.7	4.6
Brazil	271.1	4.1
Russia	218.3	3.3
Japan	146.5	2.2
Pakistan	127.7	1.9
Nigeria	127.2	1.9
Vietnam	120.0	1.8
World	6,627.4	-

Source: World Bank WDI (Accessed on March 10, 2016).

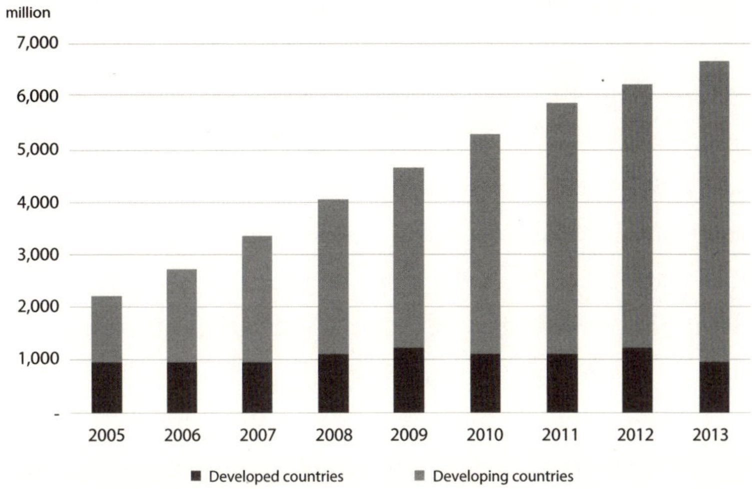

Figure 4. Mobile phone subscriptions in developing and developed countries, 2005-2013

Source: ITU WTI Database.

million subscribers, followed by the US, Indonesia and Brazil (see Table 8).

The growth of mobile subscriptions has been striking in developing countries over the last decade or so. The proportion of developing countries grew from about 30% of the world total in 2000 to nearly 78% in 2013 (Figure 4). Now they represent a bigger market for the global mobile service sector in terms of subscriptions.

Geographic and organizational concentration of mobile phone production

Nowadays global mobile phone exports are highly concentrated geographically. As shown above, almost three-quarters of world exports come from the five largest exporting nations and 90% from only a dozen countries. Four-country concentration ratio (CR4) and eight-country concentration ratio (CR8) rose from

45% to 70% and from 70% to 83% in 2001-2012, respectively. In the meanwhile, most of the other countries experienced declining exports or short-lived booms. Exports drastically declined in many former centers of mobile phone production, such as Germany, Finland and Sweden. Some emerging economies like Mexico, Hungary and Malaysia failed to keep their export momentum by the end of the 2000s. Others like India and Romania marked a rapid growth during the last few years, despite a recent sign that they might be the latest victims of concentration trends.

The geographic concentration in mobile phone GVCs can be attributed to multiple factors. First, it was accelerated by the consolidation of lead firms. A smaller number of lead firms made greater influence on the geographic distribution of production. By 2006, the total share of the world's five leading producers of mobile phones increased to over 80% of market sales. This market consolidation forced many branded firms out of business, including Siemens (Germany), Alcatel and Sagem (France) and Phillips (Netherlands), and some of their assets were sold to Asian firms, accelerating the shift of production to Asia (O'Brien 2005). Second, market survivors concentrated their production into a handful of emerging countries. Nokia moved its German factory to Romania in 2008, and eventually its production to China in 2011 (Thorpe 2011). Samsung Electronics established oversea factories in China, Vietnam, India and Brazil since 1998, but nearly 80% of its mobile phones are now produced in three factories in China and Vietnam (Kim 2012). Finally, production sharing by CMs also facilitated the concentration of mobile phone production locations. To meet the scale and speed of production required by consolidated buyers (Sturgeon and Lee 2005), multinational mega-suppliers like

Table 9. Top 5 firms' market share in the key segments of mobile phone GVC (unit: %)

Smartphone sales (2015)*		Smartphone OS (4Q2015)*		EMS service (2010)**	
Samsung	23	Android (Google)	81	Foxconn	44
Apple	16	iOS (Apple)	18	Flextronics	15
Huawei	7	Microsoft OS	1	Jabil Circuit	8
Lenovo	5	Blackberry OS	0.2	Celestica	4
Xiaomi	5	Other OS	0.2	Sanmina-SCI	4
Top 2 total	39	Top 2 total	99	Top 2 total	59

Sources: * Gartner (2016b), ** NIPA (2011).

Foxconn have combined production orders from different global brands, channeled into a few strategically located production sites. For instance, Foxconn International Holdings (FIH), the mobile phone subsidiary of Foxconn, operates just five Chinese cities and three other cities each in India, Brazil and Hungary to serve many different global brands like Apple and Nokia (FIH Mobile 2014).

At the same time, the mobile phone GVC is increasingly driven by a fewer lead firms and key intermediaries. Table 9 shows that the majority of global markets in the key segments of the chain are dominated by a handful of firms. In fact, two leading firms control a big portion of each market while their competitors fall behind by a wide margin, indicating the rise of oligopolistic market structures in the GVC. This concentration among branded manufacturers is related to severe consolidation in the smartphone operating system (OS), a core software program for advanced mobile devices. Google's Android and Apple's iOS together represented over 90% of the mobile phones sold in the 4Q of 2015 (Gartner 2014b), undermining the ground for other OSs. This indicates a mutually reinforcing pattern of market power between device and OS platform segments.

Co-evolution of value chain actors

Another important development is the co-evolution of OEMs and EMS in terms of supply chain consolidation. In 2000-2010, the market share of the five leading EMS providers rose from 53% to 75%, and just two leading EMS firms, Foxconn and Flextronics, commanded 59% of the entire EMS market in 2010 (NIPA 2011). As the OEM segment became more concentrated, EMS firms, to remain competitive, needed to match the scale and speed of production required by big OEM buyers, and they sought economies of scale by acquiring other EMS firms and exiting OEMs (Sturgeon and Kawakami 2011). The rise of more capable suppliers, along with an increasing level of standardization and commodification in mobile technology, has facilitated OEM buyers to contract out manufacturing of more sophisticated product lines to consolidated EMS firms. In this way, the consolidation in the OEM segment facilitated consolidation its key upstream node. The rise of Foxconn as the leading EMS provider is emblematic. Since its adoption of an EMS model in 2001, the sales of FIH, its mobile phone manufacturing unit, surged from $7.6 million to $10.7 billion in 2007. The growth of Foxconn relied on a few big buyers like Apple. In 2008, 91% of FIH's sales came from three largest buyers with Apple believed to be one of them.[3]

As a result, fewer and fewer of global lead firms and key intermediaries now dictate the geographies of production and exports. A country's export performance is significantly associated with the production locations of lead firms and their key suppliers. China, Mexico, Hungary and Brazil are where Nokia, Samsung and other lead firms expanded significantly from the mid-1990s, and India, Vietnam and Romania, which hosted their new factories, experienced significant export growth more recently.[4] In 2009, 82% of Nokia's total output came from China and India, while Finland contributed just 3% of its output (FCRI 2009). Similarly, China and Vietnam accounted for 80% of Samsung's total production capacity of mobile phones, while Korea represented only 9% of the total output (Kim 2012).

The effect of organizational concentration on geographic concentration amplified as a result of the co-location of component suppliers and their buyers (Lee and Gereffi 2013). As OEMs or EMS firms moved their factories abroad, their key component suppliers tended to come along. For example, Finnish component suppliers moved to China and later India to follow Nokia, often locating in the same special export zones (SEZs). Many Korean suppliers also moved to China and Vietnam along with their key buyers, Samsung and LG.[5]

While those suppliers are independently owned and the co-location decision is their own, at least in principle, multiple factors can make such a decision compelling, if not inevitable, to the suppliers. First, the demand for shorter lead times from design to market and tighter buyer–supplier coordination increases the incentive for both buyers and suppliers to get closer to each other. The CEO of a Finland-based supplier explained why he followed Nokia to China: "We are here because our customers are here. It is necessary for us to be logistically closer to them. The pace of production is so intense that it is not possible to ship components from the other side of the world" (Helsingin Sanomat 2005). Apple reportedly requires key component suppliers to keep two weeks of inventory within a mile from its assembly plants in Asia (Satariano and Burrows 2011). Second, co-location is also prompted by the hollowing-out of production in the home country. For example, Samsung's continuing expansion overseas has generated great concerns among Korean suppliers about the potential loss of orders and jobs (*Chosun Ilbo* 2012). Thus, co-locating in Samsung's new factories abroad, despite the burden of investment, could be a better option than staying at home, especially considering Samsung's robust position in global markets. Finally, the agglomeration of capable suppliers as a result of co-location creates positive externalities, increasing the incentive for other OEMs or EMS firms to move along and take advantage of clustered supplier bases.

Despite the concentration in both OEM and EMS segments, there is a great deal of disparity in mobile phone GVCs in terms of how much value can be captured in each chain segment. Value capture tends to strongly favor OEMs and high-end component suppliers, with much smaller value captured by contract manufacturers and low-end component suppliers (Kraemer *et al.* 2011). Such disparity of value capture has implications for value distribution between regions and countries. Apple's iPhone is an exemplar. While the product is manufactured and assembled primarily in China, China captures much less value than advanced economies like Japan, Korea and the US where multinational high-end component suppliers are headquartered (Xing and Detert 2010). Similarly, in the case of Nokia's N95 model assembled in China, Asia's share (mostly for manufacturing) is just 16% of the total value (Ali-Yrkkö *et al.* 2011).

Integration to and Economic Upgrading in the Mobile Phone GVC

The stages of economic upgrading and required functional capabilities in mobile phone production are illustrated in Table 10. While conventional distinctions in manufacturing are generally applicable, the increasing complexity and globalization of mobile phone production demands a more elaborated distinction to identify the positions where countries and firms are placed within the chain. The presence of sizeable local component production distinguishes domestic VC-driven assemblers from GVC-driven assemblers. ODMs are distinctive from these assemblers in that they

Table 10. Economic upgrading stages and functional capabilities in mobile phone production

Upgrading stages	Functional capability		
	Product design	Component supply	Assembly
Non-entry	None	None	None
Component supplier	None	Imported + local supply	None
GVC-driven assembler	None	Mostly imported (+ locally supplied low-tech parts)	Local assembly
Domestic VC-driven assembler	None	Mostly local supply (+ imported key parts)	Local assembly
ODM	Locally designed for OEM or MNO	Local supply (+ imported parts)	Local assembly; or offshoring
EMS	Designed by OEM	Global supply	Global assembly
Low-end OEM	Locally designed for own brands	Local supply (+ imported parts)	Local assembly; or offshoring
OEM	Locally and globally designed	Locally supplied key parts (+ imported low-tech parts)	Assembled locally or regionally; or outsourced to EMS
IT-based OEM	Globally designed	Globally outsourced (to EMS)	Globally outsourced (to EMS)

Source: Authors.

are involved in product design for OEMs and MNOs. Meanwhile, EMS providers can have their ODM unit to accommodate the buyer's need for product design (Wilde and de Hann 2006).

Some ODMs have attempted to design and sell their own brand products while maintaining their ODM contracts for global buyers. It would require substantial investment in sales, branding and marketing to compete with a much bigger global OEMs, but as observed in many Taiwanese IT contract manufacturers, the strategy of playing a dual role – ODM and OEM – can generate a synergy of learning from global buyers and making their own (Lee and Chen 2000).

However, not everyone has been successful. In 2005, a Taiwanese ODM, BenQ, boldly acquired the then ailing mobile phone unit of Siemens to become the sixth largest mobile phone maker with a new brand, BenQ-Siemens. But, the experiment was short-lived. The new mobile unit, BenQ Mobile, filed for bankruptcy in 2006 when its parent, BenQ, had discontinued its funding. It is reported that BenQ Mobile had had conflict with its major OEM client, Motorola, after launching its own brand, although it is unclear whether it played any role in the fate of the company (Wilde and de Hann 2006, 22-23).[6] And the difficulty HTC later confronted in the global smartphone market as a branded manufacturer was another example (Troianovski 2012).

Countries' changing positions in the mobile phone GVC

To examine countries' positions in the mobile phone GVCs based on the framework on trade patterns and GVC roles as presented in Chapter 3 (Figure 4), we analyzed the trade performance of 25 major trading countries that were listed to the top ten largest exporting or importing countries at least for one year between 2007 and 2013 in mobile phones or parts.[7] In 2013, they accounted for 92% of the world's exports, and 80% of the imports in mobile phones, and 93% and 91% of the world's mobile phone parts exports and imports, respectively.

For the sake of brevity, trade positions are presented only for two years, 2008 and 2013, in Figure 5 (2008 in triangle and 2013 in square). The horizontal and vertical axes represent trade balance (in US$ billion) respectively in mobile phones and parts. As a country is located in the upper right corner, it is positioned as GENERALIST, marking a trade surplus both in the end product and parts. Those in the lower left corner are generally considered as CONSUMER that rely on imports for both items. The upper right and lower left corners are occupied by SPECIALISTS but in different value chain positions: parts production and assembly.

As shown in Figure 5, most of the countries are populated in the crowded center (zoomed in Figure 6), indicating the relatively small size of their trade balances compared to those of four economies, China [CN], Korea [KR], the United States [US], and Hong Kong [HK], whose positions are discernable. China is clearly located in the generalist position, and its position strengthened in 2008-2013 as their trade surplus increased in both final goods and components. Korea also moved within the generalist territory. The country suffered but managed to keep the balance in the black in mobile phone exports, and its trade surplus in components significantly improved. In contrast, both the US and Hong Kong are located in the consumer position. For the US, it was mainly due to a rising deficit in the final good; for Hong Kong, it was attributed

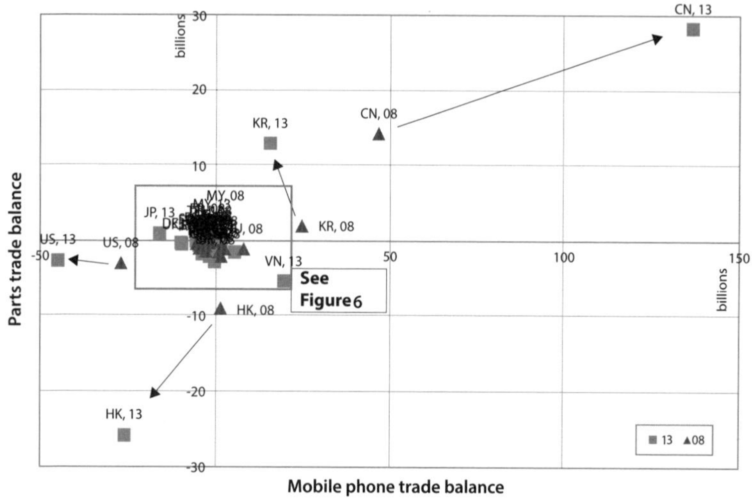

Figure 5. Mobile phones and parts trade positions, 2008 and 2013

Source: Compiled from UN Comtrade.

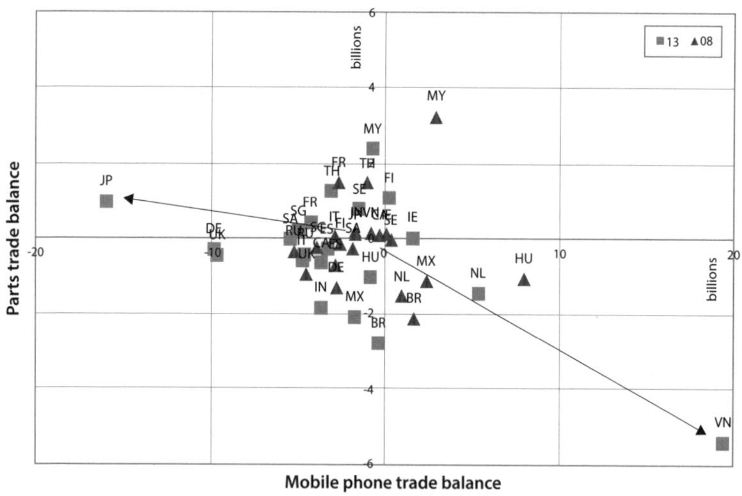

Figure 6. Mobile phones and parts trade positions (part), 2008 and 2013

Source: Compiled from UN Comtrade.

to trade deficits in both the final good and components, mainly in its trade with mainland China (see below).

In Figure 6, the crowded center area was zoomed to trace the positional change of the other countries. The scale of the change is much smaller, given a relatively small amount of their trade surplus or deficit compared to those of the four big traders. Overall, the left side is more crowded than the right side, suggesting many are mostly the importers of mobile phones. But as for component trade, they are distributed relatively evenly between the surplus and the deficit area while the size of surplus or deficit is much smaller compared to mobile phone trade (note the difference in the scale of the axes). Yet, two Asian countries are notable here; Japan [JP] improved trade surplus in components while its deficit in the mobile phone increased significantly, as the country imported more mobile phones, mainly from China (see Chapter 5). Meanwhile, Vietnam [VN] moved in a different direction. Its mobile phone exports increased considerably with its expanding trade surplus, but the country also imported more parts, moving deeper into the specialist domain in final assembly.

A further examination, with additional data point of 2011, illuminates several distinctive patterns of positional changes. In Figure 7, each panel highlights some of the movements.

Generalist position: China and Korea are the two notable examples. The two countries clearly strengthened their surplus positions in both parts and final product trade [see (a) of Figure 7].

Assembly Specialist position: Vietnam is the most prominent and the only case. The country rapidly expanded its surplus in mobile phone trade with a considerable increase in component imports, indicating the country's mobile phone exports are largely based on imported parts, or a GVC-driven assembler role in Table 10 [see (a) of Figure 7].

Paths out from Assembly Specialist position: some countries that used be in the assembly specialist position experienced the recent decline of their mobile phone exports. Hungary [HU] and Mexico [MX] are the prominent examples. A trade deficit in components was reduced in both countries in 2011-2013, but that was accompanied by a much greater decline of a trade surplus in mobile phones. In fact, the two countries' trade balance went into the red in both mobile phones and components in 2013, putting them now into the consumer territory [see (b) of Figure 7].[8]

Parts Specialist position: countries like Malaysia [MY] and Thailand [TH] are not particularly strong in mobile phone trade but maintain a surplus in components trade. Sweden [SE] and Singapore [SG] also moved into the territory of parts specialist while their deficit extended in the trade of final products [see (b) of

(a) China, Korea and Vietnam

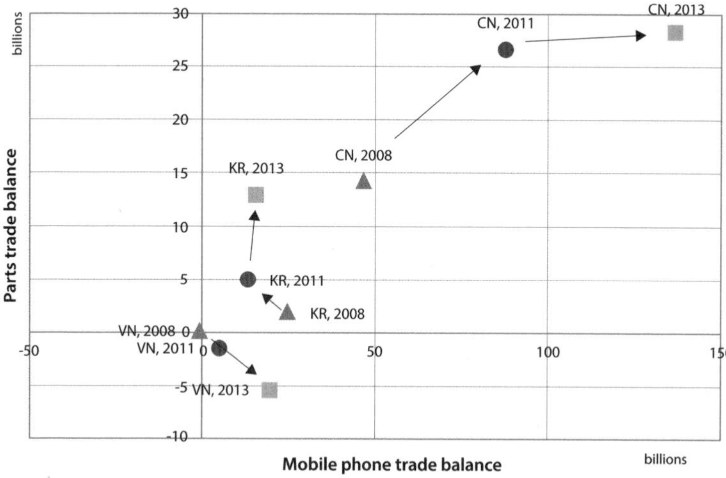

(b) Finland, Hungary, Malaysia, Mexico, Singapore, Sweden and Thailand

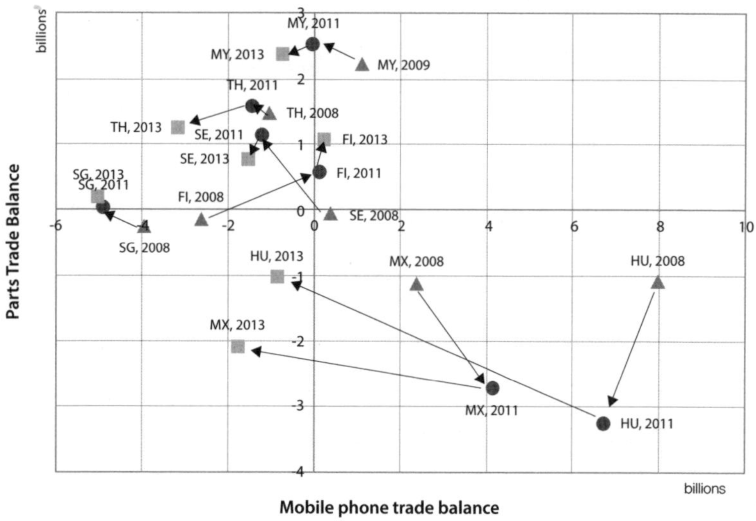

(c) Canada, Germany and United Kingdom

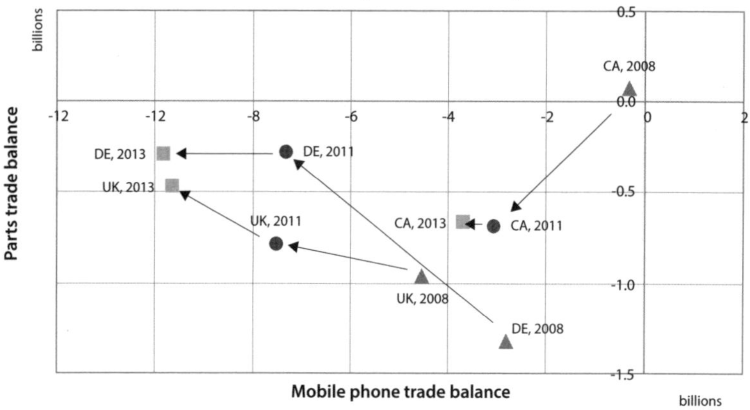

Figure 7. Trade position changes of major trading countries (parts), 2008, 2011, 2013

Notes: scales are different in the charts. Malaysia's trade balance in 2009 instead of 2008 was used because the data was unavailable.
Source: compiled from UN Comtrade.

Figure 7]. Japan also increased its surplus in components, but the growth of its deficit in mobile phone was much greater than any other countries in this category (see Figure 6).

Consumer position: many advanced industrial countries formerly known as the major exporters of mobile phones are now in this category as firms in the countries suffer in global markets or outsource their production to overseas. The United States is one of them, as shown above. The others include Germany [DE], Canada [CA] and UK [see (c) of Figure 7]. Hong Kong is also in this category, but it moved in the different direction because its deficit in parts declined much drastically (see Figure 5).

Conclusion

This chapter has examined the structure of the mobile telecom GVCs and the key trends and dynamics in the chains since the global economic crisis of 2007-2008. It has also identified the distinctive paths or modes of integration to and upgrading in the GVCs at the country level.

To sum, the entire process of delivering a mobile telecom service to the consumer requires multiple steps across several subchains in the mobile telecom GVC. In the mobile phone GVC, the OEM with brands generally controls much of the value chain from R&D through sales and distribution, while MNOs play a key role in offering mobile service to the end user. Simultaneously, growing vertical specialization through outsourcing results in the rise of a new value chain actors, such as contract manufacturers specializing in most of the mid-stream of the value chain.

The growth of mobile phone production and trade decelerated over the last few years as many emerging economies experienced economic slowdown. Some of the developments since the global economic crisis significantly changed the dynamics of the mobile phone GVCs. Mobile phone production has considerably concentrated geographically and organizationally. Geographically, it has been clustered in East Asia, which provides robust regional value chains and supplier bases. Organizationally, the global mobile phone market has witnessed a few large OEMs like Samsung and Apple to consolidate their positions in the market while many others suffered from competition. At the same time, the rise of consolidated OEMs has also led to the fast growth of contract manufacturers like Foxconn, which provide manufacturing service to multiple different brands. Many CMs are based on East Asia, further facilitating the concentration of production to the region.

While growing vertical specialization opens up multiple entry points for GVC participation, not every segment of the value chain is equal in terms of how much value can be captured. This makes upgrading critical for countries and firms to advance their position in value capture. In particular, moving up to OBMs is highly sought after, but it turns out to be challenging given required resources and capabilities as well as tightened competition among global prominent brands.[9]

Our analysis using international trade data shows the dynamic change of countries' position in the mobile phone GVC. The major trading countries are positioned in different segments and their positions changed over the last several years in different directions. China and Korea consolidated their generalist position, so did Vietnam as an assembly specialist. In contrast, Mexico and Hungary moved to the consumer position. A few countries have entered the parts specialist area, while others moved to the consumer domain. Vietnam's rise as the world's second largest mobile phone exporters was accompanied by the country's growing imports of parts and components, deepening its trajectory for the assembly specialist based on imported intermediate goods (see Chapter 5). This is a similar path took by Mexico in 2008-2011, but declining mobile phone exports later pushed the country out to the consumer position. Such a transition was shared by another major production hub, Hungary, as the country experienced a shift of production away from Europe. In addition, our analysis shows that some of Asian countries like Japan, Malaysia, and Singapore moved to the parts specialist position as more assembly production migrated from these countries to China and Vietnam, implying a different impact of production migration on a country's GVC position.

Notes

1. Because of the complexity, some suggest that it cannot be fully analyzed with a "chain" concept, alternatively proposing a "network" concept (Basole 2009; Funk 2009; Hess and Coe 2006).

2. Some CMs play a dual role in the chain. For example, Flex generates significant revenues from its own mobile phone ODM unit (Wilde and de Hann 2006, 55). Another example is HTC. It was originally established as a smartphone ODM but later sold products with its own branded smartphones (Einhorn 2010).

3. Based on FIH's annual reports in 2005 and 2007 through 2009.

4. While it is possible that the choice of production locations by lead firms is based on the export performance of a given country, the examples of Vietnam and India suggest otherwise. The two countries had virtually no meaningful exports in mobile phones before lead firms made initial investments, which boosted these countries' exports. Vietnam's exports surged to $10 billion (6.1% of the world's total exports) in 2012 from $0.3 billion in 2009, when Samsung started its first mobile phone production in Vietnam.

5. Out of 60 part suppliers for Samsung's Bac Ninh mobile phone factory, 55 of

them are Korean-owned businesses, which are housed in the same high-tech park as Samsung (Tuoi Tre News 2013).

6. In fact, a potential conflict with their OEM buyers is cited in GVC literature as one of the challenges that suppliers faces when trying to upgrade to OBM (Humphrey and Schmitz 2002).

7. The countries include: Brazil, Canada, China, Finland, France, Germany, Hong Kong, Hungary, India, Ireland, Italy, Japan, Malaysia, Mexico, Netherlands, Korea, Russia, Saudi Arabia, Singapore, Spain, Sweden, Thailand, UK, US, and Vietnam. Taiwan is not included in this part of analysis because Taiwan's trade data are not available.

8. See Chapter 5 for Vietnam's trade with other Asian mobile phone parts exporters.

9. In this sense it is notable that Chinese and Indian mobile phone brands made significant inroads into each of their domestic markets in the last few years. See Chapter 7 for more on the latest development.

Chapter 5

East Asia in Mobile Phone Trade Networks: Inter- and Intra-regional Linkages

Introduction

The rise of GVCs, a fragmented, cross-national production system, illuminates the increasing interconnection and interdependence in the global economy (Dicken 2011; Gereffi 2005). Countries and firms are increasingly engaged in the global economy by assuming a specialized role at a specific production stage in a GVC. Many developing countries are also pursuing export and employment growth by promoting GVC participation as a new mode of industrial upgrading, with an anticipation that an initial entry to a GVCs as a simply assembly specialist can be leveraged for further upgrading to higher value-added activities, such as full-packaged production and own brand manufacturing (OECD *et al.* 2014; WTO and IDE-JETRO 2011).

In this decentralized production system with a sophisticated international division of labor, the roles played by countries and firms can be diversified as they position themselves in different parts of the chain even in the same GVC. Countries may be similar in term of export intensity, but their positions in the GVC can be different as one focuses on exporting end products at the downstream of the chain while others specialize in intermediate goods such as parts and components at its mid-stream. This chapter analyzes the differentiation of regions' and countries' roles in international trade, specifically *inter-* and *inter-regional* trade in the mobile phone GVCs, and, the role of East Asia in those trade networks, and the divergent positions of East Asian countries in this high-tech sector.

East Asia has been playing an important role in the mobile phone industry. Over the last two decades, the geography of mobile phone production dramatically shifted to East Asia and emerging economies like Mexico, Brazil and Hungary. And it has changed the trade patterns of the mobile phone GVCs as new countries joined the production networks of mobile phones as the final product as well as mobile phone parts as intermediate goods (Lee and Gereffi 2013; Yeung *et al.* 2006). And, as countries move up and down in the GVCs, not only inter-regional trade networks but also the intra-regional division of labor among East Asian countries have changed. Thus, this chapter examines how the roles of major exporting and importing countries have changed in the evoling inter- and intra-regional trade networks, focusing on the diverging and emerging positions of East Asian economies in the GVCs. Particularly, focusing on a post-crisis period, 2007-2013, the analysis illuminates how the structure and dynamics of GVCs changed in the aftermath of the global economic crisis of 2007-2008 (Cattaneo *et al.* 2010a; Gereffi 2014).

The chapter is organized as follows. The next section discusses data and methods used in the analysis in detail. Then, findings from three sets of analysis are presented: (i) the key exporting and importing trends of mobile phones and parts, focusing on major trading countries and the change of their trading partners; (ii) inter-regional trade patterns of mobile phones and parts; (iii) intra-Asia trade networks and their changes over the period. The chapter concludes with a discussion of the implications of the findings in terms of convergence and divergence of global integration in East Asia.

Data and Methods

To analyze international trade flows in mobile phone GVCs, this analysis used the bilateral trade data compiled from the United Nations (UN) Comtrade dataset (http://comtrade.un.org), one of the most extensive database of international goods trade from 1962. To identify the product categories for the mobile phone and the parts used for it, the paper used Harmonized System (HS) codes at the six-digit level, the most disaggregated level with internationally comparable product classification. For mobile phones, HS 2007 classification code 8517.12 ("telephones for cellular networks or other wireless networks") was used along with its 2002 classification code 8525.20 ("transmission apparatus for radio-telephony incorporating reception apparatus"). For mobile phone parts, HS code 8517.70 is used.[1]

To measure the amount of bilateral trade (nominal value in US $), the chapter used trade data reported by the *importing* country since import data are usually considered more accurate than data reported by exporting countries (Escaith 2011). The analysis covers a post-crisis period from 2007 to 2013, focusing on the effect of the global financial crisis and the ensuring recession. Included to the analysis are all the countries that reported their imports in the aforementioned product categories at least once during the seven-year span.[2]

To analyze intra- and inter-regional trade flows as well as trade between and within developed and developing economies, countries are aggregated by geography and income level. The regional and income-level aggregations follow the World Bank country classification, where the world is divided by geography to seven regions, i.e., East Asia and Pacific (East Asia hereafter); South Asia; Europe and Central Asia (Europe hereafter); Middle East and North Africa (MENA); Sub-Saharan Africa (SSA); North America; Latin America and the Caribbean (Latin America hereafter). By income level, countries are grouped into developed countries (high-income OECD; and high-income non-OECD countries) and developing countries (low; upper-middle; and lower-middle ncome countries).[3]

International Trade of Mobile Phones and Parts

East Asia's strong performance in mobile phone trade

The world's exports of mobile phones nearly doubled from $131 to $230 billion in 2007-2013 despite a dip in 2009 caused by the global economic crisis. During the period, China consolidated its position as the leader of the world exports as its share climbed up from 35% to nearly 60%. Shown in Figure 1, East Asia has also strengthened its position as the top exporting region; its share in the world exports increased from 59% to 78% in the period as a result of strong performance by China as well as Vietnam and Korea.

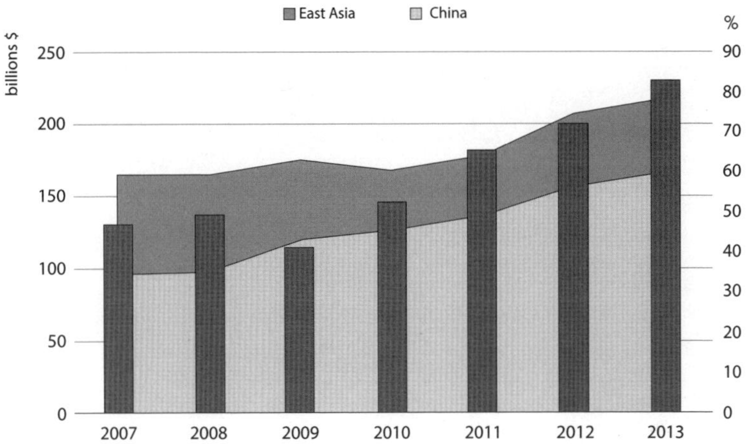

Figure 1. The world's mobile phone exports (value), 2007-2013

Source: Compiled from UN Comtrade.

The three countries together represented 74% of the world mobile phone exports in 2013, indicating the high degree of region- and country-level concentration in mobile phone exports.

By contrast, other regions suffered; e.g., Europe lost its share by 16% and Latin America's share also dropped to 2% from 5% in the seven-year period. A handful of countries like China and Vietnam emerged as the winner, whereas many other countries that used to be the major mobile phone producers and exporters dropped out, to name a few, Finland, Germany, Hungary and Malaysia.

Table 1 shows the change of the leading exporting countries over the period. Even in Asia, Malaysia and Singapore are no longer on the leaderboard, whereas Vietnam has emerged as the leading exporters in the last few years, indicating the fast changing landscape of mobile phone trade.

Table 1. World's leading mobile phone exporting countries, 2007-2013 (unit: %)

2007		2009		2011		2013	
China	35	China	43	China	49	China	60
Korea	16	Korea	16	Korea	9	Vietnam	9
Finland	7	Mexico	7	Taiwan	7	Korea	7
Hungary	7	Hungary	6	Mexico	5	Netherlands	4
Germany	5	Taiwan	4	Hungary	5	Taiwan	3
Malaysia	4	Finland	3	Vietnam	3	Mexico	2
Mexico	3	US	3	Netherlands	2	US	2
US	3	India	2	US	2	Germany	1
Taiwan	3	UK	2	UK	2	India	1
Singapore	2	Canada	2	Ireland	2	Hungary	1
ROW	16	ROW	13	ROW	14	ROW	10

Notes: East Asian countries are shaded. ROW: the rest of the world.
Source: Compiled from UN Comtrade.

While Asian countries have risen as the center of the world's mobile phone exports, our analysis shows that their export destinations changed over the period. Table 2 summarizes the changes in the four leading Asian mobile phone exporting countries in 2007-2013, i.e., China, Vietnam, Korea and Taiwan.

China's mobile phone exports more than tripled, from $45 billion to $138 billion, just in the seven years. The US remains China's leading destination for mobile phones. At the same time, China's exports to its regional neighbors increased; in 2013, 32% of the exports headed for East Asian countries, up from 28% in 2007, mainly due to the rise of Japan as one of the top destinations for China, indicating a closer trade linkage between the two economies. By contrast, Europe has lost its position as the leading destination of mobile phones as its share in China's exports decreased to 22%. While China's exports to developed economies suffered

Table 2. Major exporting countries and their leading export destinations (unit: %)

2007		2009		2011		2013	
China							
US	26.4	US	28.6	US	25.6	US	27.2
Hong Kong	12.1	Hong Kong	9.4	Hong Kong	10.6	Hong Kong	12.3
Singapore	8.3	France	5.6	Japan	8.1	Japan	10.6
Germany	6.0	India	4.9	Germany	4.2	Mexico	4.1
India	5.7	Japan	4.3	India	4.1	Germany	3.8
Netherlands	5.2	Singapore	3.9	France	4.1	India	3.3
Russia	3.3	Mexico	3.8	UK	3.7	France	3.2
Mexico	2.9	Germany	3.6	Mexico	3.1	Russia	2.4
France	2.7	Australia	2.9	Singapore	2.9	Canada	2.1
Finland	2.5	Indonesia	2.2	Australia	2.9	Singapore	2.1
Vietnam							
Hong Kong	92.5	South Africa	24.2	Germany	12.9	Germany	9.7
Singapore	4.9	Hong Kong	23.5	Russia	10.9	UK	8.5
Ghana	2.0	India	19.9	France	9.4	Saudi Arabia	7.8
Malaysia	0.2	Thailand	16.2	UK	9.3	Italy	5.6
Korea	0.2	Indonesia	6.3	India	6.0	France	5.6
US	0.1	Turkey	4.4	Spain	6.0	Hong Kong	5.3
Kuwait	0.1	Singapore	3.3	Italy	4.9	Slovakia	4.8
UK	0.0	Cambodia	1.3	Thailand	4.1	Thailand	4.7
South Africa	0.0	Malaysia	0.2	Australia	3.7	Malaysia	4.6
Indonesia	0.0	Germany	0.1	Malaysia	3.7	India	4.5
Korea							
US	30.9	US	44.3	US	49.7	US	36.8
UK	7.9	China	6.3	Japan	10.7	Japan	8.3
France	6.7	France	5.0	Germany	3.1	Slovakia	7.7
Russia	4.9	Japan	3.4	India	2.9	Germany	5.3
Germany	4.7	Hungary	2.9	Saudi Arabia	2.8	Canada	4.3
Singapore	3.9	Spain	2.9	Canada	2.6	France	3.9
Italy	3.8	Germany	2.9	France	2.2	Sweden	2.8
China	3.5	Netherlands	2.6	UK	2.1	Saudi Arabia	2.4
Hungary	3.3	Australia	2.5	Hong Kong	1.8	Hong Kong	2.4
Mexico	2.8	India	2.1	Mexico	1.7	Netherlands	2.2

Taiwan							
US	37.3	US	53.6	US	49.4	US	27.3
Mexico	8.1	Hong Kong	4.3	UK	7.8	China	15.1
Germany	5.2	China	3.8	China	5.3	Singapore	7.4
China	4.1	Mexico	3.7	Hong Kong	5.1	Germany	5.4
Japan	3.9	Singapore	3.5	Singapore	4.6	UK	4.7
Thailand	3.9	Japan	3.3	Germany	4.4	Japan	4.1
Hong Kong	3.3	Germany	2.9	France	1.9	Hong Kong	3.7
Spain	2.8	Netherlands	2.6	Australia	1.9	Indonesia	2.6
Canada	2.8	France	2.4	Korea	1.8	Australia	2.4
Denmark	2.8	Italy	2.1	Russia	1.5	Mexico	2.3

Note: East Asian countries are shaded.
Source: Compiled from UN Comtrade.

slightly right after the economic crisis, it was recovered; in 2013, 83% of China's exports were destined to high-income country markets. Overall, China's exports are distributed relatively evenly across three major import markets: East Asia, Europe and North America, but their relative importance changed.

Meanwhile, Vietnam has risen fast to be the world's second largest exporter of mobile phones. Its share in the world exports jumped from less than 1% to 9% in 2007-2013 as its exports amounted to $21 billion in 2013. In 2007, Vietnam exported a merely $60 million worth of mobile phones and more than 90% of them went to Hong Kong. Since 2008, its export destinations diversified dramatically. In 2013, Europe was Vietnam's leading export destination to represent 55% of the country's exports, followed by East Asia (23%) and Middle East and North Africa (MENA) (11%, respectively). At the same time, more exports from Vietnam headed for developed economies; 74% of its exports in 2013 went to high-income countries, such as Western European markets like Germany, UK, Italy, and France.

For much of the early 2000s, Korea was one of the mobile phone producing countries that expanded its world exports share. However, its mobile phone exports marked a steady decline over the period, from $21 billion to $16 billion, reflecting rising offshore production by firms like Samsung and LG in China and Vietnam. The country's export destinations fluctuated a little during the period, but North America and major European markets like Germany remained the largest import partners of Korea's mobile phones. Korea was also consistently less reliant on its regional market than other Asian exporters; East Asia's share were less than 20% for all the years other than 2012. At the same time, Korea relied more on developed country markets. The share of high-income countries in Korea's exports increased from 84% to 94% in 2007-2013 as Korea increased its exports to the US and Japan, Korea's two largest importing partners in 2013.

Finally, Taiwan's exports grew significantly from $3.5 billion to $13.4 billion in 2007-2011, but dropped sharply in 2012 to $8.9 billion as exports to major Western markets such as the US, Germany and UK suffered drastically. The US market played a key role in Taiwan's mobile phone exports in the early growth, and was still the largest importing country of mobile phones from Taiwan as of 2013. However, as its exports to other Asian countries like China, Japan and Singapore increased from 2012, East Asia (37%)has become the largest importing region for mobile phones from Taiwan, followed by North America (29%) and Europe (25%).

East Asia's growing role in mobile phone GVCs is also noticed in our analysis of key mobile phone import markets. While Europe is the largest importing region, representing 33% of the world's imports, its share decreased from 40% in 2007-2013. Meanwhile, East Asia's share as the second largest import market rose from 19% to 29%. By country, the US is still the largest importer of mobile phones, representing 22% of the world imports in 2013. Other top importers include Hong Kong (11%), Japan (7%), Germany (5%) and UK (5%). The developed economy market (particularly OECD countries) is still the major importer group, accounting for 82% of the world imports, indicating the persistent importance of South-to-North trade.[4]

One notable change over the last several years was the rise of Japan as the third largest importer; the country that used to be a major exporter of many advanced electronics goods now imports much more than exports mobile phones ($16.5 billion of imports vs. $514 million of exports in 2013). Japan's imports drastically increased in recent years and more than tripled in 2010-2013, suggesting the rising popularity of foreign brand phones like iPhones as well as growing outsourcing by Japanese mobile phone brands to China, which represented 88% of Japan's imports in 2013.

Our analysis of the four major import markets shows an interesting competitive dynamic between Asian exporters (see Table 3). China's position as the leading exporter in many of the key markets was strengthened at the expense of other East Asian countries like Korea and Taiwan. It is likely to reflect the effect of increasing production in China for exports by non-Chinese firms (e.g., exporting by Korean firms' factories in China), but also the rising competitiveness of Chinese firms like Lenovo and Huawei in many key import markets.

In the US market, mobile phone imports nearly doubled to $50 billion in 2007-2013. During the period, China's share in the

Table 3. Leading exporting countries in major mobile phone import markets (unit: %)

2007		2009		2011		2013	
US							
China	46.5	China	41.7	China	53.6	China	75.6
Korea	24.5	Korea	24.6	Korea	18.3	Korea	12.2
Mexico	10.1	Mexico	20.1	Taiwan	15.6	Mexico	4.6
Taiwan	5.1	Taiwan	6.4	Mexico	9.4	Taiwan	4.0
Malaysia	4.2	Canada	3.0	Malaysia	1.1	Malaysia	1.6
Japan							
China	47.6	China	70.6	China	78.5	China	88.8
Korea	27.0	Korea	21.0	Korea	18.2	Korea	8.3
Malaysia	16.3	Taiwan	4.4	Taiwan	2.0	Taiwan	1.8
Taiwan	8.4	Malaysia	2.1	Malaysia	0.9	Malaysia	0.9
Canada	0.2	Hungary	1.4	Mexico	0.2	Mexico	0.1
Germany							
China	37.6	China	40.2	China	43.2	China	45.7
Hungary	17.6	Hungary	14.5	Viet Nam	8.8	Vietnam	17.3
Korea	13.5	Korea	12.2	Taiwan	6.8	Korea	7.8
Finland	10.5	UK	6.0	Netherlands	6.0	Poland	4.4
Netherlands	4.9	Finland	5.4	India	5.7	Czech Rep.	3.9
UK*							
Korea	23.5	Korea	23.4	China	30.5	Netherlands	30.1
Netherlands	18.1	Finland	20.1	Hungary	15.4	China	25.1
Finland	15.8	Netherlands	15.8	Luxembourg	13.2	Vietnam	15.3
Germany	14.2	Hungary	13.4	Taiwan	9.7	Ireland	6.6
Hungary	7.2	China	8.4	Netherlands	7.4	Hungary	5.7

Notes: * UK's import data for 2009 are not available; instead, data for 2008 is presented.
East Asian countries are shaded.
Source: compiled from UN Comtrade.

world's largest market jumped from 47% to 76%, widening the gap with Korea, which lost its share significantly, down to 12% from 25%. Other major exporters to the US market, notably Mexico, Malaysia and Taiwan, all experienced the drop of their share. By region, the share of imports from East Asia went up to 91% in 2013 thanks to the strong performance of China whereas Latin America became a big loser. Similarly, in the Japanese market, China's share also increased in a wide margin, from 48% to 89%, while the share of other major Asian exporters like Korea, Taiwan and Malaysia all dwindled to a single digit in the third largest market. This does not mean that imports from these countries declined in total value since Japan's imports increased rapidly over the period; in fact, imports from Korea and Taiwan increased. However, they were overwhelmed by imports from China, which increased over 18 times in just seven years.

In major European markets, along with China, Vietnam made a big inroad to one of the major regional markets. In Germany, China's share increased from 38% to 46%, and Vietnam emerged fast as the second biggest exporter, accounting for 17% of German's imports in 2013. Meanwhile, other former major exporters suffered, including Finland, the home of former Nokia, and Hungary, a major production location of mobile phones in Eastern Europe, as well as Korea. In the UK, imports from the Netherlands played a leading role in recent years, amounting to 30% of UK's mobile phone imports, although there is a possibility that most of the imports were re-exports.[5] China accounted for 25% of UK's imports in 2013, followed by Vietnam (15%). By contrast, Finland, Korea and Germany, all the major exporters that, combined, had represented more than a half of UK imports in 2007, lost their shares in the ensuring years. In 2013, these three countries together accounted for merely 6% of UK's imports.

Overall, this analysis of mobile phone international trade illustrates the increasing role of East Asian exporters in the world's mobile phone trade, particularly the consolidation of China's position and the fast rise of Vietnam as the leading exporters worldwide as well as in the major import markets. While Korea and Taiwan remained to be major exporters, as our import market analysis illustrates, their positions (at least as the direct exporter) were increasingly undermined by China and Vietnam in major import markets,[6] not to mention those of other non-Asian exporters like Finland, Germany and Mexico.

Shifting production locations and changing flows of mobile phone parts trade

The international trade of mobile phone parts and components steadily increased in 2007-2013, from $59 billion to $119 billion despite a dip in 2009 (see Figure 2). Similar in mobile phones, East Asia performed strongly in mobile phone parts; four out of the top five exporters in 2013 were East Asian countries, i.e., China (57%), Korea (14%), Japan (3%), and Taiwan (3%), and the US was only non-Asian among the top five (Table 4), according to our trade data analysis.

Major Asian exporters, China, Korea, Vietnam and Taiwan, expanded their world market share, whereas many non-Asian countries that used to be strong in mobile phone parts production suffered the loss of their world market share, notably, the US, Mexico, Germany, Canada, and Finland. Regions' performance reflects the rise of East Asia as well. East Asia expanded their share in the world's mobile phone parts exports from 62% to 82%, while both Europe and North America experienced a drastic erosion of their position in the world market.

In some countries, performance in the trade of final products and parts appears to be closely intertwined, meaning that the

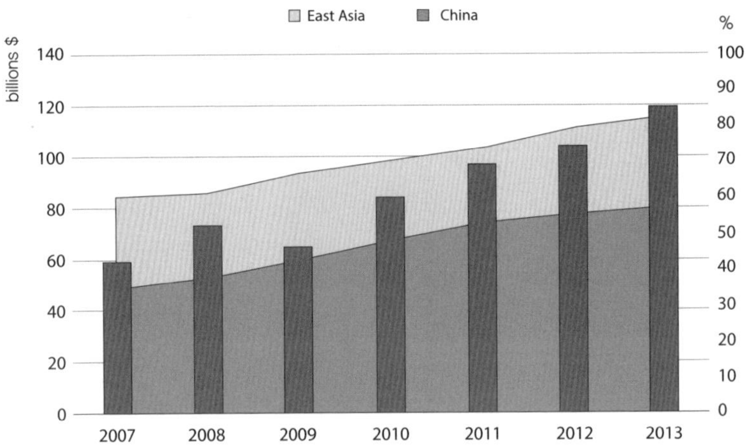

Figure 2. The world's mobile phone parts exports, 2007-2013

Source: Compiled from UN Comtrade.

Table 4. The world's leading exporting countries of mobile phone parts, 2007-2013

(unit: %)

2007		2009		2011		2013	
China	34.9	China	42.5	China	52.7	China	57.1
Korea	7.2	Korea	7.0	Korea	8.2	Korea	13.5
US	6.0	Japan	6.0	US	4.1	Japan	3.4
Japan	5.7	US	5.7	Japan	3.8	Taiwan	2.7
Mexico	5.1	Mexico	4.1	Malaysia	3.0	US	2.6
Malaysia	4.9	Malaysia	3.9	Taiwan	2.9	Malaysia	2.2
Germany	3.8	Sweden	3.0	Sweden	2.6	Mexico	1.7
Canada	3.1	Taiwan	2.8	Mexico	2.6	Sweden	1.5
Finland	3.0	Thailand	2.6	Thailand	2.0	Vietnam	1.4
Thailand	2.7	Germany	2.5	Germany	1.9	Thailand	1.3
ROW	23.7	ROW	19.9	ROW	16.3	ROW	12.5

Notes: East Asian countries are shaded. ROW: the rest of the world.
Source: Compiled from UN Comtrade.

change of mobile phone exports affects that of the parts as well. Illustrative is the case of Finland; the home country of former Nokia lost its world export share in mobile phone parts by 7% as its finish good exports plummeted to $9 billion to less than $1 billion in 2007-2013. During the same period, the world share of the country's parts exports shrunk from 3% to less than 1%.

Our analysis of the export destinations of the major parts exporters displays some interesting trends regarding the geographical shift of the mobile phone GVCs (see Table 5). First, as more production concentrated to China, component exports from China to other major production countries, such as Mexico, Korea, Japan, Brazil, Finland and the US, declined. However, China's parts exports to Vietnam, an emerging production center, increased $29 million to 4.8 billion in 2008-2013. Still, the largest portion of China's parts exports is re-imports (exports to China mostly via Hong Kong) and exports to Hong Kong for re-exports to a third destination, respectively 32% in 2013.[7] The share of these two trade flows declined to 50% in 2010, but it have expanded since, suggesting the increasing importance of the Greater China trade.

Second, there is an interesting similarity and difference among three major parts exporters in East Asia, i.e., Japan, Korea and Taiwan. For all the three, China and Hong Kong are the major destinations of their exported parts. However, the relative importance of the Great China area changed over time as well as differed among the three. For Japan, exports to the Great China area drastically increased, from 48% to 75% in 2007-2013. In the meantime, its exports to the US and Singapore declined substantially. For Korea, while China and Hong Kong continued to be the major trading partners, accounting for 68% of its parts exports in 2013, Vietnam and Brazil emerged to the second and third largest export partners (14% and 6% of Korea's parts exports in 2013). These two countries (in addition to China and India) are the key offshore produc-

Table 5. Major exporting countries of mobile phone parts and their trade partners

(unit: %)

2007		2009		2011		2013	
China							
China	28.3	Hong Kong	28.9	China	26.9	China	32.0
Hong Kong	27.8	China	21.7	Hong Kong	26.4	Hong Kong	31.5
Japan	8.2	Mexico	7.2	Mexico	5.9	Viet Nam	7.1
US	7.8	Japan	6.4	Hungary	5.6	US	3.5
Finland	5.3	US	6.1	US	4.2	Mexico	3.0
Korea							
China	64.3	China	57.3	China	58.2	China	63.9
Japan	11.2	US	9.0	Viet Nam	8.1	Viet Nam	13.7
US	5.8	Brazil	6.9	Brazil	5.7	Brazil	5.8
Hong Kong	5.8	Hong Kong	6.1	US	4.8	Hong Kong	4.5
Finland	5.6	Japan	4.4	Hong Kong	4.1	India	3.2
Japan							
Hong Kong	26.5	Hong Kong	30.6	Hong Kong	41.6	China	44.8
China	21.7	China	30.6	China	25.5	Hong Kong	29.7
US	13.9	Korea	10.2	US	8.7	Korea	9.9
Singapore	9.8	US	9.5	Korea	5.6	US	5.2
Korea	7.9	Netherlands	3.3	Mexico	2.4	Mexico	1.8
Taiwan							
China	36.4	China	31.5	China	33.5	China	40.5
Hong Kong	28.8	Hong Kong	17.1	Hong Kong	25.0	Hong Kong	28.8
US	11.7	Mexico	11.2	US	13.1	Mexico	7.1
Japan	4.5	US	10.3	Mexico	7.7	US	6.8
Korea	4.0	Korea	5.8	Hungary	2.0%	Japan	3.4

Note: East Asian countries are shaded.
Source: Compiled from UN Comtrade.

tion locations for two Korean mobile phone manufacturers, Samsung and LG. The recent rise of investment in Vietnam by Samsung contributed significantly to the expansion of the country's mobile phone exports. The fact that this involves the increase of parts exports from Korea to Vietnam indicates the close relationship between offshore production and the trade of parts and component (see Chapter 7). Finally, China and Hong Kong accounted for 70% of Taiwan's parts exports. While the share dropped to below 60% in 2008-2010, it has been since recovered to the current level. At the same time, Taiwan's parts exports to other major production locations like the US Mexico, Korea and Brazil decreased, indicating the gravitating effect of Taiwan's parts exports to China.

Finally, the growing importance of China as the destinations for parts exports is also shown in other major parts exporters. For example, for the US, Mexico was still the largest importers of mobile phones parts from the US (17%), but the Greater China area's share increased from 20% to 26% of the US's parts exports. At the same time, the US's exports to other traditional production locations like Canada, Japan, Germany, Singapore and Finland declined significantly.

On the side of importing mobile phone parts, China and Hong Kong are the leading. Combined, these two represented 55% of the world's mobile phone parts imports in 2013, up by 18% from 2007. Vietnam has emerged as the third largest importer as it became a major center of mobile phone production. The US is still an important importer but its share dwindled from 14% to 5% of the world's imports in 2007-2013. Other major producing and exporting countries filled the bottom of the leaderboard, including Korea, Japan, Brazil (3%, respectively) and India (2%). These eight leading importers accounted for 80% of the world's mobile phone parts imports. By region, East Asia accounted for 70% of the world imports as it consolidated its position of the global factory for the mobile phone. And, more and more parts are imported to developing countries. In 2013, 52% of parts products were imported by developing countries, up from 26% in 2007, indicating their rise as the center of mobile phone production.

In China and Hong Kong, bilateral trade between the two has become more important than trade with other partners. More than a half of China's imports in 2013 were re-imports, mostly likely via Hong Kong. At the same time, imports from China became the bigger part of Hong Kong's parts imports (81% in 2013 from 66% in 2007). Among the leading parts exporters, Korea only expanded their exports to China to 26% from 20%; all the other major ones like the US and Finland lost their share. In Hong Kong, only Thailand gained slightly (from 0.9% to 1.6%) whereas other key partners, suffered including Japan, Korea, Taiwan and the US.

In Vietnam, parts imports increased sharply from $247 million to $14 billion during the period, reflecting the country's growing production of mobile phones. China and Korea, the two largest parts exporters to Vietnam, consolidated their positions, accounting for 68% and 31% respectively in 2013, while imports from Hong Kong and Singapore declined drastically, from 14% and 10% to less than 1% (see below).

In the US market, China's share doubled while neighboring Mexico and Canada all suffered the loss of the share. In Korea, imports from China and Japan are substantial but the most noticeable change is a fast rise of imports from Vietnam (5.4% of Korea's imports in 2013), suggesting the strengthened trade linkage of intermediate goods between the two. In Brazil and India where Samsung and LG have their own mobile phone factories rising imports from Korea were also noticeable. While China is the leading import partners for both countries, Korea's share increased significantly, from 17% to 32% in Brazil in 2007-2013, and from 6%

Table 6. Major mobile phone parts importers and their trade partners, selected years

(unit: %)

2007		2009		2011		2013	
China							
China	42.1	China	42.8	China	47.5	China	54.7
Korea	19.8	Korea	18.6	Korea	18.6	Korea	25.9
Finland	5.5	Japan	8.5	Taiwan	4.6	Japan	4.5
Japan	5.3	Taiwan	4.2	Japan	6.2	Taiwan	3.2
US	4.4	Malaysia	3.8	Malaysia	3.6	Hong Kong	1.8
Hong Kong							
China	66.1	China	70.6	China	74.1	China	80.7
Japan	10.4	Japan	10.5	Japan	9.1	Japan	4.5
Taiwan	4.9	Taiwan	2.8	Taiwan	2.8	Taiwan	3.4
US	3.3	US	2.7	US	3.3	Korea	2.7
Singapore	3.2	Korea	2.5	Korea	2.2	Thailand	1.6
Vietnam*							
China	23.6	China	35.9	China	57.6	China	67.6
Hong Kong	13.6	Korea	32.7	Korea	36.5	Korea	31.0
Spain	10.7	Hong Kong	5.0	Japan	1.6	Sweden	0.3
Singapore	10.7	Malaysia	4.8	Taiwan	1.4	Philippines	0.3
Sweden	6.6	Taiwan	4.8	Malaysia	0.7	Taiwan	0.2
US							
Mexico	25.9	Mexico	27.7	China	35.5	China	41.4
China	19.7	China	27.3	Mexico	18.6	Mexico	19.1
Canada	13.2	Malaysia	7.1	Malaysia	7.8	Malaysia	9.4
Malaysia	12.8	Korea	6.6	Korea	6.3	Korea	6.7
Japan	5.7	Japan	6.0	Taiwan	6.1	Thailand	3.9
Korea							
China	43.6	China	41.4	China	55.3	China	55.7
Japan	14.3	Japan	15.8	Singapore	8.3	Japan	12.7
US	9.0	US	7.5	US	6.9	Malaysia	6.0
Malaysia	6.6	Malaysia	6.4	Japan	6.8	Vietnam	5.4
Singapore	4.3	Singapore	4.9	Malaysia	3.8	Singapore	4.1

Notes: * Vietnam's import data for 2007 is not available; instead, data for 2008 are presented.
East Asian countries are shaded.
Source: Compiled from UN Comtrade

to 19% in India in 2008-2013. Korea was the second largest parts exporter to each of the two countries, only behind China.

Overall, East Asian countries advanced their competitive positions in the global market and increased intra-regional trade among them. Particularly, the position of China – both the largest exporter and importer of mobile phone parts – significantly consolidated in most of the major import markets over the seven years, with its trade with Hong Kong through re-exports and re-imports expanding. At the same time, Korean mobile phones manufacturers' offshore production played a key role in boosting the country's parts exports to countries like Vietnam, Brazil and India.

Inter- and Intra-regional Trade Networks in the Mobile Phone GVC

Our previous analysis shows two interesting dynamics. First, East Asian economies are increasingly trading one another, strengthening regional value chains. Second, as particularly noticeable in Korea's parts trade, the offshoring of mobile phone production affected the trade patterns of mobile phone parts. To examine how these dynamics played out in the inter- and intra-regional trade networks of the mobile phone, we analyzed the changing patterns of bilateral trade among world-regions, and among Asian economies.

Inter-regional trade networks of mobile phones and parts

The changes in the inter-regional trade flows of the mobile

phone are illustrated in Figure 3. In 2007-2013, first, intra-regional trade grew strongly in East Asia [EAP], from $21 billion to $55 billion, and from 16% to 24% of the world's mobile phone trade. This is attributed to the rise of East Asia as the center of mobile phone production as well as consumption. Second, East Asia's exports

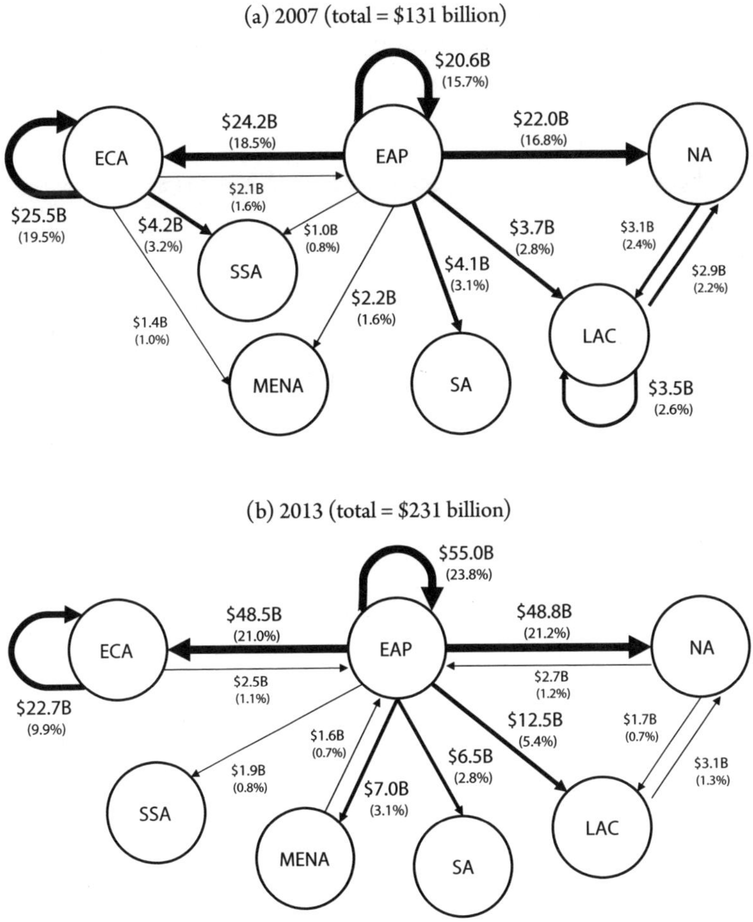

Figure 3. Inter-regional trade flows of mobile phones, 2007 and 2013

Note: Only appeared are the trade linkages with more than 0.5% of the world trade.
Source: Compiled from UN Comtrade.

to all the other six world-regions amounted to more than a half of the world trade (54% of the world trade in 2013), indicating the concentration of mobile phone production in East Asia. Taken together, East Asia's intra- and inter-regional trade accounted for 82% of the world trade in 2013, up from 62% in 2007, illustrating the rising importance of the region in the mobile phone GVC. Third, as imports from East Asia played a bigger role in mobile phone GVCs, intra-regional trade in other regions declined; intra-European [ECA] trade decreased from $25 billion to $22 billion, now 10% of the world trade, and trade within Latin America [LAC] also declined $3.5 billion to $0.5 billion in 2007-2013. Europe's exports to Sub-Saharan Africa [SSA] and the Middle East and North Africa [MENA] also declined as those regions shifted to imports from East Asia, mostly China. Similarly, inter-American trade linkage, between North and Latin Americas, weakened as both regions more relied on imports from East Asia.

Compared to mobile phone trade flows above, mobile phone parts trade flows show some similarities, such as the growing importance of East Asia's intra-regional trade in the world trade, as well as some differences, such as the stagnation of exports from East Asia to Europe and North America. The key findings are summarized as follows (see Figure 4): first, intra-regional trade within East Asia increase significantly to $76 billion, 64% of the world's mobile phone part trade in 2013, from 41% in 2007. Second, while the rise of East Asia in mobile phone trade increased the region's exports to Europe and North America (see above), it had a different effect on parts trade, stagnating East Asian exports to the other two regions, where mobile phone manufacturing is declining. This suggests that the most of the recent growth in East Asia's parts

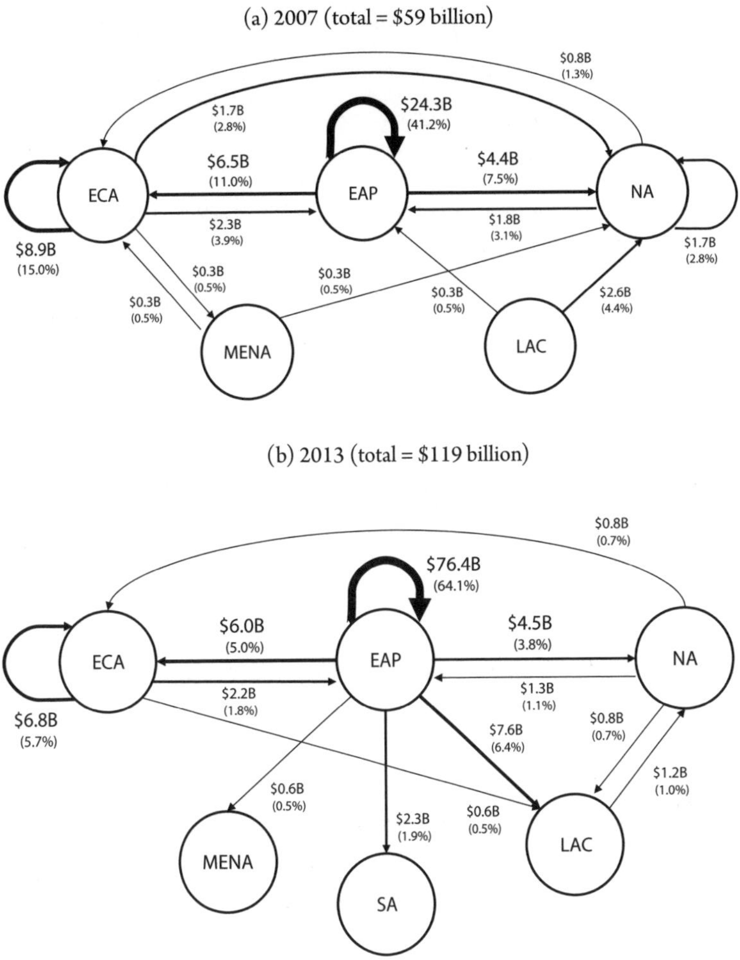

Figure 4. Inter-regional trade flows of mobile phone parts, 2007 and 2013

Note: Only appeared are the trade linkages with more than 0.5% of the world trade.
Source: Compiled from UN Comtrade.

trade was attributed to *intra-Asian* trade. Third, intra-regional parts trade was declined in Europe and North America; for example, Europe's intra-regional trade shrunk by $2.1 billion in 2007-2013. This is likely related to the decline of mobile phone manufacturing in those regions and the rise of offshore outsourcing to East Asia and Latin America. Finally, exports from East Asia to Latin America and South Asia rose significantly. Exports to Latin America also increased from North America and Europe. This is likely associated with the growth of mobile phone manufacturing in countries like Brazil and India and the trade linkage between these emerging production centers and East Asia. It also reflects the growing investment of East Asian firms like Samsung, LG and Foxconn in countries like Brazil and India, which facilitated parts exports from East Asia to these countries (see chapter 7).

Intra-Asian trade networks of mobile phones and parts

The analysis thus far highlights the importance of East Asian economies in the global trade of mobile phones and parts, and the growing significance of trade within Asia. The final segment of our analysis further focused on the dynamics of intra-Asian trade.[8] Mobile phone trade within Asia rose from $26 billion to $65 billion in 2007-2013 and the region's share increased from 20% to 28% of the world's total mobile phone trade. In mobile phone parts, trade among Asian countries more than tripled, from $26 billion to $81 billion over the same period. The share of intra-regional trade flows in the world's parts trade rose from 43% to 68%, indicating that intra-Asian trade has more intensified in parts trade than the trade of the final good.

Figure 5 shows the changing pattern of mobile phone trade between Asian countries in 2007-2013. The only bilateral trade linkage whose value exceeds 1% of the intra-regional trade in a given year is represented. In 2007, the largest trade linkage in this trade network was China's exports to Hong Kong (21%), fol-

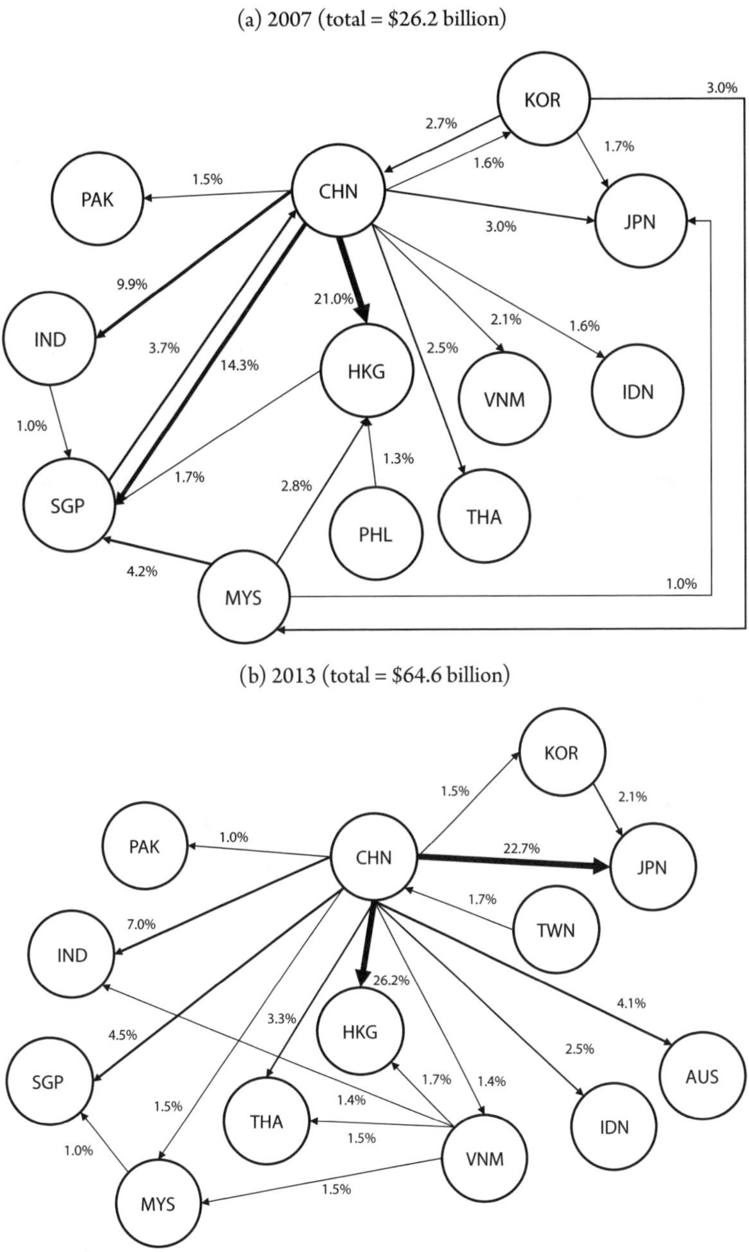

Figure 5. Intra-Asian trade network of mobile phones, 2007 and 2013

Note: Only appeared are the trade linkages exceeding 1.0% of the intra-Asian trade.
Source: Compiled from UN Comtrade.

lowed by China's exports to Singapore (14%) and India (10%). Including these, China's export linkages to other Asian countries amounted to a total of 58% in 2007. At the same time, albeit to a much smaller scale, there were other intra-regional exporters; for example, Korea exported to China, Japan and Malaysia (combined, 7.4% of the entire intra-regional flow), and Malaysia's exports to Singapore, Malaysia, and Japan (8%). Also, Singapore's exports to China amounted to 3.7%. In this sense, while China was by far the largest exporter in the intra-regional trade network, other several major exporters also played a significant role.

The trade flow in 2013 is distinctive in that such multi-polarity significantly demised. While China's exports to other Asian countries increased to 76% of the total intra-regional trade, the role played by countries like Korea, Malaysia and Singapore dwindled. The *non-Chinese* export ties that remained meaningful in 2013 were from Korea to Japan, and from Malaysia to Singapore. In addition, two notable new developments took place: first, China's exports to Japan significantly increased, and now this trade link accounted for 23% of all the intra-regional trade. As noted above, it is likely attributable to the growing popularity of foreign mobile phones in Japan, including the iPhone (mostly produced in China), as well as Japanese phone makers' increasing offshore outsourcing to China. The other key development is the rise of Vietnam as an exporter to multiple countries. While its share was much smaller compared to China's (7%), the emerging production center has developed export linkages to countries like India, Thailand and Malaysia as well as Hong Kong. As a result, the 2013 trade flows show that one big (China) and one smaller (Vietnam) exporters play a key role as regional production hubs in the intra-Asian trade linkages in mobile

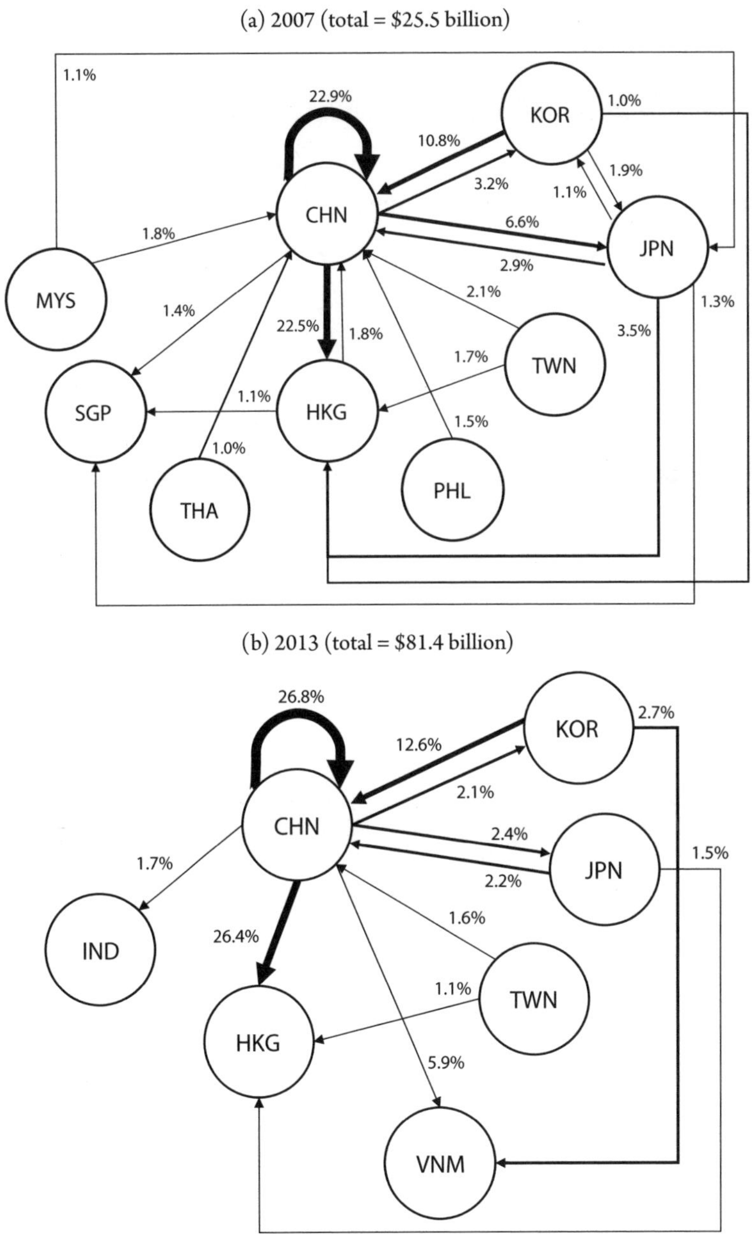

Figure 6. Intra-Asian trade of mobile phone parts, 2007 and 2013

Note: Only appeared are the trade linkages with more than 1.0% of the intra-Asia trade.
Source: Compiled from UN Comtrade.

phones.

The intra-Asian trade patterns of mobile phone parts illuminates another interesting dynamics. As shown in Figure 6, the largest trade linkage was in 2007 and remained in 2013 China's re-imports (mostly via Hong Kong).[9] The share of the re-imports increased from 23% to 29% of the total intra-Asian trade of mobile phone parts. China's exports to Hong Kong remained the second biggest linkage, accounting for 27% in 2013. The parts trade network also illustrates the intensity of Northeast Asian trade, among Korea, Japan and China. In 2007, these three countries traded mobile phone parts with one another, accounting for 12% of intra-Asian parts trade. In 2013, the Korea-Japan linkage became insignificant, but the two countries' linkages with China were still important.

On a broader scale, a more interesting picture arose in China's changing trade relations with other Asian countries. In 2007, China was mainly the importer of parts from other Asian countries, which include Korea (11% of the entire intra-regional trade), Japan (3%) and Taiwan (2%) as well as from Malaysia (1.8%), Hong Kong (1.8%), the Philippines (1.5%), and Thailand (1%). In turn, China exported parts for mobile phones to Japan (7%) and Korea (3%), where some of major global mobile phone brands are headquartered. In 2013, the number of China's Asian trading partners for parts imports reduced to just three, Korea (13%), Japan (2%) and Taiwan (2%). By contrast, China's export partners diversified, including in 2013 Vietnam (6%) and India (2%) as well as Korea and Japan. This suggests that China's domestic parts production increased significantly during the period, whether it was due to the relocation of parts producers from other Asian countries like

Malaysia to China, or Chinese firms' substitution of imported parts with domestically produced ones, or both. At the same time, China is now able to export parts to Vietnam and India, the countries where mobile phone assembly are expanding fast. This indicates the fast changing countries' positions in the Asian regional trade and production networks.

Conclusion

This chapter has examined the changing patterns of inter-regional and intra-regional trade and the shifting positions of countries in the mobile phone GVCs, focusing on the shifting roles of East Asian countries in the trade networks. The findings of the chapter affirm some of earlier findings on the changes in the mobile phone GVCs, such as a growing consolidation of mobile phone production in East Asia and China. At the same time, our regional-level analysis sheds light on an interesting interaction between inter- and intra-regional trades. Mobile phone trade within a region outside East Asia has become less significant as many region bolstered a cross-regional trade linkage with East Asia, as shown in the decline of intra-regional trade in Europe and Latin America as well as inter-American trade. This suggests a replacement effect of intra-regional trade by inter-regional trade with East Asia.

A similar effect is found in mobile phone parts trade; for example, the intra-regional trade of mobile phone parts declined in Latin America while imports from East Asia considerably increased. These changes are likely to be affected not only by trade but also through foreign direct investment; for example, a growing investment by Asian firms such as Samsung, LG and Foxconn in Latin America has likely led to the growth of parts import from East Asia. This raises the question whether regionalized production has any future in these regions in the face of a growing concentration of mobile phone GVCs in Asia.

Finally, our analysis affirms the importance of the China-Hong Kong tie in mobile phone trade networks within Asia. China's leading role in the networks is prominent in both final products and the parts. At the same time, it shows that Vietnam has begun to develop its own exporting network, partly supported by imported parts from China and Korea as well as by foreign investment from Korea as well as from Singapore and Malaysia. These findings also illuminate the possibility of China's upgrading in parts production as it moved from importers to exporters to major emerging production hubs like Vietnam and India.

Notes

1. A separate category for the mobile phone, 8517.12, was first established in the HS 2007 classification codes. Countries began to classify the mobile phone according to the new HS codes in different years and until then, the mobile phone was included to HS 2002 code 8525.20, which also included other types of non-cellular wireless phones, such as code-less phones. HS 8517.70 was first introduced in the HS 2007 codes to designate parts for mobile phones.

2. In the UN Comtrade dataset, the data of trade with Taiwan are unavailable, despite its strong position in the mobile phone industry. However, countries to export to or import from Taiwan attribute the trade to the partner category of "Other Asia, not else specified" (code 490). In reality, according to the UN International Trade Statistics Knowledgebase, only trade of Taiwan is included under the code, except for several countries that include in this category their trade with unidentified Asian countries (http://unstats.un.org/unsd/tradekb/Knowledgebase/Taiwan-Province-of-China-Trade-data). Thus, in this analysis, we consider all the trade included for that residual code as Taiwan's trade.

3. For more on the classification, see http://data.worldbank.org/about/country-and-lending-groups (July 2015).

4. It should be noted, however, that this import flows do not take into ac-

count production in developing countries for their domestic markets, such as mobile phones produced in China for domestic consumption.

5. In fact, exports data reported by the Netherland indicate a much lower export figure to the UK (e.g., $3.4 billion in UK's import data vs. $50 million in the Netherland's exports data in 2013). The Netherlands does not report any re-import or re-export data to UN Comtrade.

6. Some of the change is related to Korean or Taiwanese-owned firms' increasing production in and exports from China and Vietnam to the world.

7. China's imports from (or exports to) China are partially explained by re-imports. More than 90% of China's reimports are produced in China, exported to Hong Kong, where many MNEs' distribution centers are located, and then re-imported in China, a process of the transshipment of Chinese intermediate goods from one Chinese location to another, principally from one EPZ to another (http://www.trademap.org/stFAQ.aspx). See also WTO and IDE-JETRO (2011, 24-26).

8. For this analysis, we included countries in the following two categories: East Asia and Pacific [EAP] and South Asia [SA]. As in the previous analyses, trade to/from "Asia n.e.s" was counted toward Taiwan's trade

9. See notes 7 above.

Section III

Convergence and Divergence in Mobile Asia

Chapter 6

Divergent Paths of GVC Integration and Upgrading in the East Asian Mobile Telecom Industry

Introduction

Economic globalization has challenged how industrial development takes place.[1] Over the last few decades, cross-national flows of trade and investment have been liberalized, with many barriers lowered and new neo-liberal norms, regulations and institutions established. Particularly, the emergence of GVCs has transformed the context in which industrial development occurs in a global economy (Gereffi *et al.* 2001b; UNCTAD 2013). Production activities have been fragmented into value-adding tasks and are conducted across national boundaries through offshore outsourcing (Arndt and Kierzkowski 2001; Milberg and Winkler 2013). A GVC refers to "the full range of activities that firms and workers perform to bring a specific product from its conception to its end use and beyond" (Gereffi and Fernandez-Stark 2011). Similar concepts have been introduced to understand the growing fragmentation and geographic dispersion of production, notably the "global production network" (Coe and Hess 2013; Henderson *et al.* 2002). Earlier, the "new international division of labor" had been used by (Fröbel *et al.* 1980; Marin 2006). Despite their differences these concepts commonly regard the emergence of the new form of fragmented production as one of the defining features of economic globalization (see Sturgeon 2001). A new generation of industrializing countries, notably China, India, Brazil and South Africa, has entered global production networks as major suppliers, changing competitive dynamics in global industries. Nowadays, industrial development can be pursued through multiple entry points in the value chain by engaging in specific segments of the chain and moving to higher value activities (Kaplinsky 2000; Lee 2010).

An earlier debate on globalization and development, centered on whether or not neo-liberal economic globalization would lead to the convergence of development models across countries (Fourcade-Gourinchas and Babb 2002; Guillén 2001), has evolved into how increasingly fragmented and decentralized production shapes development paths and outcomes (Gereffi 2009; UNCTAD 2013). Some value chain activities have a more positive impact than others on exports and employment, and the country's position in the value chain can determine development outcomes. The question about the effects of GVC participation on development has become complicated in the post-recession global economy (Cattaneo *et al.* 2010a; Neilson *et al.* 2014). The growing consolidation of production into a few large emerging economies and the increasing importance of developing country markets as end markets could further generate divergent prospects for industrial development.

In East Asia, the major industrialized economies – Japan, Taiwan and Korea (hereafter Korea) – while often considered together under the umbrella of an East Asian development model, exhibited marked differences in the ways they organized industrial development during the post-war high growth era (Biggart and Guillen 1999; Fields 1997). The question is whether and how the patterns of industrial development have changed as these economies have confronted globalization over the last few decades. Are the countries converging or diverging, and how have their linkages to global industries changed? Answering these questions is made more intriguing by the integration of China with global industries. This integration has affected the choices of China's neighboring countries, which in turn have influenced China's responses, highlighting the interactive aspect of industrial development in the region (Baek 2005).

This article attempts to address these questions by examining the development paths of China, Japan, Korea and Taiwan in mobile phone manufacturing. Drawing from a GVC approach, the study proposes an analytical framework to discern different trajectories of industrial development, focusing on the position of a country's firms in the mobile phone GVC and their orientation toward global markets. Mobile phone manufacturing is particularly interesting. It is one of the highly technology-intensive, advanced manufacturing sectors in which many countries are eager to excel. Also, in East Asia, mobile phone manufacturing is part of the electronics sector, which has played a key role as a major source of exports, jobs and innovation for each of the countries in different periods of history (Hobday 1998). As shown below, the countries remain the forerunners in the global mobile phone industry, and their positions have been strengthened in recent years (Lee and Gereffi 2013).

Our findings first point to a significant divergence among the four East Asian countries. A striking difference is found among

Japan, Korea and Taiwan. Firms in each country are successful in some chain segments or geographical markets but less successful in others, thereby positioning themselves in different market niches of the value chain. We also find that the development trajectory of China, in comparison to those of the other three countries, is more complex and internally diversified. Despite some commonalities with its neighbors, China also has a unique element that points to the possibility of a multi-path strategy of industrial development in mobile phone manufacturing.

The rest of the article is organized as follows. The next section examines theoretical issues regarding globalization and industrial development in general and in East Asian contexts with an introduction to our analytical framework. After outlining our data and methods, we discuss how globalization has changed mobile phone manufacturing and the trajectories of the four East Asian countries from a comparative angle. The final section discusses the implications of our findings in terms of the future of industrial development in East Asia.

Data and Methods

This study uses a case-based comparative method, following a well-established tradition of the literature that examines the development trajectories of East Asian countries from a comparative perspective (Evans 1995; Hamilton and Biggart 1988). The literature has compared the patterns of development across East Asia and how they were affected by the rise of China, the Asian economic crisis, post-crisis dynamics and other changes (Hsieh

2011; Lee and Kwak 2009). This article combines this country-level comparison with GVC analysis, which typically focuses on in-depth examination of a single sector and countries' and firms' value chain position therein (Lee 2010).

The study used mainly the UN Comtrade dataset to collect the trade figures of mobile phones.[2] Mobile phone subscription data were compiled from the World Development Indicators database.[3] Market share data were obtained from various publications, including market research reports. Trade journals, government reports, newspaper and magazine articles and other secondary data sources were also used.

The Globalization of Mobile Phone Manufacturing and East Asia

The mobile phone industry has changed significantly as a result of globalized production and consumption over the last two decades. Mobile phone production has shifted geographically from advanced economies, its traditional center of production and consumption, to emerging economies (Lee and Gereffi 2013). In 2001, the majority of mobile phones (52%) were exported from five developed countries: Germany, the UK, Korea, the US and Finland. In 2011, the top five exporters consisted of China, Korea, Hungary, Hong Kong and Mexico, accounting for 73% of the world's mobile phone exports. Only Korea has managed to stay at the top as developing and transitional economies have emerged as major exporters.

This shift is based on a growing level of fragmented production and the rise of global value chains (Hess and Coe 2006; Lee and Gereffi 2013). Mobile phone production used to be vertically integrated by branded manufacturers, such as Nokia and Motorola, with most of the production tasks from design to assembly conducted in a single – mostly industrially advanced – country. Now, as a result of rising offshoring and outsourcing, more mobile phones are produced by third-party contract manufacturers, so-called OEM suppliers and electronics manufacturing service (EMS) providers. These third-party manufacturers specialize in manufacturing and assembling parts and components for branded manufacturers. This trend, which offers labor cost advantages to manufacturing sectors, is mostly conducted in developing countries (Lüthje 2002). For instance, iPhones are designed by Apple in the US but are assembled almost entirely in China by Foxconn, a Taiwanese contract manufacturer, with hundreds of components imported from Germany, Korea and other advanced economies. This form of international division of labor is now common in the manufacturing of consumer electronic devices (Dedrick *et al.* 2010).

As the production of mobile phones has changed, so has consumption. The most notable change is the increase of mobile phone use in developing countries. In 1995, high-income countries accounted for 87% of the world's users. In 2010, by contrast, 77% of users lived in middle- or low-income economies, indicating a shifting end market toward developing countries. The number of mobile phone users has increased much faster in developing countries. From 2005 to 2010, the number of mobile phone users increased by 706% and 659% in low-income and less developed economies, respectively. Meanwhile, growth has remained stagnant in many advanced markets, with the number of mobile phone users increasing by just 37% in high-income markets.

This global expansion of mobile phone production and consumption has generated new competitive dynamics. First, as a result of the fragmentation and decentralization of production, there are multiple different paths through which countries and firms can be integrated into global industries. While the international division of labor is nothing new, the process has become more sophisticated at the level of value-adding tasks, giving rise to a new form of international trade known as "trade in task" (WTO and IDE-JETRO 2011). And, some countries or firms capture more gains than others by conducting higher value-added tasks (Ali-Yrkkö *et al.* 2011). In the iPhone case, China assumes largely labor-intensive tasks like the final assembly of the product with relatively small economic gains, and the overwhelming majority of the value from the iPhone is captured in the form of brand, marketing and technology rents by the US (most by Apple) and Japan, Korea and Germany where high-end component suppliers such as Toshiba, Samsung and Infineon are headquartered (Dedrick *et al.* 2010).[4] Second, the performance of mobile phone producers increasingly relies on their competitiveness in global markets. In the past, mobile phone producers dealt with a small number of advanced-country markets, mostly their own domestic and regional markets. Now, competition takes place at a global level, particularly in rapidly growing emerging-economy markets. This poses a challenge, even for leading global firms, to adapt strategies to market dynamics in foreign, particularly developing, countries (Rooney 2012).

Overall, East Asia has emerged as a strong center of global mobile phone production as a result of increasing production in

Table 1. Mobile phone exports and subscribers in East Asia

	Mobile phone exports (US$)[a]			Mobile phone subscribers[b]		
	2001	2011	2011 global market share	2001	2010	Per 100 people[d]
China	4.6 billion	63.2 billion	41.7%	145 million	859 million	64
Japan	1.8 billion	27.1 million	0.02%	75 million	121 million	95
Korea	7.5 billion	15.1 billion	10.0%	29 million	51 million	104
Taiwan[c]	2.7 billion[d]	10.6 billion	7.0%[e]	22 million	27 million	118

Sources: (a) compiled from UN Comtrade, (b) The International Telecommunication Union's World Telecom Indicators, (c) Taiwan's Bureau of Foreign Trade (http://www.trade.gov.tw/) for exports data, (d) based on data from the year 2000, (e) based on the world's total exports ($151.5 billion).

China and the strong performance of East Asian firms in global markets. Well-developed regional supply chains provide a strong incentive for global firms to move production to the region. In 2011, China and Korea accounted for 52% of the world's exports, and more than two of five mobile phones exported worldwide were manufactured in China. On the consumption side, mobile phone users in East Asia increased in number from 25 million to 1.7 billion between 1995 and 2010, representing 31% of the world's mobile phone users in 2010. The growth was particularly astonishing in China, where mobile phone users increased in number nearly six-fold between 2001 and 2010 (see Table 1).

Amid the rise of East Asia in the global mobile phone industry, striking differences among these four countries became apparent, also shown in Table 1. On the production side, while each of the four countries touted prowess in manufacturing mobile phones and other electronic devices, their export performance diverged as Japan failed to keep pace with the others. In 2011, Japan accounted for less than 1% of global mobile exports, a surprisingly low figure for the one-time giant in the electronics industry. Meanwhile, China, the world's leading producer and exporter of mobile phones, increased its superiority over the other countries. Second, China's domestic market grew significantly, overwhelming the other three countries. The mobile market in China is yet to be saturated, with only 64 mobile phone users for every 100 people as of 2010. Compare this to Japan, Korea and Taiwan, where nearly everyone has at least one mobile phone and a full array of advanced mobile services is offered.

Divergent Paths of Mobile Phone Manufacturing in East Asia

A further examination shows that Japan, Korea, Taiwan and China took strikingly distinctive trajectories in response to globalization in mobile phone manufacturing. The difference is illustrated in Figure 1, based on the proposed framework above and our quantitative and qualitative assessment of each country's mobile phone industry. Korean and Taiwanese firms emerged as key players in global markets but in different parts of the value chain: Koreans more as branded manufacturers and Taiwanese mainly as specialized suppliers. Their common orientation toward global markets is in striking contrast to the strong position of Japanese branded manufacturers in the domestic market and their inability to translate this local success overseas, which contrasts with the very strong position of Japanese component suppliers in foreign markets. Finally, firms in China have concurrently engaged in different parts of the GVC and different end markets, a unique multipath industrial development.

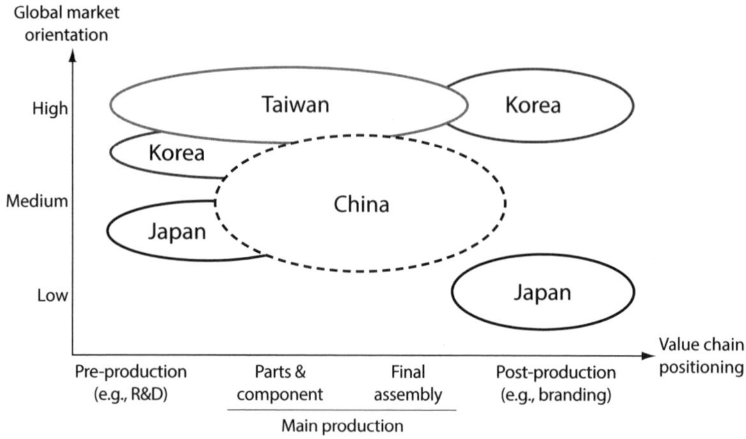

Figure 1. Development trajectories in mobile phone manufacturing

Note: The positions of the countries in the diagram are based on the authors' qualitative and quantitative assessment of each country's competitive strength.
Source: Authors.

Korea and Taiwan: Two different pathways to going global

Korea and Taiwan have been frequently compared with regard to post-war export-oriented industrial development, in which electronics manufacturing was one of the key sectors that drove exports and employment (Evans 1995; Feenstra and Hamilton 2006; Sato 1997). While their strong orientation toward global markets and success therein continued in the manufacturing of mobile phones, Korean and Taiwanese firms responded differently to the globalization of mobile phone production, engaging in different segments of the mobile phone GVC. Korean mobile phone manufacturing was driven by large branded manufacturers backed by conglomerates, known as *chaebol*. Korean firms quickly established global production and marketing prowess based on an initial success in a virtually protected domestic market for mobile phones. In contrast, globalization in Taiwan was spearheaded by specialized manufacturers and SMEs, while the domestic market was dominated by foreign brands. Duplicating their success model with other electronics such as computers, Taiwanese firms were introduced as key suppliers to major foreign buyers and capitalized on their geographic and socio-cultural proximity to supply chain bases in China.

Korea was a latecomer in mobile phone manufacturing. When Korea tried to join the trend in the early 1990s, the sector was dominated by US and European firms, which were little interested in transferring technology to Korean firms that had already challenged Western firms in consumer electronics such as televisions and microwaves. Facing this obstacle, the Korean government and local firms decided to adopt a digital cellular technology called Code Division Multiple Access (CDMA), then little known and initially developed by Qualcomm, an American start-up company. A state-led consortium was formed by a major government research institute and a handful of large domestic electronic makers, notably Samsung and LG, to facilitate Korea's technological learning (Park 2013). By awarding CDMA-only mobile service licenses, the government protected local producers in the domestic market from competition with global brands, such as Nokia and Ericsson, most of which had opted for Global System for Mobile Communications (GSM) standard technology (Kushida 2008).[5] The dominance of local producers in the Korean market has little changed. As shown in Table 2, of the four countries in this study, the share of domestic brands in the local market is highest in Korea (Euromonitor International 2013). Japan is the only other country wherein domestic brands have the majority share in the local

Table 2. Mobile phone market shares in selected East Asian markets (unit: %)

Country	Korea		Taiwan		Japan*		China	
Year	2006	2011	2006	2011	2006	2011	2006	2011
Domestic brands	87.5	83.1	14.4	10.0	64.7	62.7	17.6	23.9
Foreign brands	6.0	14.0	68.7	82.0	3.4	16.7	75.7	62.4

Notes: * Sony-Ericsson, a Japanese-Swedish joint venture, is considered a domestic brand (7.5% in 2011). The sum is not equal to 100% because the category of "Other" is not counted.
Sources: Euromonitor International (2012a; 2012b; 2013a; 2013b).

market. In Taiwan and China, the situation is quite the opposite, with domestic brands holding a much weaker position than foreign brands.

Building upon accumulated domestic capabilities and the secured home market, Korean firms first exported CDMA phones to mostly North American markets, but quickly caught up by learning and utilizing GSM technology and expanding their exports to a much wider range of foreign markets. This expansion contrasts Japanese firms' embrace of their own local standard, called Personal Digital Cellular (PDC), which limited their ability to export.[6] Korean firms had little experience in offshore outsourcing for foreign mobile phone buyers, unlike Taiwanese firms. Instead, they started as branded manufacturers. By 2001, Samsung and LG, two major Korean conglomerates, represented 9.6% of the world's mobile phone market, respectively ranked fourth and tenth worldwide. As shown in Table 3, their combined global share increased to 19.4% in 2005, and in 2010, Samsung and LG became the world's second and third largest mobile phone brands, respectively, in unit sales, with a combined share of 24.7%. In 2012, Samsung unseated Nokia as the largest mobile phone producer in the world.

These leading Korean producers are highly export-oriented in sales and are globalized in production. The Korean market only

Table 3. Top 5 leading mobile phone producers and their global market shares

(unit: %)

2005		2007		2010		2012	
Nokia	32.5	Nokia	37.8	Nokia	28.9	Samsung	22.0
Motorola	17.7	Motorola	14.3	Samsung	17.6	Nokia	19.1
Samsung	12.7	Samsung	13.4	LG	7.1	Apple	7.5
LG	6.7	Sony-Ericsson	8.8	Apple	2.9	ZTE	3.9
Sony-Ericsson	6.3	LG	6.8	Sony-Ericsson	2.6	LG	3.3

Note: Firms based in East Asia in bold (including joint ventures).
Sources: Gartner (2006; 2008; 2012; 2014b).

accounts for about 5% of Samsung's and LG's mobile phone unit sales, respectively (Samsung Electronics 2010; LG Electronics 2009). Given the small size of domestic market (1.5% of total global unit sales in 2010), the rapid growth of these companies is mainly attributable to their active engagement in global markets through exports. Furthermore, the production of Korean firms is increasingly conducted outside Korea. In 2011, 77% of Korean firm phones were produced abroad, mainly in China and Vietnam (Ministry of Knowledge Economy 2012). Korean firms have also invested in overseas R&D capabilities in order to absorb advanced technology and market trends (*Chosun Ilbo* 2004).

In addition to their strong global orientation, Korean leading mobile phone producers are highly vertically integrated. In 2011, LG was estimated to outsource only 13% of its mobile phone production, and Samsung produced all of its mobile phones in-house. This contrasts with the average for industry-wide outsourced production, which is approximately 30% (NIPA 2011). Furthermore, many of the key components in Samsung and LG mobile phones are supplied by their related companies. For example, Samsung Electronics and its associated firms under Samsung Group manufacture a wide range of high-end components, from memory chips to mobile displays, for Samsung-branded mobile phones.

However, this strong tendency toward vertical integration through the *chaebol* network has led to the relative underdevelopment of local contract manufacturing. Many local component suppliers are under a dependent relationship with these domestic buyers, which are much bigger, more globalized and in a dominant market position. Contract manufacturers in Korea are not only very few in numbers with weak global profiles (see Table 4), but also struggle with a dearth of opportunity in a market dominated by vertically integrated manufacturers like Samsung and LG.

Taiwan firms also entered into global mobile phone manufacturing in the 1990s. Unlike the Koreans, however, many Taiwan firms began as outsourcing suppliers for foreign firms. Many started as small component producers for mobile phones, from cases to keypads, and some firms later became OEM suppliers for foreign buyers by assembling mobile phones according to the designs and specifications of buyers. Some Taiwan firms evolved into higher value-added segments of the chain by further accumulating capabilities in technology and scale, either by becoming EMS providers specializing in large-scale manufacturing and supply chain management for global brands or by adding product design functionality to become ODMs that provide full-package services from design to assembly. Many of the rest of the firms continue to focus on supplying a variety of high value-added components based on strong R&D competency. The increase of offshore outsourcing in the early 2000s increased the growth of Taiwan's mobile phone exports, from 4.7 million to 36 million units in 2000 and 2005, respectively (Ministry of Economic Affairs 2008). The overwhelming majority

Table 4. The world's leading contract electronic manufacturers (EMS/ODM), 2006

Rank	Company	Headquarters	Total revenue (unit: US$ million)
1	Hon Hai Precision	Taiwan	40,527
2	Flextronics	Singapore	17,708
3	Asustek	Taiwan	17,196
4	Quanta Computer	Taiwan	16,503
5	Solectron	US	11,200
6	Sanmina-SCI	US	10,955
7	Jabil	US	10,300
8	Celestica	Canada	8,800
9	Inventec	Taiwan	7,890
10	TPV Technology	Hong Kong	7,176
11	Wistron	Taiwan	6,800
12	BenQ	Taiwan	6,094

Source: EDN Staff (2007).

of Taiwan's exports in the mid-2000s was based on GSM/GPRS standards, widely adopted in global markets (KOTRA 2006).

Taiwan's distinctive path is evident in the strong competitiveness of Taiwan firms in the global contract manufacturing market, including both EMS and ODM firms. As shown in Table 4, three Taiwanese firms have been ranked among the world's top five contract manufacturers. The combined revenues of seven Taiwan firms at one point accounted for 54% of the total revenue of the world's top 20 contract manufacturers. No Korean firms made it into the top 100 contract manufacturers list, in stark contrast to the 11 Taiwan firms on the list. Taiwan firms, in particular, have benefited from the shift of mobile phone manufacturing to China. By leveraging their geographical proximity and combining high-tech R&D capabilities in Taiwan and large-scale, lower-cost manufacturing in China, Taiwan firms have become key players in mobile telecom production networks in East Asia, linking suppliers in Taiwan and China to global brands in the US and Europe. The rise of Foxconn (Hon Hai Precision's trade name) as the leading EMS provider is illustrative of Taiwan's global importance. With origins as a little-known component supplier in the 1970s, Foxconn introduced an EMS model in 2001 to serve major global electronics makers such as Dell, Hewlett-Packard and Apple. Building on its lengthy experience in manufacturing and supply chains in mainland China, the company rose to be the world's largest EMS provider in 2005. In 2010, Foxconn managed to capture 44% of the global EMS market and became the largest private employer in China.

The rise of Taiwan as a specialized supply base, however, contrasts with the country's difficulty in nurturing a global brand. Despite their prowess in manufacturing, Taiwan firms failed to produce a globally competitive mobile phone brand. One notable example of this difficulty is the story of BenQ Corporation. With beginnings as an ODM spin-off of Acer, a well-known PC maker, BenQ made an aggressive move to become a global brand manufacturer by acquiring the then struggling Siemens's mobile phone unit. The move caused BenQ Mobile, the company's mobile phone business unit, to quickly become the world's sixth largest mobile phone maker by the mid-2000s. The upgrading effort, however, could not be sustained in the face of financial difficulty. BenQ Mobile eventually filed for bankruptcy in 2006. In the absence of local manufacturers with strong global brands, the domestic market in Taiwan is now dominated by foreign brands, unlike the Korean market, which is dominated by strong local brands (see Table 2).

In sum, while mobile phone firms in Korea and Taiwan have had a common strong orientation toward global markets, there was a critical difference between the two countries. In Korea, globalization was driven by branded manufacturers that were supported by large and highly diversified conglomerates like Samsung and LG. The manufacturers were successful in leveraging their dominance in an insulated domestic market to globalize sales, as well as production and brands, although their strong control over supply chains undermined the opportunity for growth of local SMEs specializing in components and contract manufacturing. In Taiwan, by contrast, globalization was driven by specialized suppliers, which were successfully inserted into several different production nodes in the value chains of foreign brand manufacturers. The flip side of this success among Taiwan firms has been their difficulty in establishing globally recognized brands and a domestic market dominated by foreign brands.

Japan: Lost in globalization?

In comparison to Korea and Taiwan, a major difference of the Japanese mobile phone industry is its strong orientation toward the domestic market and the near absence of Japanese brands in global markets. The difference is all the more striking because consumer electronics brands such as Sony and Panasonic have long been known for their global success. The fact is also astonishing because the Japanese mobile telecom market is famous for early adoption of innovative mobile technologies and services, such as 3G mobile broadband services.

By 2010, Japan represented less than 1% of the world's mobile phone exports after continuous slippage from 3.3% in 2003 (see Table 1). As in Korea, several major global electronics makers, including NEC, Panasonic and Toshiba, dominated mobile phone production in Japan. These mobile phone producers were globally competitive in the analogue era; in 1990, five of nine of the world's largest manufacturers were Japanese. Over the next two decades, however, their global profile shrank. One reason for this is that the adoption of PDC as Japan's 2G standard significantly hampered global competitiveness. By 2006, the world market share of the five leading Japanese phone makers was less than 5%, lower than the individual share of Samsung or LG. Since the early 2000s, the majority of Japanese mobile phone makers have retreated from overseas markets – including China – instead relying heavily on the home market (Kushida 2008). However, even domestic demand, once robust, has begun to decline, as Japanese consumers have remained tight-fisted. In 2013, 22 million units of mobile phones were shipped for sales in Japan by domestic manufacturers, 58% lower than in 2007 (see Figure 2).

The failure of Japanese phone makers in their efforts to globalize is evident in the following two examples. The first example is the attempt to globalize i-mode, a mobile Internet service provided by NTT DoCoMo, the largest mobile network operator in Japan. In 2000, NTT DoCoMo acquired 15% of KPN Mobile, a Dutch mobile network operator, in an effort to export its i-mode service, one of the world's first 3G mobile broadband services, to European markets and beyond. This move heightened the expectation that, after their failure to globalize because of the adoption of the isolated local standard in 2G, Japanese phone makers could pre-empt overseas markets with their Internet-enabled devices (Young 2002). The hope, however, did not materialize amid the burst of the dot-com bubble and the lukewarm reception of the i-mode service in Europe. In 2005, DoCoMo finally retreated from

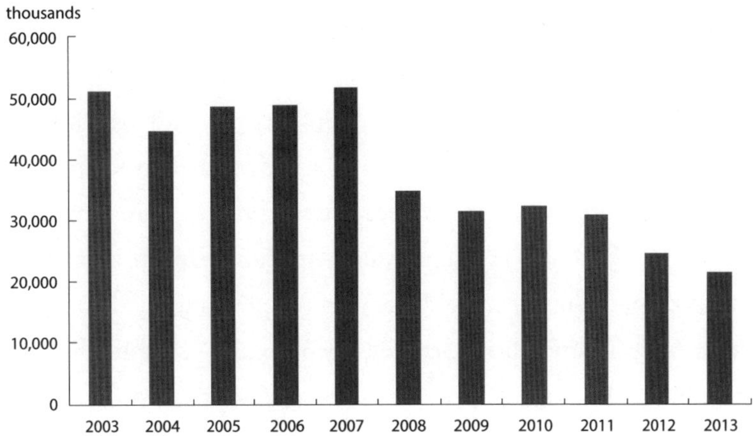

Figure 2. Mobile phone domestic shipments in Japan
Source: JEITA (2014).

the overseas venture with a huge loss and great disappointment for Japanese vendors.

Another example of failed attempts was Japanese manufacturers' Chinese venture (Marukawa 2009). Japanese firms encountered a market dynamic different from that in Japan. Unlike Japan, where 80% of mobile phones sold in 2010 were bundled with monthly subscription contracts and are branded by the operator and sold through the sales outlets of operators, in China, 84% of phones were sold separately from contracts (Euromonitor International 2011; Euromonitor International 2012b). In comparison to Japan, where operators strictly control competition, the unbundling system of China reduces entry barriers for phone makers and intensifies competition. By 2006, after years of difficulty gaining ground, all Japanese phone makers withdrew from China, the world's largest mobile phone market. This blow further increased Japanese reliance on a stagnant home market.

Compared to mobile phone production, Japanese firms remain much stronger in production of components, although their dominance has weakened recently. According to a study in 2000 by Deutsche Bank Research, 29 of 36 component makers supplying nine key enabling components for mobile phones were Japanese (cited in Fingleton 2012). Japan's share in global exports of mobile phone components decreased from 6.4 to 1.9% between 2007 and 2012. Also, Japanese firms account for just 0.5% of the total retail value of the iPhone, compared to 4.7% for Korean firms (Kraemer *et al.* 2011).

In sum, Japan's trajectory in mobile phone manufacturing has been different from those of Korea and Taiwan because of its heavy reliance on the domestic market. In particular, Japanese phone makers, despite their globally-recognized brands and proven manufacturing prowess, have failed to translate their advanced domestic products into global success and maintain the same level of success abroad as their Korean competitors.

China: Multiple trajectories of industrial development

Compared to the other three countries, China is a late-latecomer to mobile telecommunications. In 2004, only one of four Chinese people had a mobile phone, while more than 70% of people in Korea and Japan were using mobile phones.[7] In the same year, China's exports accounted for just less than 15% of total world exports; today, the country is the largest mobile phone exporter in the world, accounting for 42% of the world's exports.

Like Japan, China has a large domestic market and is a major exporter like Korea (albeit on a much larger scale); however, unlike the other countries, China is characterized not by a singular development path, but by multiple paths. As shown below, China shares commonalities with each of the other three countries, which represent China's three development paths. However, increasing mobile phone exports to developing countries, particularly in low-end market segments, illustrates its fourth development path.

First, its large domestic market allows China to follow the Japanese path with a strong orientation toward the domestic market. One notable example is China's effort to develop its own standards. Motivated by the idea of reducing its dependence on foreign technology, logic suggests that the domestic market of China is large enough to sustain proprietary standards, even if the standards prevail only in the Chinese market. In 3G, the Chinese government has been working with domestic and foreign vendors to facilitate the development of TD-SCDMA, its home-grown 3G standard, as an alternative to W-CDMA, the most widely adopted global 3G standard. The government has granted a TD-SCDMA 3G license to China Mobile, the country's largest mobile network operator, in order to ensure that the indigenous standard was sufficiently backed with financial and technological resources to be competitive with the more mainstream standards supported by foreign firms. The Chinese 3G scenario was not exactly the same as when Japan selected its own 2G standard or when Korea opted for CDMA instead of the mainstream GSM. Regardless, the idea of having proprietary home-grown standards would be inconceivable without the existence of a massive domestic market, and the venture could incentivize even foreign vendors to develop TD-SCDMA handsets, although there is little chance of success outside China.

Second, the recent expansion of Chinese mobile phone manufacturers to global markets indicates that China may have locally-branded manufacturers that are as successful in global markets as Samsung or LG. The notable examples are ZTE and Huawei. Over several years, these two firms posted strong growth in the Chinese market despite the fierce competition of major foreign brands (see Table 3). In 2011, ZTE and Huawei were tied for third place after Nokia and Samsung in China's mobile phone sales with each representing 7.5% of the domestic unit sales, up from 2.5% and 2.9%, respectively, in 2006 (Euromonitor International 2012a). Building upon the rapid growth at home, these firms have significantly advanced their standings in global markets with their own brand phones. While much of these sales occurred within China, the share of global sales has steadily increased. In 2010, 53% of the mobile phone unit sales of ZTE and 43% of the unit sales of Huawei came from overseas markets, compared to 42% and 34% in 2009 (Euromonitor International 2011; Gartner 2012). In 2012, ZTE and Huawei accounted for 3.9% and 2.7% of global mobile phone sales (unit-based). These firms are particularly aggressive in developing country markets, as well as in low-end segments of advanced economy markets, typically neglected by big global brands. For example, Huawei ranked seventh among the top 10 smartphone sellers in the US market in 2011 by supplying low-cost smartphones to smaller, regional mobile network operators, which tend to target low-end markets (Troianovski 2012).

A third trajectory in China's integration to global mobile phone production is its strong presence in component production and assembly, somewhat similar to Taiwan's path. China is strong in exporting mobile phones but also in exporting parts for mobile

Table 5. Leading exporters and importers of mobile phone parts, 2011

(unit: US$ million)

Exporters	Trade value	Share (%)	Importers	Trade value	Share (%)
China	38,246	38.6	China	22,245	25.0
Hong Kong	21,493	21.7	Hong Kong	18,144	18.7
Korea	8,959	9.0	United States	6,222	6.4
Mexico	4,760	4.8	Mexico	5,210	5.4
US	4,581	4.6	Hungary	3,914	4.0
Others	20,965	21.2	Others	39,228	40.5

Notes: Based on HS code 851770 (parts of telephone sets, including telephones for cellular networks/for other wireless networks). Taiwan is not included in the UN Comtrade database.
Source: UN Comtrade.

phones. The inflow of foreign contract manufacturers and component suppliers, particularly from Taiwan and other Asian countries, has turned China into a hotspot for global mobile phone manufacturing with strong supply bases in China. Many components are imported to and assembled in China and then subsequently exported all over the world. Table 5 shows the key role of China in the global trade of mobile phone parts. China leads the world in both the export and import of mobile phone parts, followed by Hong Kong, which plays a gateway role for China's international trade. In 2011, China and Hong Kong together accounted for 60% of exports of global mobile phone parts and 44% of the imports.

Each of the three aspects of China's mobile phone manufacturing has some similarities with the strategies of Japan, Korea and Taiwan, resulting in a much more complex and internally diverse development model. Compounding the complexity is that China is not only integrated in the value chain targeted at advanced-economy markets, but is also linked to the value chain for emerging markets.

The growing importance of emerging markets is illustrated

Table 6. Mobile phone export destinations of China and Hong Kong in 2007 and 2011

China exports to:			
2007	Share (%)	2011	Share (%)
US	26.4	**China, Hong Kong SAR***	39.3
China, Hong Kong SAR*	17.3	US	15.7
Germany	7.1	Rep. of Korea	6.4
India	5.8	Japan	4.2
Singapore*	5.7	United Kingdom	2.5
Hungary	3.3	Netherlands	2.3
Finland	2.9	**India**	2.1
United Kingdom	2.7	Germany	1.7
France	2.1	**Mexico**	1.6
Australia	1.9	**United Arab Emirates***	1.5
Hong Kong exports to:			
2007	Share (%)	2011	Share (%)
US	26.8	**China**	21.6
Japan	13.2	**India**	14.9
United Arab Emirates*	9.4	US	13.7
Singapore*	7.0	**United Arab Emirates***	5.6
France	4.8	**Indonesia**	4.3
Spain	3.2	**China, Macao SAR***	2.8
India	3.0	**Singapore***	2.4
China, Macao SAR*	1.9	**Mexico**	2.4
Philippines	1.8	**Bangladesh**	2.3
Other Asia, not elsewhere specified	1.8	**Paraguay**	2.1

Note: Countries and administrative regions not classified as "high-income OECD countries" according to the World Bank's classification list are in bold ("high-income countries" are marked with an asterisk) (http://data.worldbank.org/about/country-and-lending-groups, Accessed February 25, 2014).
Source: UN Comtrade.

by the changing destinations of China's mobile phone exports. As shown in Table 6, most of China's exports in 2007 were concentrated in the US and other high-income OECD countries, with only the non-high-income countries of India and Hungary among the top 10 export destinations. In 2011, additional emerging markets joined the list of China's major export destinations, which included India, Mexico and the United Arab Emirates, as well as Hong Kong. The shift was more obvious in the mobile phone export of Hong Kong.[8] In 2007, the US accounted for 27% of Hong Kong's mobile phone exports, with only India and the Philippines representing non-high-income economies in the top 10 export destinations of Hong Kong. By 2011, many of Hong Kong's exports headed for India, the United Arab Emirates, Indonesia, Mexico, Bangladesh, Paraguay and other emerging economies, indicating the increasing importance of these markets for the exports of China and Hong Kong. The exporting destinations of China, and particularly its exports via Hong Kong, contrast with those of Korea and Taiwan. In 2011, the percentage of non-high-income-OECD markets in the exports of the two countries was 17% and 24% respectively, while the percentage for Hong Kong was 53%.[9] In both Korea and Taiwan, the share of the US market, the largest importer of mobile phones for each, increased from 27% to 54% and from 42% to 50%, respectively, between 2007 and 2011.[10]

What further distinguishes China from its neighbors is that Chinese firms actively cater to a growing market for low-end mobile phones in emerging and low-income countries. Illustrating this point is the success of so-called "Shanzhai" mobile phones in China and, to an increasing extent, abroad (Gao 2011; Zhu and Shi 2010). Most of these phones are unbranded, targeting low-end markets. They are produced by a large number of fragmented producers in dense inter-firm networks in order to meet the rapidly changing consumer appetites for affordable mobile phones in many low-income countries. Originating as a local phenomenon in China, the unbranded "white-box" manufacturers have quickly expanded beyond China. The rapid expansion has even threatened established brand manufacturers like Nokia in developing country markets (Gartner 2010a).

In sum, the trajectory of China's mobile phone manufacturing shows a much more complicated picture than the development trajectories of its East Asian neighbors, showcasing the possibility of simultaneous industrial development through multiple different paths. Similar to Japan, China has an inward orientation based on its large domestic market and proprietary standards. It also has manufacturing capabilities established by foreign firms in both assembly and component production (similar to the model in Taiwan). Lately, Chinese firms have increased their export profiles on the merits of their own brands, similar to the success of some Korean firms. Finally, unlike Taiwan and Korea, the Chinese mobile phone industry also actively utilizes its unique domestic experience to pursue growth opportunities in emerging economies and low-end market segments.

Conclusion

This article has examined how globalization has affected the development paths of mobile phone manufacturing in China, Japan, Korea and Taiwan. Significant divergence among the countries was found with regard to both the position in the global mobile phone value chain and market orientation. The study shows that the rise of a fragmented production system, specifically GVCs, provides countries and firms with the opportunity to hold differentiated roles in the chains, leading to the divergence of development paths. Even within the same industry, the East Asian countries have taken different paths, focusing on different parts of the value chain and market niches. A growing specialization in mobile phone manufacturing, for instance, has offered firms a unique chance to engage in the GVC as specialized suppliers of global brands with little concern for sales and branding. The opportunity has been well utilized by Taiwanese firms whose path is distinctive from those of many Korean and Japanese firms, as branded manufacturers.

In addition, the findings confirm that a more sophisticated framework — such as the one we have proposed — is needed in a global economy where production is increasingly organized through GVCs. Our framework can differentiate the trajectories of industrial development within and across countries, moving beyond a simple dichotomy of whether or not a country is open to foreign investment or whether it follows EOI or ISI. Some Chinese firms have been successfully capitalizing on their domestic experience with low-end consumers to take advantage of the rapid expansion of mobile phone demand in other developing countries. The outward-oriented path is distinctive from the EOI of many Korean or Taiwanese firms whose key export markets are advanced economies. The framework also allows us to identify the simultaneous development of multiple trajectories in China's mobile phone industry and to compare them with those of neighboring countries.

At the same time, this study highlighted the importance of a more nuanced understanding of industrial development paths. It illustrates the difficulty of comparing countries in terms of simple success or failure in industrial development. For example, similar to a recent debate surrounding the post-1989 Japanese economy (Westra 2012), Japanese firms' weak profile in global mobile phone markets and the increasing disconnection between global and local markets — coined the "Galapagos" syndrome (Kushida 2011) — may not be simply understood as the firms' failures given the fact that Japanese consumers are enjoying some of the worlds' most advanced mobile services, enabled by the mobile handsets manufactured by domestic firms, in addition to the strong presence of Japanese component suppliers in global markets. Also, while the embrace of globalization by Korean and Taiwanese firms has led both countries to notable success in different areas, each country appears to be constrained by its own success. Korea's *chaebol*-driven path has marginalized many SMEs specializing in components, whereas Taiwanese firms, with limited financial resources and branding experience, are still struggling to upgrade to OBMs, as exemplified by BenQ Mobile and HTC (Troianovski 2012).

This growing complexity of development paths and often contrasting outcomes have significant implications for various aspects of industrial development, such as technological capabilities and employment. While these topics are not fully addressed in the article, uneven gains across countries with different paths and sub-sectors in different GVC nodes are exhibited in our analysis. Although East Asia is the center of mobile phone manufacturing, largely benefitting from the globalization of the mobile phone GVC, the increasing concentration of production in China (and Vietnam lately) has generated a series of concerns about the 'hollowing-out' of local industrial bases and job losses in other Asian countries, as exemplified by the fact that two-thirds of Korean mobile phones are produced abroad. Moving up the value chain to capture rents from higher value-added activities such as R&D is a constant challenge in the GVC characterized by rapidly changing technological, geographical and corporate terrains. The East Asian countries succeeded in some areas but not in others.[11]

Another question that is important yet not explored systematically in this article is which drivers and mechanisms generated the observed cross-national differences. Why was Korea successful in nurturing a handful of highly capable global brands while Taiwan and Japan failed to do so? How does a country's relative strength in one segment of the value chains relate to its weakness in others? What has driven the internal divergence of development paths in China? To answer these questions, more in-depth analysis is necessary with a focus on the institutional and organizational aspects of each country, as well as the strategic decision-making of various economic actors, including key domestic and foreign firms, within and outside of the mobile phone sector.

Finally, this study identified the concurrent development of multiple trajectories in China's mobile phone industry with some overlap in value chain niches with its neighboring countries. One question is whether such parallel development is transient — meaning it will eventually disappear — or whether it will remain a distinctive characteristic of China's industrial development. Although it is too early to answer, both options seem plausible at this point. The rise of established local brands such as ZTE and Huawei, for example, may undermine the popularity of low-end "Shanzhai" phones, which would eventually decrease the diversity of these concurrent paths. However, given the significant regional and social disparity of economic growth within China, low-end markets may persist even after these major local brands become more prominent at home and globally. Moreover, diverse forms of institutional elements and corporate organizations in China, from large state-owned enterprises to foreign-owned firms and private start-ups, together with the country's strategy of combining different forms of competitive advantages for the sake of comprehensive economic improvement, might enable the co-existence of multiple different forms of development strategies (Appelbaum *et al.* 2011; Rasiah *et al.* 2012).

Another uncertainty is the impact of China's multi-path development. The economic divergence of Korea, Taiwan and Japan generates little competition among these countries because firms in these countries are positioned in relatively distinct market niches. Indeed, the entry of China on the scene has thus far helped many of these firms in different ways, due to the fact that China provides lower-cost production locations and a large number of new consumers for its neighbors to utilize to improve their global competitiveness. This structural diversity at the regional level has so far created a somewhat complementary relationship in the East Asian mobile phone production network at large, consistent with other findings based on a broader set of sectors and countries (WTO and IDE-JETRO 2011). The question for the future is whether such complementarity will persist as Chinese firms try to move up the value chain. The rise of ZTE and Huawei as global brands may threaten the positions now held by Samsung or LG in global markets. The upgrading of Chinese suppliers is likely to generate more direct competition with Taiwanese SMEs. The increasing power of

China's proprietary standards could likewise undermine the position of foreign firms in the Chinese market in favor of local firms. Thus, the question of the future of industrial development in East Asia warrants further research.

This article contributes to the literature of industrial development in East Asia by highlighting a diverging pattern of development paths in the region as well as the internal complexity of the Chinese trajectory. It underscores the importance of a sophisticated framework informed by the GVC literature in understanding diversity across and within countries in fragmented and decentralized global industries. There are limitations, however, that should be addressed in future research. While we use international trade and market data, researchers can further benefit from utilizing more primary data, such as interviews with key corporate actors, particularly to delve into the drivers and mechanisms of path divergence across and within countries. Also, firm-level analysis combined with an inquiry of national institutional and organizational configurations can help to better explain the persistence and change of global-local linkages and development paths.

Notes

1. This chapter has been published in *Journal of Contemporary Asia*. Joonkoo Lee, Jong-Cheol Kim and Jinho Lim. 2016. "Globalization and Divergent Paths of Industrial Development: Mobile Phone Manufacturing in China, Japan, Korea and Taiwan", *Journal of Contemporary Asia* 46(2), 222-246, copyright © Journal of Contemporary Asia, reprinted by permission of Taylor & Francis Ltd., www.tandfonline.com on behalf of *Journal of Contemporary Asia*.

2. For mobile phones, we used Harmonized System (HS) code 851712 (telephones for cellular networks/other wireless networks, other than line telephone sets with cordless handsets) in the 2007 classification and 852520 (transmission apparatus for radio-telephony incorporating reception apparatus) in the previous HS classifications. For mobile phone components, we used HS code 851770 (parts of telephone sets, including telephones for cellular networks/for other wireless networks) in the

2007 classification.

3. For more on these databases, see the relevant websites: http://comtrade.un.org; and http://data.worldbank.org/data-catalog/world-development-indicators. These databases are the sources for the statistical data that follows.

4. According to Kraemer and colleagues (2011), the total wholesale price of the iPhone ($549) in 2010 was split as follows: Apple profits (58.5%); cost of labour in China (1.8%) and outside China (3.5%); cost of material inputs (21.9%); profits for firms in Korea (4.7%), EU (1.1%), Japan (0.5%), Taiwan (0.5%), non-Apple US firms (2.4%); and unidentified profits (5.3%).

5. CDMA, or IS-95 to be precise, is a second-generation (2G) digital cellular standard developed by Qualcomm. In 1995, Korea became the world's first country to deploy a CDMA-based commercial mobile network. Meanwhile, GSM is the widely adopted 2G digital cellular standard, developed by the European Telecommunications Standards Institute (ETSI). By 2005, GSM networks accounted for more than three-quarters of the worldwide cellular network market, serving 1.5 billion subscribers.

6. PDC is one of the second-generation digital mobile telecom standards, similar to GSM and CDMA. It was exclusively adopted in Japan, unlike the other two standards, which had a global presence.

7. In actual number of users, China, with 334 million users, was four times larger than Japan in 2004. By 2010, China had 859 million mobile phone users, 64% of its population, making it by far the largest mobile phone market in the world.

8. Hong Kong's mobile phone exports were almost entirely re-exports (99.99% in 2011), and the majority of them were from China (57% in 2011), according to the UN Comtrade dataset.

9. The share of non-OECD markets in China's mobile phone exports decreased from 30% to 18% between 2007 and 2011, but it appears to be in part because an increasing number of mobile phones from China to non-OECD markets were exported through Hong Kong, which accounted for almost 40% of China's mobile phone exports in 2011.

10. This is also affected by the relocation of production by many Korean and Taiwanese mobile phone firms to countries like China and Vietnam, which is particularly the case for the products targeting developing countries.

11. For the points made in this and the next paragraph, we are indebted to our two anonymous reviewers. Despite the importance of the topics, it is beyond the scope of our current paper, a task we leave for future research.

Chapter 7

Evolving Firm Strategies and Regional Value Chains: Samsung, Apple, and Shanzhai

Introduction

Multinational enterprises (MNEs) play a key role in advancing regionalization. They significantly affect the structure and dynamic of regional trade relations and supply chains through FDI and offshore outsourcing (WTO and IDE-JETRO 2011). Their FDI strategies involve the decisions regarding what they seek to capture – resource, market, or strategic assets (Dunning 1992), and which region or country a specific function is located in. The level and scope of offshore outsourcing set by MNE lead firms deeply influence what types of suppliers and jobs are selected. Their governance strategies with suppliers set the conditions of GVC participation and value distribution (Gereffi and Lee 2012). In this sense, MNEs play a role as a facilitator and governor of regional connection and interaction by engaging in global and regional value chains. And, as highlighted in Chapter 3, extra-regional firms can also shape regional value chains as buyers, suppliers and partners for collaboration.

This chapter aims to highlight the important role of MNEs and their value chain strategies in shaping the structure of regional value chains in Asia and presenting various opportunities and constraints in economic and social upgrading for countries, firms and workers in the region. It also illuminates that the rise of emerging economies as the center of production and consumption in the mobile phone GVC can disrupt the existing market structure and the competitive landscape, and that such disruption can be based on a new form of regional division of labor, facilitated by technological and organizational innovation.

To illustrate these points, the chapter examines three cases from the mobile phone industry: a) Samsung Electronics (SEC) as the leading regional and global mobile phone brand and producer; b) Apple, Foxconn, their trans-regional relationship that has dramatically changed the mobile phone industry; and c) the case of *unbranded* mobile phones in China, known as 'Shanzhai', and the quick surge of local brands in emerging economies like China and India. The first case illustrates that SEC governs its value chain primarily in a vertically integrated manner, and how the governance form, in addition to its strategy of supplier co-location, affects the dynamics of regional value chains. The second case focuses on the role of Apple as an extra-regional actor in influencing the East Asian supply chains in mobile phones and how its influence is amplified through its close relationship with Foxconn, a Taiwanese firm leading the world EMS market. The final case shows how the Shanzhai phone and the ensuing rise of more established local brands in China and India is deeply embedded in well-developed regional value chains and inter-firm, inter-country trade networks in East Asia.

Integrated Value Chains, Co-location and Regionalization: The Case of Samsung

Samsung Electronics, Co., Ltd. (SEC hereafter) is the world's largest mobile phone manufacturer. In 2015, it sold more than 320 million units of smartphones, accounting for 23 % of the total worldwide sales (Gartner 2016b). The Korean MNE is known for offering diverse electronic products, from semiconductors to microwaves and refrigerators. The mobile phone has been the mainstay of the company's business in recent years and played a significant part in generating revenues and profits. Its Galaxy S line of smartphones offers some of the most advanced functions, only matched by a few competitors like Apple. Figure 1 shows SEC's revenue trends in 2012-2015. Its revenue peaked in 2013 with $217 billion and since has decreased to $177 billion in 2015.

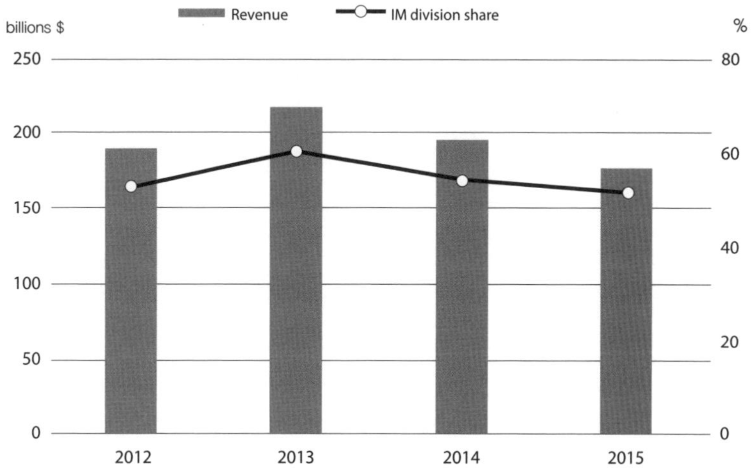

Figure 1. SEC's annual revenue, 2012-2015

Source: Compiled from SEC's annual consolidated financial statements.

Among the company's three business lines, the company's IT and Mobile Communications (IM) division produces mobile phones, tablets, laptops as well as network equipment.[1] In 2015, the division accounted for 52 % of the total revenue.

SEC was founded in 1969, initially as a trading company. While it had had a long history as a well-established electronic maker in the domestic market, its mobile phone business only began in the mid-1990s as Korea entered manufacturing of mobile phones for the first time. SEC was one of the Korean companies that participated in a government-industry consortium to develop and commercialize a mobile phone based on then nascent CDMA technology, backed by US-based Qualcomm (Lee 2003). In 1994, SEC launched its first analog mobile phone with the brand of '*Anycall*', and instantly became one of the leading mobile phone brands in Korea. In 2001, it entered the GSM market, which accounted for the majority of the global market. This expansion significantly boosted its sales globally; in 2003, SEC became the world's third largest mobile phone company in unit sales for the first time. Since then, the company's leading position in the global market has been solidified as it became the world's largest mobile phone producer in 2012, surpassing Nokia (Gartner 2013), and made a global success with its Android-based Galaxy series in a rapidly expanding smartphone market.

In its early years, SEC had an experience as an outsourcing supplier for Western electronic brands like General Electric (GE) for microwaves and other electronics products, and quickly moved up the value chains to become an OBM in many products. Thus, when it was entering the mobile phone business, its brands were firmly established at home although they were much less so in global markets. While relying on imported technology, like Qualcomm-backed CDMA, SEC started to produce and sell mobile phones with its own brand without any prior experience of OEM or ODM in the mobile phone business. In the ensuing years, a number of upgrading efforts were made, including its entry to the GSM market and catching-up more advanced standards and technologies, as well as developing and manufacturing many high-end, key components like semiconductors and high-resolution, energy-saving display modules by itself or through other related companies in Samsung Group. Also, SEC has made a huge investment in designing, global marketing and branding. In 2015, Samsung ranked 7th in Interbrand's Best Global Brands, with $45 billion of brand value.[2]

SEC's value chain governance and regional expansion through FDI

Shown in Chapter 4, the mobile phone value chain has a complex structure, and each mobile phone brand governs the complexity in a different way. One of the most distinctive aspects in SEC is that the company relies heavily on in-house production, which contrast with an increasing use of outsourcing and contract manufacturers in mobile phone manufacturing and electronics in general (see Chapter 4). SEC's mobile phones are manufactured almost entirely in the company's assembly factories in Korea and abroad. The company considers this vertically integrated form of mobile phone assembly, and maintaining the organizational and geographic proximity between manufacturing and other functions like R&D, as one of key factors that sustains its competitive advantage (Nam 2009). Furthermore, SEC has its own semiconductor

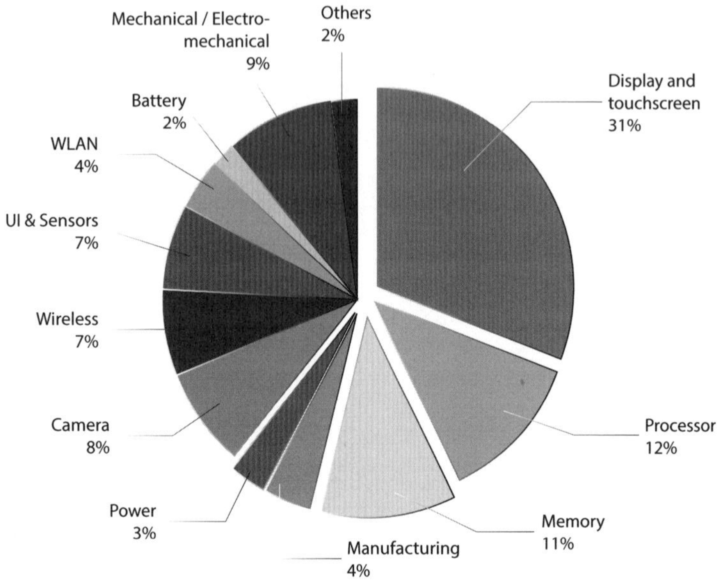

Figure 2. Samsung Galaxy S4 bill-of-materials estimates

Source: Based on iSuppli.

business which supplies key components like microprocessors and flash memory chips to its mobile device division.

This high level of vertical integration is reflected on the composition of parts and components in SEC's products. Figure 2 presents the share of each component's estimated costs in the bill-of-materials (BOM) of the Galaxy S4, the company's flagship model. As in other mobile phones nowadays, a dozen of high-end components account for the overwhelming majority of the costs (see Dedrick *et al.* 2011). Display and touchscreen are the two most expensive component, together representing 31 % of the total BOM. These are followed by processors (12%) and memory chips (11%). And, all these three expensive components, along with power components (3% of BOM), are supplied in-house or by its related firm in Samsung Group. In total, 61% of the Galaxy S4's BOM is accounted for by SEC and its related firms, indicating a high-level of vertical integration at the level of SEC and Samsung Group.[3] This is particularly contrasting to the fact that Apple, SEC's chief competitor in smartphones, relies considerably on third-party contract manufacturers like Foxconn and Pegatron for assembly of its products, as well as other major component manufacturers, including SEC, one of Apple's major suppliers (Vascellaro and Ramstad 2012).

Since the mid-1990s, SEC's production networks have been expanded geographically. As of 2014, the company produced mobile phones from six different countries, including Korea, China, Vietnam, Indonesia, India and Brazil. Given its high level of vertical integration, its global expansion of production networks was mainly through establishing its own subsidiaries abroad via FDI, and used them as an export platform. Many key parts and components are imported from Korea and other countries to be assembled in those factories and many of final products are exported to other regional and global markets.

Korea's exports of mobile phone parts, as presented in Chapter 5, increased to the countries where Korean companies, notably SEC and LGE, operate their assembly factories. In 2013, 91% of Korea's mobile phone parts exports headed for the top five destinations, China (64%), Vietnam (14%), Brazil (6%), Hong Kong (4%), and India (3%). And, SEC has its own mobile phone manufacturing facilities in all of these countries except for Hong Kong, which is used as a gateway of trade with China. Notable is Vietnam's case. As shown in Table 1, until 2008 Vietnam amounted

Table 1. Mobile phone parts trade between Korea and Vietnam

	2008	2009	2010	2011	2012	2013
Korea's exports to Vietnam (mil US$)	4.4	65.7	210.0	642.9	1,272.8	2,206.3
% in Korea's exports	0.1	1.5	3.5	8.1	10.7	13.7
% in Vietnam's imports	3.6	32.7	32.9	36.5	29.8	31.0

Source: compiled from UN Comtrade.

to less than one% of Korea's mobile phone part exports. In 2009, SEC started its first mobile phone production in Vietnam, and since then the exports rapidly increased, from $66 million to $2.2 billion in 2009-2013. For Vietnam, Korea became the second largest import partner of mobile phone parts, accounting for 31% of Vietnam's fast growing mobile phone parts imports (China is the largest with 68%)

In addition to FDI-based expansion, SEC also utilizes the strategy of co-locating Samsung affiliates and its key Korean suppliers near the company's production facilities. For instance, 55 out of about 60 part suppliers for SEC's Bac Ninh mobile phone factory in Vietnam were Korean-owned, housed in the same industrial park as SEC was located (Tuoi Tre News 2013). SEC tend to request its key suppliers in Korea to move their production to its offshore locations to replicate its domestic supply chains overseas. For many SMEs, such co-location involves a great deal of investment and risk, but given a shrinking volume of production at home (see Table 2) as well as SEC's well-established position as one of the world's leading mobile phone brands, it is also not easy for them to decline such a request.

On one hand, with co-location, SEC can quickly ramp up production even in a location with a weak local supplier base like

Vietnam. And, the host country can expect to boost employment quickly because co-located suppliers provide additional opportunity for the growth of employment and tax revenue. On the other hand, it is not always the best for local firms' upgrading. With more capable suppliers locating nearby, MNE lead firms may be less incentivized to invest in building up local capabilities. Moreover, high quality standards and rapid change in today's mobile phone market makes localization a constant moving target that is hard to reach. In fact, in Vietnam, locally owned suppliers for SEC are only a few, and contribute very little; most of them assume simple tasks like packing and wrapping in SEC's supply chains (Tuoi Tre News 2013), while many advanced tasks are conducted by Korean-owned suppliers with a special relationship with SEC.[4]

East Asia and SEC: Regionalized production and key markets

As SEC expands globally its value chain activities, including manufacturing, the share of offshore production has increased significantly. As of 2014, the company's mobile phone production was concentrated in six country hubs: Korea, China, Vietnam, India, Brazil, and Indonesia. In the early years of offshore production, China played a central role in SEC's production network. Mobile phone factories were established in Tianjin, Shenzhen, and Huizhou, respectively, in 2001, 2002, and 2007. By 2008, China finally surpassed Korea as the center of production, accounting for 54% of SEC's mobile phone production, followed by Korea (41%).

As the costs for production arouse in the Chinese coastal regions over the last several years, SEC gradually shifted production to other offshoring locations. Table 2 shows SEC's mobile phone

Table 2. SEC's mobile phone factories and annual production capacity

(unit: US$ million)

Country	City	Establishment year	2011		2012		2014	
			Volume	Share	Volume	Share	Volume	Share
Korea (HQ)	Gumi	1996	38.4	9%	38.4	8%	40.0	8%
China	Huizhou	2007	120.0	29%	120.0	25%	50.0	9%
	Tianjin	2001	81.6	20%	84.0	17%	100.0	19%
	Shenzhen	2002	10.2	2%	-	-	-	0%
Vietnam	Bac Ninh	2009	120.0	29%	180.0	37%	120.0	23%
	Yen Binh	2014	-	-	-		120.0	23%
India	Gurgaon	2006	28.2	7%	48.0	10%	50.0	9%
Brazil	Campinas	1998	18.0	4%	18.0	4%	5.5	1%
	Manaus	1995	-	-	-	-	6.5	1%
Indonesia	Cikarang	2015	-	-	-	-	40.0	8%
	Total		416.4	100%	488.4	100%	532.0	100%

Sources: Compiled from Kim (2012b) and Lee (2015).

factories and their annual production capacity since 2011. Its Shenzhen factory has no longer produced mobile phones from 2012, and the production capacity in the other Chinese factories was also curtailed considerably. China now accounted for less than a third of SEC's mobile phone production capacity. Meanwhile, thanks to the second mobile phone factory in Yen Binh near Hanoi, Vietnam has become the largest production country for SEC mobile phones since 2014 in terms of production capacity. At the same time, production capacity increased in India and a new factory was established in Indonesia near Jakarta in 2015, whereas production in Brazil was reduced in recent years. And, as a result of this continuing expansion of offshore production, the share of SEC's domestic production has declined significantly. In 2014, its Gumi factory only amounted to 8% of the company's production capacity although it mostly focused on high-end mobile phone products.

The importance of Asia in SEC's production networks and the intra-regional shift of production locations is also reflected in SEC's employment. Overall, SEC's worldwide employment more than doubled over the last decade, from 137,400 in 2005 to 319,208 in 2014, indicating the continual growth of its business. At the same time, the share of overseas employment continued to grow; in 2005, it accounted for 34% of the company's total employment, and in 2014 it amounted to 69%. This shows that the center of employment growth has shifted to its overseas units, and domestic employment grew but could not catch up the growth abroad.

Figure 3 presents the shift of the company's employment by geography. It shows that China led the growth of overseas employment until 2010. By 2010, China accounted for 20% of SEC's total employment and 40% of the workforce employed abroad. But, since 2012 the share of, Other Asia, (including Japan) began to surpass China and the other regions. And in 2014, the Other Asia category became where SEC was employing most, representing 35% of the total SEC employees. While the data do not allow a further break-down of the employment figures by country, the rise of employment in this part of Asia is likely to reflect the company's increasing presence in countries in Vietnam, India and Indonesia in recent years.

It is not a simple task to exactly measure the direct effect of SEC's production networks on a specific country in Asia. It is hard to estimate exactly the effect on China, for example, given that many local and multinational firms, including SEC, engages in China's mobile phone production and exports. Meanwhile, Vietnam is a little different because SEC's move to Vietnam has significantly affected Vietnam's export performance not only in mobile phones

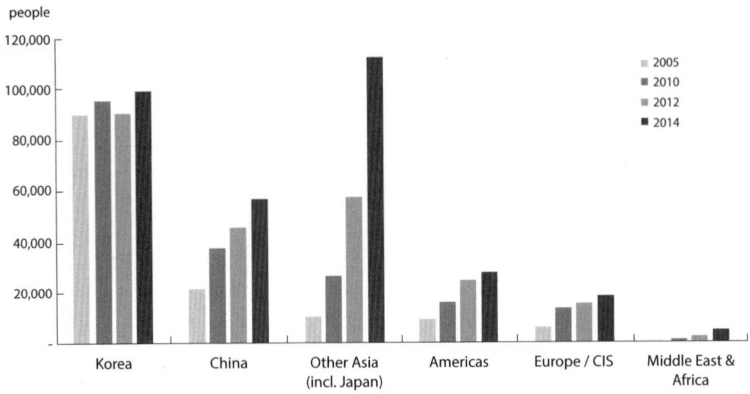

Figure 3. SEC's employment by geography, 2005-2014
Source: Samsung Electronics' annual sustainability reports.

but also in the overall manufacturing exports. In 2012, a year after SEC expanded its first Vietnamese factory at Bac Ninh, the factory alone produced more than 100 million units of mobile phones, over 95% of which was exported to the EU, the Middle East, Russia and other Asian nations, recording $12.7 billion of revenue, which amounted to 11% of Vietnam's total export turnover (Hung 2013). SEC is planning to expand the two plants with a new investment of US$3 billion, which would make their production capacity to expect to grow to 270 million units per year (Cho 2015).

SEC engages in Asia not only through production but also marketing and sales at the downstream of its value chains. As noted in Chapter 4, Asia is one of the most dynamic markets in the global mobile phone industry, and includes the world's biggest single country market (China), highly sophisticated mobile service markets like Japan and Korea, as well as some of the fast growing developing country markets in Southeast Asia. The Asian market as a whole is the largest market for the company, representing 36%

Table 3. SEC's market shares in Asian mobile phone markets

Country	2015 total unit sale ('000)	SEC's market share (%)						SEC's rank
		2011	2012	2013	2014	2015	% change	
China	474,918	18.7	21.8	22.1	13.8	11.0	-7.7	3
India	171,839	19.0	13.8	23.8	22.1	21.5	2.5	1
Indonesia	47,057	23.3	22.0	20.8	22.2	25.1	1.8	1
Japan	38,420	5.2	6.2	6.1	3.9	4.0	-1.2	5
Philippines	23,618	23.9	24.0	19.6	15.5	12.3	-11.6	3
South Korea	20,711	51.9	62.7	58.0	61.3	64.6	12.7	1
Vietnam	15,806	25.3	28.1	30.1	28.4	27.4	2.1	2
Thailand	15,212	11.2	15.2	26.0	31.7	30.2	19.0	1
Taiwan	9,889	15.9	20.7	23.2	17.5	17.8	1.9	2
Malaysia	9,246	29.2	37.8	41.0	41.7	38.9	9.7	1
Hong Kong	7,437	22.7	37.8	34.0	33.8	32.2	9.5	2
Singapore	3,685	28.7	43.6	48.8	35.1	34.3	5.6	1

Source: Compiled from Euromonitor International.

of the company's 2015 revenue, and the importance of the region is much bigger when Korea is included (10% of the revenue) (Samsung Electronics 2015, 10). In this sense, Asia is not only SEC's key production centers but also its key mobile phone markets.

Furthermore, in this dynamic and diverse regional market, SEC has been one of the market leaders in most of the national markets in the region. Table 3 shows SEC's performance of mobile phone sales in key Asian national markets. In 2015, SEC was one of the top three leading mobile phone brands in market share in each of all the markets in Asia except for Japan, where local brands are still in a strong position, and SEC was the market leader in six national markets, including India, the world's second largest national market in unit sales. This market-leading position was strengthened considerably over the last half decade, particularly in the countries like Thailand and Malaysia.

However, SEC has recently confronted a challenge from its global rivals, notably Apple, but also an increasing number of local brands. In China, the world's largest market, SEC was ranked the 3rd but in the face of strong challenges from many local brands like Huawei and Xiaomi as well as its global rival, Apple. Its share has suffered a decline from 19% to 11% of the market over the last five years. Also, notable is the case of the Philippines. As low-end local brands, so-called "Pinoy phones," notably Cherry Mobile and MyPhone, surged in the domestic market, SEC's market position was undermined, and its market share decreased by 12% points in 2011-2015.

In sum, SEC has built an extensive production network across Asia through FDI-based offshoring and with co-located key suppliers. Its highly integrated value chain, from key components to design and branding, plays a key role in differentiating itself from its competitors and helps the company capitalize on its resources and capabilities across different segments of the value chains, strategically spread across East Asia and beyond. At the same time, through its extensive regional value chain, SEC plays an important part in integrating regional economies and industries, significantly affecting the trade patterns of final and intermediate goods across the region as well as a country's integration to GVCs and economic upgrading therein.

Role of Extra-regional Actors in Regional Value Chains

Regionalization and the emergence of regional value chains is attributed to various actors' engagement in an effort to form and manage a web of regional economic exchange of goods, services as well as knowledge and information. And, not only regional actors but also 'external' actors — in a sense that they are based outside the region — play a significant role in shaping regional value chains through their presence in the region as a producer, seller, buyer, consumer, or both. In mobile phones, the rise of the offshore outsourcing model has been spearheaded by Western MNEs and their presence as a buyer have become noticeable in East Asia as the region emerged as the primary location of outsourced production for many non-Asian brands as well as Asian ones.

One of the interesting aspects of the regional value chains in the East Asian mobile phone industry is the rise of contract manufacturers in correspondence to the concentration of offshore outsourcing to the region. And, some of the third-party suppliers have grown fast and big, consolidating outsourcing orders from multiple global buyers. It has created a pattern of co-evolution of value chain concentration in the two key segments at the mid-stream (assembly manufacturing) and down-stream (branding and sales) of the mobile phone GVCs (Lee and Gereffi 2013). These large transnational first-tier suppliers pool outsourced production from multiple buyers, improving the economies of scale. The increasing capacity of these suppliers and their capabilities to serve multiple buyers simultaneously has facilitated the further increase of brands' outsourcing as the latter's confidence in outsourcing and sharing production with other brands grew (Appelbaum 2008; Sturgeon and Lee 2005). East Asia has been a breeding ground for contract manufacturing, particularly in Taiwan, as exemplified by the rise of Foxconn (see Chapter 6).

In short, offshore outsourcing by non-Asian electronics firms and the ensuring rise of East Asian contract manufacturers highlights that regional value chains are not solely driven by intra-regional actors, such as Asian MNEs. Inter-regional linkages do play a significant role in shaping intra-regional connections and interactions. In the following, this point is illustrated with the example of Apple and Foxconn and their trans-regional linkages.

Apple and the East Asian supply base: Inter-regional value chain linkage

While SEC has maintained a vertically integrated form of supply chains, Apple's supply chains, its major rival in the global smartphone market, have evolved in the opposite direction, extensively combining offshoring and outsourcing. Apple focuses on conducting in-house some of upstream activities such as R&D and product design and downstream tasks like sales and marketing, while it extensively uses third-party suppliers for components and assembly across a wide range of product lines from its desktops to smartphones.

Based on the BOM analysis of one of Apple's flagship products, Figure 4 illustrates the supply chains of the iPhone4s and the value distribution therein between the countries involved. As with many other mobile phones, the product consists of a few hundreds of components, but high-end components like mobile processors, memory chips and display units come from some of major mul-

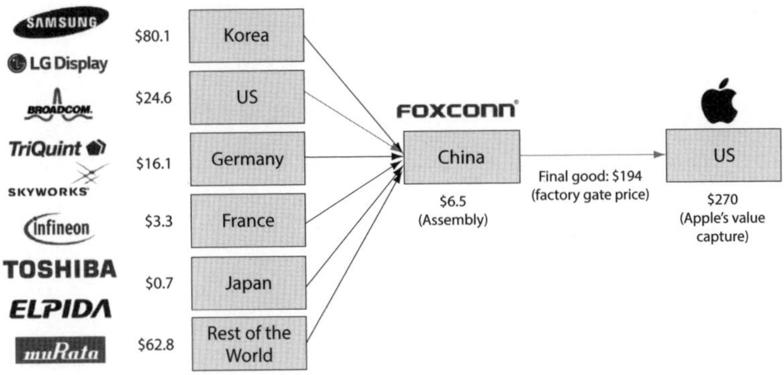

Figure 4. Apple's supply chains of the iPhone4s

Source: Based on OECD (2011).

tinational electronics companies, which include SEC, Broadcom, Skyworks and Toshiba. When the value of parts and components is considered, suppliers from Korea account for $80, the largest share for any single country, out of the factory gate price ($194), followed by the US ($25) and Germany ($16). Most of the products are finally assembled by Foxconn at some of its Chinese locations to take advantage of lower labor costs. Indeed, China as the location of final assembly contributes only a small fraction ($6.5) of the product's retail value.[5] Importantly, most of the remaining part of the value is captured by Apple for high value-added activities like R&D and branding as well as for its role in organizing and governing the entire supply chains.

The fact that many of the key components for Apple products are supplied by MNEs, mostly from affluent Western and Asian countries, belies the importance of regional supply chains in East Asia. According to Apple's Supplier List in 2013, more than 600 firms out of 748 Apple suppliers listed were located in Asia and 331 in mainland China (CihinaFile 2013). A considerable number of suppliers are clustered in mainland China and neighboring Asian countries. Some firms are Chinese but many others are foreign-owned companies or Chinese subsidiaries of MNEs from Korea and Japan as well as the US and Europe.[6] In this way, Apple's supply chains are embedded in a strong supplier base in the East Asian region. Indeed, several years ago in the midst of an intense public debate on offshoring and job losses in the US, Steve Jobs was confronted a question by President Obama whether Apple could bring back, or 'back-shoring,' manufacturing jobs in the supply chains to the US According to a *New York Times* report, the late Apple founder answered negative (Duhigg and Bradsher 2012), implying that the supplier network the company relied on in Asia could not be replicated in the US in a similar scale or scope. Apple has tried to keep all the suppliers closely located suppliers in and around China to capitalize on the 'just-in-time' (JIT) supply of key materials and components (Satariano and Burrows 2011).

The presence of Apple's value chains in East Asia has not only helped the company's competiveness in global markets, but also boosted East Asian suppliers. Taiwanese, Korean and Japanese suppliers have experienced a rise of revenue and stock prices over the last several years by being a supplier to Apple (Cheng and Chien 2016; Kotaro 2016). Given Apple's strong performance in sales and forerunning in innovation in design and technology, the status of Apple's supplier granted them a prospect for revenue growth as well as a sign of highly competent suppliers in this fast changing high-tech industry. Indeed, Apple accounted for the overwhelming majority of profits in the industry over the period (with a fraction shared by SEC), whereas many other brands failed to capture any significant portion of the profits (Dediu 2012).

At the same time, being in the same boat with Apple means that if Apple's sales suffer, these suppliers are hit as well. In 2016, Apple posted a disappointed result in the first-quarter sale of iPhone 6 series, leading to its first quarterly revenue decline in 13 years. It sent a shock wave across suppliers in Asia. In addition to the shrinkage of the overall mobile phone demands, the effect was amplified by the consolidation of smartphone markets, where many capable suppliers rely on a handful of brands like Apple and SEC. Japan Display, for instance, suffered a 24% decline of sales in the first quarter, posting an operating loss of 7 billion yen. The Apple supplier's sales and profits already showed a decline as Apple reduced orders to suppliers in the face of the lukewarm reception of the iPhone 6 series in the market. Sharp, another display supplier, also posted an operating loss of 92 billion yen in the first quarter as it witnessed a drop in Apple's sales (Kotaro 2016).[7] The effect was also felt in Taiwan; according to a news report, major Taiwanese suppliers' sales to Apple rose in the first quarter of 2015 an average of 17% year-over-year, but their sales dropped by 7% during the same period in 2016, putting major suppliers like Largan Precision, Catcher Technology, and Pegatron in Apple-induced slump (Cheng and Chien 2016).[8]

In short, Apple's decentralized supply chains relying on a wide range of third-party suppliers have facilitated the growth of specialized suppliers in East Asia, which has bolstered Apple's competiveness as well. The US-based company plays a key role in organizing a regional supply chain which includes both Asian and Western suppliers located regionally. While Apple suppliers in East Asia have been successful over the last several years thank to their linkages to Apple, the inter-regional linkage has also revealed its downside in the face of the recent slump of Apple's sales.

Foxconn: Growing by supplying global brands

As discussed in Chapter 4, the co-evolution of global brands (or OEMs) and contract manufacturers in terms of supply chain consolidation is one of the key recent developments in mobile phone GVCs (Lee and Gereffi 2013). In 2000-2010, the market share of the five leading EMS providers rose from 53% to 75%, and just two leading EMS firms, Foxconn and Flextronics (now Flex), commanded 59% of the entire EMS market in 2010 (NIPA 2011). As the OEM segment became more concentrated, EMS firms, needed to match the scale and speed of production required by big brand buyers, and they sought economies of scale by acquiring other EMS firms and exiting OEMs (Sturgeon and Kawakami 2011). The rise of more capable suppliers, along with an increasing level of standardization and commodification in mobile technology, has facilitated OEM buyers to contract out manufacturing of more sophisticated product lines to consolidated EMS firms, which expanded their domains in the mid-stream part of the mobile phone GVCs. In this way, the consolidation in the OEM segment has facilitated consolidation its key upstream node.

Emblematic is the rise of Foxconn, the tradename of Taiwan-based Hon Hai Precision, as the leading EMS provider. Until 2001, it had been mainly engaged in relatively simple assembly of electronic products based on inputs and components supplied by buyers or larger manufacturers. Since 2001, when it adopted an EMS model, the sales of Foxconn International Holdings (FIH) Mobile, Foxconn's mobile phone manufacturing unit, surged from \$7.6 million to \$10.7 billion in 2007. While FIH Mobile suffered the slow-

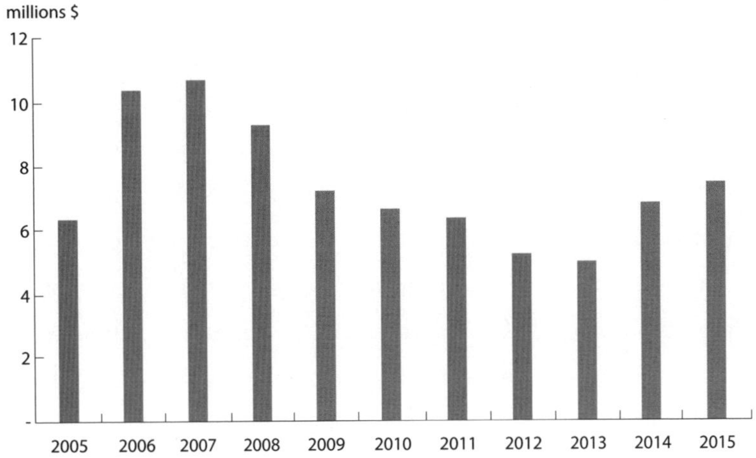

Figure 5. FIH Mobile's revenue, 2005-2015

Source: FIH Mobile annual reports.

down of business in the face of sluggish demand growth after the global economic crisis, its sales and profits began to bounce back, and in 2015, it recorded $7.5 billion of revenues and $297 million of operating profits (FIH Mobile 2016).

The main business of FIH Mobile is providing a vertically integrated manufacturing services for mobile phone brands worldwide. The company's operations consist of three regional segments based on the location customers: Asia, Europe and Americas. The company caters to customers worldwide through its production facilities in Asia (China and India), Europe (Hungary) and Latin America (Brazil), employing more than 110,000 people worldwide.[9] Yet, most of its production is conducted in multiple manufacturing plants spread across mainland China. The largest among them are factories in Shenzhen, Zhengzhou and Chengdu. Two Shenzhen plants hire approximately 400,000 employees to make iPhones and iPads as well as products for other electronics makers, and Foxconn factories in Zhengzhou and Chengdu, each with about 100,000 employees, respectively focus on iPhones and iPads (Luk 2014).

In this way, Foxconn plays a critical role in linking China's labor and East Asian suppliers to brand buyers in North America and Western Europe.[10] Its key capability lies in managing a large scale of production internally and through supply chains to serve multiple global and regional brand buyers at the same time, although the company's growth has been largely attributed to a few big buyers like Apple.[11] In other words, when China is playing a role of a 'global factory' in the world economy, it is supported organizationally by companies like Foxconn that play a bridging role in the mid-stream of the GVCs for many global brands.

At the same time, Foxconn has made a continuing effort to upgrade their position in the global electronics industry. As an EMS provider, the company's margin is generally low: 5.2% of gross margin in 2015 (FIH Mobile 2016), which is much lower than the industrial average. It is because the primary motivation of global brands outsourcing assembly and related services to EMS providers was to lower production costs, and given Foxconn's reliance to a handful of big buyers, the latter is likely to have an upper hand in their bargaining relationship. While the EMS market is significantly concentrated, concentration has also taken place at the brand segments, which intensified EMS firms' dependence on a smaller number of brand buyers (see Chapter 4).[12] In response, Foxconn has increased the level of vertical integration to key technology and components so as to make up a thin margin in its EMS business with higher margins in component production. At the same time, by producing some of the key components in-house, it can expect to secure a stable supply of these components as well as reducing production costs by controlling production by itself, both of which would not only benefit Foxconn but also satisfy its buyers. Foxconn is also trying to upgrade to high-end component manufacturing as well, as shown in a recent acquisition of Sharp, a troubled Japanese display manufacturing firm.

Another upgrading effort is moving up to the brand segment of mobile phones and other electronics value chains. Yet, Foxconn's effort of selling its own branded phones locally has not been successful so far, and this is not particularly surprising given that Taiwanese mobile phone manufacturers are known for their difficulty in upgrading to branded manufacturers (see Chapter 6), and suppliers' move to branding is not generally welcomed by their branded buyers due to a potential conflict in the final product market (Humphrey and Schmitz 2002). However, in the face of decreasing orders from its key buyers like Apple, Foxconn made a more effort to diversify their markets and buyers. One of the latest was to acquire Microsoft Mobile's entry-level phone unit, a part of the business that Microsoft acquired from Nokia in 2014. The acquisition included Nokia Vietnam's plant in Bac Ninh (Greene and Verbergt 2016). This indicates that Foxconn is expanding its production base beyond mainland China to the rising center of the global mobile phone production. Also, Foxconn can capitalize on the value of the Nokia brand in many emerging country markets, where feature phones remain an important market segment and the Nokia brand still resonates with many consumers. Foxconn also can avoid a potential conflict with some of its key buyers, whose focus is now in the expanding smartphone segment.

The focus of our discussion above lies on the economic side

of regional production networks and the role of intra- and extra-regional actors in bridging transnational relationship in value chains. The importance of external actors in regional value chains, however, is also evident in their impact on social conditions, specifically conditions for workers integrated to the chains.

The Apple and Foxconn case is also emblematic in this regard. In 2010-2012, a series of workers' suicides took place in Foxconn's factories in China where Apple products were produced. The ensuring news reports and investigations by labor watchdogs revealed a series of violations of labor standards, including low wages, excessive overtime, and compromised workplace safety (Chan 2013; SACOM 2010). While Apple initially refused to hold any accountability for the conditions at its supplier factories and the workers it did not directly employed, much of the criticisms and pressures, mounted from CSOs, the media and the public, including its loyal customers, over Apple, whose brand image was tied less to sweatshops than innovative and sleek products. Eventually, Apple and Foxconn jointly announced in 2012 to allow a third-party organization to investigate labor conditions in some of Foxconn's factories in China and promised to improve working conditions, including raising wages.

This case highlights some of the important aspects of regional value chains and its effect on socio-economic conditions in the region. First, it shows the key role of extra-regional actors not only in the rise of East Asian suppliers but also shaping labor conditions in the regional supply chains. The engagement of non-Asian actors like Apple is not limited to the economic aspects of regional value chains but extended to their social impacts. Second, the case also highlights the importance of large transnational suppliers like Foxconn in affecting labor conditions of the region. It is well known that Foxconn's presence in a region or city significantly affects the labor market conditions for the region or city, including the rapid rise of employment opportunities and the sudden influx of migrant workers from nearby regions (Chan *et al.* 2013). A sheer size of employment generated by such a mega-supplier indicates the outsized influence of a specific value chain actor in many aspects of labor relations in a given region or country (Appelbaum 2008; Lee and Gereffi 2015).

Market Disruption, New Entrants and Regional Value Chains

The growth of mobile phone consumption in developing countries has significantly affected the mobile phone GVC. One of the interesting related developments is the rapid increase of *non-branded* mobile phones, targeting at the less quality- and more price-conscious consumers in developing countries, or so-called 'bottom of the pyramid' (BOP). As shown in Chapter 4 (see Table 1), the portion of the 'Others' category in the market share statistics compiled by Gartner, an IT market analysis consultancy, remained less than 20% of global shipments until 2009, but it reached 31% in 2010 and rose to 34% in 2014. The category includes less prominent brands outside the top 10 sales list (in 2014, with a market share with less than 2% of the global sales), but it also contains unbranded, or so-called 'white-box', mobile phones. And, according to many market analysts, the rise of the latter is playing a key role in the growth of the residual category (Gartner

2012).

White-box devices generally refer to the genetic models that do not carry any brand name and are created by using a turnkey solution based on application processes and reference designs and platforms. The devices are sold through legal channels but also through "gray" or underground market channels. While most unbranded white-box devices are targeted at the low-end segments of the market at affordable prices yet with key basic functions, more and more are produced in an organized manner with more advanced functions thanks to modularized technology and components and the sophistication of supplier ecosystems for such products. It expedites the process of launching an Android-based, white-box smartphone from scratch, now within just a four-week period (Gartner 2014a).

The popularity of unbranded mobile phones has bifurcated the mobile phone market into two segments: the high-end smartphone market dominated by Apple, Samsung and several other globally-branded OEMs, and the low-end phone market populated by fragmented unbranded phone manufacturers, with "Shanzhai" phones in China a notable example (Zhu and Shi 2010; Brandt and Thun 2011). The popularity of non-branded phones is even challenging lead firms in markets for basic feature phones, what is called the "low-end disruption" in the mobile phone market (Dediu 2012). Furthermore, some of the white-box makers have emerged to upgrade to an established brand, as shown below in the case of some of the fast rising Chinese local producers like Gionee.

In this regard, shifting end markets to emerging economies is likely to accompany GVC segmentation or bifurcation, presenting new opportunities and challenges to value chain actors in terms of

GVC participation and upgrading. In the following, we examine the growing importance of market disruption originated in the emerging economy, and the rise of new entrants and the role of regional value chains therein, focusing on the recent dynamics in the Chinese and Indian markets.

Shanzhai, MediaTek, and regional value chains

Originally, "Shanzhai" (literally "mountain village" in Chinese) handsets refer to mobile phones cloned after branded products that are sold at knock-down prices without legitimate authorization and registration. Initially emerged from Shenzhen, they created a huge buzz in the Chinese market in the late 2000s. Some estimated that there were about 150 million unregistered handsets in China in 2007 alone, produced by nearly 100 device vendors. It costed approximately a fourth or less than branded phones because it came without costs for marketing and sales, final stage testing and after-sales service (Kao and Lee 2010; Zhixiang 2008).

A host of factors has made possible for such white-box phones to flourish in China and increasingly other emerging economies. First, as mobile phone technology became mature, many components, particularly low- to mid-end ones, have become commodified in the sense that they can be easily supplied from the market and the phone producer does not need to invest in developing and manufacturing them in-house. Second, increasing standardization and modularization of components and sub-units also makes it easier for the OEM to build a mobile phone without in-depth knowledge of all the different technological elements necessary to do it. Particularly, MediaTek's turnkey solutions played a key role in the rise of white-box phones. The mobile system-on-chip (SOC) solutions developed by the Taiwanese chipset design firm basically combine application chipsets and other key hardware and software functions into an integrated system. This allows the mobile phone maker to readily deploy the solutions to develop a variety of mobile phone models only with different look and feel through quick customization.

Organizationally, modular technology facilitated the deverticalization in the value chain between integrated chipset solution providers like MediaTek and mobile phone manufacturers, or OEMs, which now focus more on product development and actual manufacturing and assembly while leaving some of the key technologically sophisticated processes to such specialized solution developers. Also, such a division of labor was helped by the emergence of independent design houses (IDHs), who specialized in product design. This has further unloaded some of the burden of extensive product development and design processes from OEMs, which makes them focus on a more agile response to changing customer preferences and market trends. At the same time, it has facilitated the entry of local firms with little technological and R&D capabilities to mobile phone manufacturing. All these factors drove the mushrooming of Shanzhai phone makers in China in the late 2000s. And as demands for affordable mobile phones rose in emerging economies, these phones were exported to Russia, India and other developing countries.

In more recent years, as the Chinese market quickly gravitated to more advanced mobile phones, including smartphones, some of the former Shanzhai phone vendors entered the mainstream market by upgrading with own brands and extensive marketing campaigns as well as offering more advanced, higher-priced products.

At the same time, the low-end market the Shanzhai phone initially developed is also increasingly targeted by mainstream brands, which also utilize modular platforms like what MediaTek provides.

These developments have intensified competition in the Chinese mobile phone market. A host of newcomers like Xiaomi, OPPO, Vivo, Tianyu, Meizu, and Gionee expanded their market share considerably in just a few years, whilst foreign incumbents like Samsung, Nokia (now Microsoft), HTC, and LG as well as even domestic ones like ZTE experienced a significant setback in their market position, as shown in Figure 26. Among incumbents, Samsung, Lenovo and Huawei managed to maintain their leading positions, but others like Nokia and ZTE drastically lost their market in 2011-2015. Now the market is filled with new local entrants, which expanded their market share drastically in such a short period. And, some of them are already feeling their growth slowing down in a highly volatile competitive landscape.

In sum, the popularity of white-box mobile phones illustrates some of the profound changes in the recent mobile phone GVCs. More and more new consumers are coming from emerging and developing countries, and the first-time users are likely to be lower in disposable income than early adopters although their aspiration for advanced devices may be a little less, highlighting the importance of targeting at emerging markets for further expansion. And, the availability of more affordable phones has facilitated the diffusion of mobile phones across the developing world, particularly among the population (Karippacheril *et al.* 2013; World Bank 2009).

At the same time, it has affected the competitive landscape in the mobile phone industry and global value chains. Thanks to modularized platforms and commodified components, it has be-

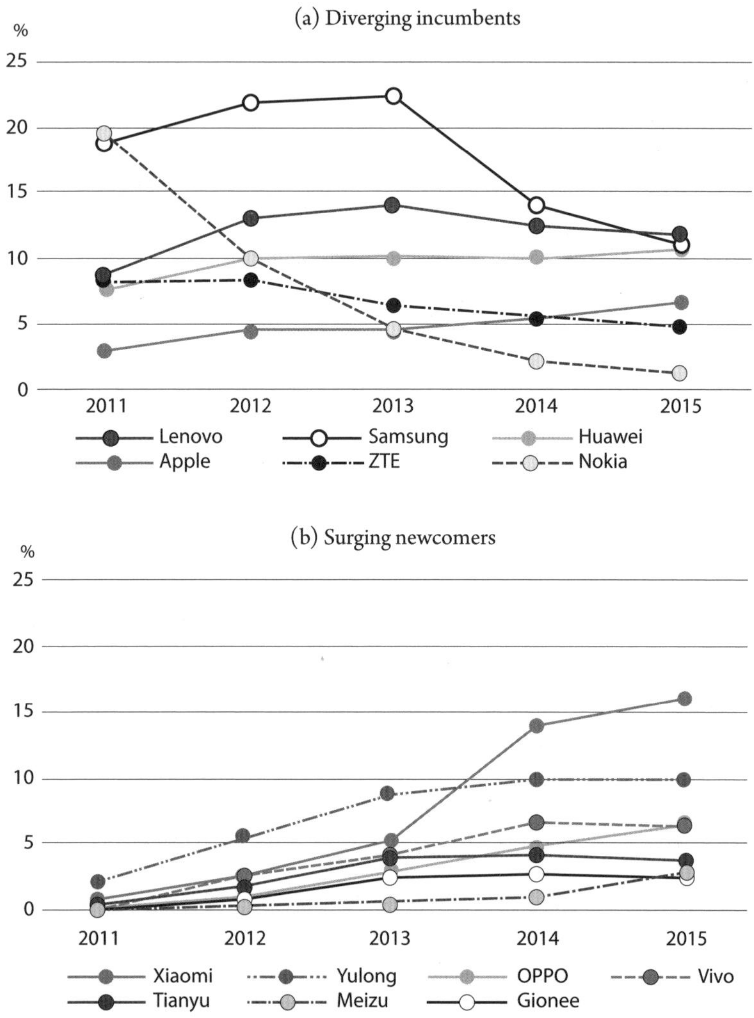

Figure 6. Mobile phone market shares by brands in China, 2011-2015

Source: Compiled from Euromonitor International (2015b).

come much easier for the OEM to launch a variety of good-quality smartphone for different markets in a short period. It has lowered entry barriers for many domestic brands in emerging markets like India and the Philippines. They emulate the Shanzhai model pioneered by Chinese firms in their own markets, as illustrated below in the Indian case. These local brands highly focus on localizing products and services (e.g., dual SIM cards and longer battery life) to outcompete global brands like Samsung and Apple, simultaneously capitalizing on the opportunities presented by deverticalization in the mobile phone GVC, for instance, extensively utilizing foreign ODM vendors and standardized reference platforms.

India's mushrooming local-brand mobile phones

India is the second largest mobile market behind China, with more than 900 million mobile phone users. The market is expected to grow further, given that its mobile subscription density, 74 out of 100 people in 2014, is still lower than China (92 out of 100 people), according to a World Bank statistics. India is now considered the next big growth market for many global mobile phone brands, which are confronting slowed market growth in advanced economy markets and tighter competition with local brands in China. Yet, as shown in Figure 7, Indian local vendors made significant inroads over the last few years into the domestic market previously dominated by foreign brands like Nokia and Samsung. The growth trend in unit sales in 2011-2013 reversed in the face of economic downturn that plagued many emerging markets, but in the tightened market, local mobile phone brands were still able to be expand their market share in the domestic market. While Samsung remains the largest mobile phone seller in India (22% of total unit sales), four leading local brands — Micromax, Karbonn, Lava and Intex — increased their combined market share from 17% to 42% in 2011-2015.

The fast growth of local brands was facilitated by multiple

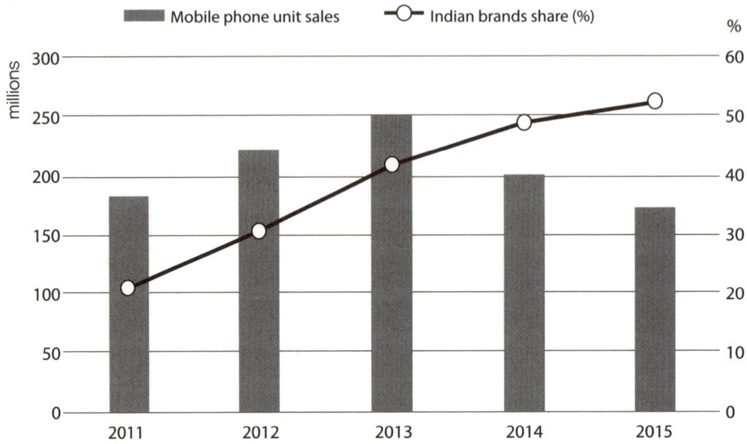

Figure 7. Mobile phone market sales and local vendors' share in India, 2011-2015
Source: Compiled from Euromonitor International (2015c).

factors. First of all, Nokia's struggle left a big hole up for grab in the Indian market. Until 2012, the Finnish company, now part of Microsoft Mobile, led the market, with 41% in 2011; however, its market share continued to slide even after being acquired by Microsoft, to 8% in 2015, opening a chance for others to capture a bigger pie in the fast growing market. Second, Indian firms made a successful entry through strong localization efforts, such as offering mobile phones with dual SIMs or supporting multiple local languages. Local vendors also effectively utilized local distribution channels, simultaneously releasing multiple phone models with advanced functions still at affordable prices. More importantly, Indian firms actively utilized imported phones and semi-assembled kits from China, Taiwan and Korea to capture the market. Similar to Chinese white-box vendors, Indian producers took advantage of modularized mobile platforms by partnering with capable OEMs and ODMs in the East Asian mobile phone value chains.[13] For example, Micromax still imports most of its products from its Chinese manufacturers, with only limited volumes (mainly tablets) manufactured locally. It is mainly because key components such as display panels have to be imported, and Micromax does not sell enough to drive down the cost as much as its Chinese suppliers can do (Euromonitor International 2015a). Still, through such a value chain arrangement, Micromax has become the second largest mobile phone seller in India. Finally, extra-regional actors like Google played an important role in facilitating the growth of local brands. Google has initiated the *AndroidOne* project, where it works with mobile phone vendors to develop affordable (as low as $100) Android-based smartphones, specifically tailored to consumers in developing countries. India is the first country that AndroidOne phones were released, and Micromax, Karbonn and Spice, three major local brands, have been participating in the project. In this sense, the India case illustrates the importance of regional value chains as well as the role of extra-regional actors in facilitating the mushrooming of locally branded mobile phones.

Built on the success at home, Indian firms are expanding their reach to neighboring countries like Bangladesh and Sri Lanka as well as other emerging economies. Micromax is the third largest smartphone vendor in Russia, for example, and planning to export smartphones to China (McLain 2016). Also, in the midst of the Indian government's 'Made in India' initiative of promoting domestic manufacturing, Indian mobile phone companies are trying to build or expand production facilities, often in partnership with foreign manufacturers. For instance, Lava International plans to expand its production facilities by 2017, and Karbonn set up a mobile phone factory with Water World Technology, a Chinese manufacturer, in 2015. Also, in an effort to upgrade, some of the leading Indian producers are trying to establish production facilities for key components like printed circuit boards (PCBs) (Aulakh 2014).

These upgrading efforts are affected by the increasing presence of Chinese mobile phone brands in India.[14] In the face of saturation at home, many Chinese brands have begun to make inroads into Indian and Southeast Asian markets, challenging Indian firms. For example, Lenovo significantly expanded its operation in India. Even new players like Gionee, Vivo, and OPPO are quickly expanding to India for production and marketing, posing a threat to burgeoning Indian local producers (Rao 2016). However, at the same time, there are increasing ties between Indian and Chinese firms. In 2015, for example, Gionee, a Chinese vendor, partnered with Foxconn, a Taiwanese, and Dixon Technologies, an Indian EMS provider, to start manufacturing mobile phones in India. Another Chinese vendor, Coolpad, joined forces with Videocon Industries, an Indian manufacturer, to produce some of the Coopad devices in the latter's Indian factories. In this way, Chinese and Indian firms are competing at one part, but cooperating at the other part of the mobile phone value chains, further expanding the geographic and organizational boundaries of Asian mobile phone value chains.

Conclusion

This chapter has examined three cases from the mobile phone industry in Asia: SEC as the leading global brand; Apple and Foxconn and their trans-regional relationship; and finally, the rise of white-box mobile phones in China and the growth of popular local brands in China and India. It illuminates the important role played by firm actors, particularly intra- and extra-regional MNEs, in shaping the structure of regional value chains. And, RVCs facilitate the rise of new forms of firm actors and market strategies.

The case of SEC shows that the company plays an important part in integrating regional economies and industries through its extensive regional value chain, significantly affecting a country's GVC integration and economic upgrading, with Vietnam a prominent example. SEC's highly integrated value chain through FDI-based offshoring and co-located key suppliers facilitates the company to take advantage of distinctive resources and capabilities across different segments of the value chains, strategically located across East Asia and beyond.

In contrast, Apple's decentralized supply chain depends on a wide range of third-party suppliers, and the rise of Apple in the mobile phone industry facilitated the growth of specialized suppliers in East Asia although the recent slow-down of Apple's iPhone sales has put many of them in slump. While Apple are not based in Asia and organizes its supply chain differently from SEC, it also deeply affects not only the rise of East Asian suppliers but also shaping labor conditions in the regional supply chains.

The final case illustrates the importance of regional value chains in the rise of new breeds of mobile phone producers in China and India. Both Shanzhai phone producers and emerging local brands in these countries are deeply associated with specialized suppliers like MediaTek, and these producers challenged global brands like Nokia and Samsung and outcompeted them in some markets by integrating specialized suppliers with their ability to quickly and flexibly address local consumer demands. Taken together, all these three cases highlight important relationships between MNEs' evolving strategies and changing dynamics in regional value chains.

Notes

1. The other two Divisions are the Consumer Electronics (CE) division and the Device Solution (DS) division. The latter is in charge of semiconductor and display businesses.

2. http://interbrand.com/best-brands/best-global-brands/2015/ranking/.

3. This does not include SEC's margins and costs from non-manufacturing activities, such as R&D, technology licensing as well as branding and marketing. As shown in the case of Apple's iPhone product, nowadays, a great deal of margins are claimed by the brand manufacturer that leads and governs its value chain (see below).

4. Even the co-located suppliers may find it difficult to keep following SEC as the latter constantly shifts its production locations from one to another. They have to either make an additional investment which can be costly, or develop alternative buyers.

5. The total value captured by China can be higher since many MNEs produce their parts and components supplied for Apple's products in China to capitalize on lower product costs as well as geographic proximity to the final assembly, which is considered important by Apple (Satariano and Burrows 2011).

6. The importance of MNEs in China's high-tech manufacturing is illustrated by the fact that they account for the majority of China's high-tech exports. In 2010, 82 percent of China's high-tech exports came from foreign-invested firms in China, which rose from 79% in 2002 (Prange 2016, 5).

7. In March 2016, Sharp was bought by Foxconn for $3.5 billion, the largest acquisition thus far by a foreign company in Japan's technology sector. It is also a major move by Foxconn to upgrade to developing and producing technologically advanced components.

8. The woe of these Taiwanese suppliers were also amplified by the fast catching-up of Chinese suppliers in mobile phone manufacturing, or the expansion of so-called 'red supply chains,' which leads to a fierce price-cutting competition among Asian suppliers (e.g., display by BOE Technology; chip production by Spreadtrum).

9. http://www.fihmb.com/about/FIHprofile.aspx. "The total employment of Foxconn amounted to 873,000 as of the end of 2016."

10. Foxconn also serves major Chinese and East Asian mobile phone brands. See Table 2 in Chapter 4.

11. In 2015, 72 percent of FIH Mobile's total revenue came from the five largest buyers, with Apple believed to be one of them. The largest buyer accounted for 26 % of the total (FIH Mobile 2016, 33).

12. In fact, this is not a phenomenon particularly to the electronics sector. As a 'smile curve' idea suggests, the lower value added in the midstream of the value chain

(production) compared to pre- (upstream) and post-production (downstream) is applied to many other manufacturing industries (Mudambi 2008).

13. Our analysis at Chapter 5 also illustrates that India's trade linkages with other Asian countries have been strengthened. In mobile phones, India expanded its major import partners to China and Vietnam in 2007-2013. And, India's imports of mobile phone parts from China significantly increased.

14. The government has begun to discourage Indian firms from using imported components, which mainly came from China, by removing some of the tax exemptions from the 2016 government budget plan (Firstpost 2016).

Chapter 8

Epilogue

Mobile Asia and the Future of Capitalism

This book has examined the landscape of global and regional mobile phone value chains, and shown that inter- and intra-regional value chains and MNEs as key participants to GVCs shape the way regional connection and interaction emerges. Built on the literatures of convergence and divergence in Asian capitalisms and global value chains, it has addressed the key trends and dynamics in global mobile telecom value chains, and the growing importance of Asian and extra-regional MNEs and regional value chains therein by analyzing the patterns of international trade networks and divergent trajectories of East Asian economies in GVC integration and industrial upgrading.

The first two chapters in Section I have discussed key theoretical and conceptual backgrounds. The first emphasizes the historical rise of Asia in the context of recent waves of globalization and regionalization, and diverging paths in Asian capitalism amid economic, social and cultural commonalities. The next has introduces the key concepts of the GVC approach and recent developments in the global economy from a GVC lens. It has proposed analytical frameworks to understand a country's development niches and paths within GVCs, and highlighted the interaction between MNEs' strategies and the dynamics of RVCs.

The subsequent four empirical chapters have, respectively, examined the structure and key dynamics of the mobile telecom GVCs and distinctive modes of integration to the GVCs (Chapter 4); the shifting patterns of inter- and intra-regional trade and the evolving positions of major countries in the mobile phone GVCs (Chapter 5); diverging integration paths among four East Asian countries in the GVCs and china's multi-path trajectories (Chapter 6); and three case studies highlighting the interaction of firm strategies and regional value chains (Chapter 7). These chapters highlight the important role of Asian economies and regional value chains in the mobile phone GVCs and the divergence and interaction of upgrading paths therein.

Key Findings: Summary and Discussion

This study highlights a *highly dynamic nature of the mobile telecom GVC*. In the chain, the entire process of delivering a mobile service to the consumer requires multiple steps across several sub-chains, with a variety of corporate and institutional actors and their relationship playing a key part. Growing vertical fragmentation through outsourcing and geographic dispersion of value chain activities significantly has changed how mobile phones are conceived, produced and delivered to the end consumer, including the rise of the developing world as the center of production (and increasingly consumption) and the emergence of new value chain actors like contract manufacturers that play a specialist role in the mid-stream of the chain.

Asia has emerged as the center of the mobile phone industry in the midst of geographic and organizational concentration of the mobile phone GVC. While the growth of mobile phone production and trade decelerated over the past few years as the market slowed down after the global financial crisis, mobile phone production has considerably concentrated geographically to Asia and organizationally to a handful of brand lead firms and transnational contract manufacturers. This dual concentration is mutually enforcing, as shown in the example that consolidated OEMs facilitate the geographic concentration of production, specifically to East Asia, and to China and Vietnam, in particular.

The rise of Asia in the global mobile telecom industry is significantly attributed to the region's internal and external connections through global and regional value chains. A dense web of inter-firm networks plays a key role in deepening regional integration in the form of regionalization but also in advancing the region's position in the mobile phone industry. The co-evolving relationship between geographic and organization concentration has helped the region and some of the regionally-based firms to consolidate their leading positions in this highly competitive sector, plagued with frequent market and technological disruptions. The agglomeration of capable suppliers in the region also helped them solidify their positions in the mobile phone GVCs.

Our analysis of international trade, however, illustrates *the dynamic change of countries' positions* in the mobile phone GVC. As shown in Chapter 4, China and Korea consolidated their generalist positions, so did Vietnam as an assembly specialist. Vietnam's rise as the world's second largest mobile phone exporter was accompanied by the country's growing embeddedness in regional trade networks of intermediate goods in East Asia. As more assembly production migrated to China and Vietnam, some of the Asian countries, notably Japan, Malaysia, and Singapore, moved to the specialist position in parts, implying a growing specialization and differentiation within Asian regional production networks.

A similar pattern is identified in our analysis of inter- and intra-regional trade network in Chapter 5. It has shown a *fast changing intra-regional division of labor* in the Asian mobile phone industry. China is leading in the Asian trade networks of final products and parts and components. Whereas much of China's parts exports are likely to be done by foreign affiliates based in China, the case of China's exports to Indian emerging mobile phone brands, as discussed in Chapter 7, illustrates the expansion of China's role in the mobile phone GVCs to an exporter to major emerging production hubs like Vietnam and India. It is also notable that Vietnam is now developing its own exporting network, partly supported by imported intermediate goods from other Asian countries, such as Korea.

These findings illuminate a continuing evolution of countries' positions in global and regional value chains and division of labor. GVCs allow countries and firms to assume differentiated roles across the chains. Our study makes a contribution to the literature of GVCs and industrial development by providing a framework to understand a country's position within trade networks or across value chains. The findings show that Asian economies are dynamically repositioning their roles in global and regional value chains. And, such repositioning is significantly affected by the location and supply chain strategies of leading MNEs, as shown in Chapter 7, although we are not able to match exactly country-level trade flows and firm-level activities. The fact that China is now firmly centered on the regional trade flows of mobile phones and parts, and its growing trade relations with India, Vietnam and other Southeast and South Asian countries indicates the expansion of Asian mobile phone RVCs beyond East Asia despite the persisting central role played by East Asian firms like SEC and Foxconn.

Our study of *intra-regional divergence* with four East Asian country cases in Chapter 6 highlights that the rise of a fragmented production system, specifically GVCs, provides countries and firms with the opportunity to assume differentiated roles in the chains, leading to the divergence of development paths. A considerable divergence among China, Japan, Korea and Taiwan was found with regard to both the position in the global mobile phone value chain and market orientation. At the same time, our study implies the limitation of comparing countries in terms of simple success or failure in industrial development, as exemplified by Japanese domestic success and Taiwan and Korea's global success, and Korea's failure to nurture SMEs. In addition, the study has identified the concurrent development of multiple trajectories in China's mobile phone industry, with some overlap in value chain niches with its neighboring countries.

Such intra-regional difference affirms the need of a more sophisticated framework beyond a simple dichotomy of whether or not a country is open to foreign investment or whether it follows EOI or ISI. More importantly, it raises a question of the effect of the increasing concentration of production in China (and Vietnam lately) has on other industrialized Asian countries like Korea, Taiwan and Japan, specifically, whether and to what extent it creates the hollowing-out of value chain activities, not only manufacturing but also R&D, as China and other developing Asian economies move up the value chain. The change could unsettle the regional division of labor between developed and developing Asia to a point that complementarity gives way to direct competition among the countries (WTO and IDE-JETRO 2011). This possibility could be realized if China continues its multi-path development tragectory to counter its neighboring economies on multiple upgrading domains, as we discuss in Chapter 6.

In addition, our inter-regional trade analysis illuminates *a replacement effect of intra-regional trade by inter-regional trade with East Asia*. Mobile phone trade within Europe and Latin America became less significant as these regions bolstered cross-regional trade linkages with East Asia. This is likely to be induced by not only trade but also foreign direct investment relationships, as shown in a growing investment by Asian firms in Latin America and the concurrent growth of parts imports from East Asia. This dynamic raises a question of whether regionalized production has any future outside Asia in the face of a rising concentration of mobile phone GVCs in Asia.

Finally, our study has highlighted *the interaction of firm strategies and regional value chains*. Firm actors, especially intra- and extra-regional MNEs, play a key role in shaping the structure of regional value chains and, in turn, RVCs facilitate the rise of new forms of firm actors and market strategies. SEC plays an important part in integrating regional economies through its extensive regional value chain, significantly affecting the GVC integration and economic upgrading of the countries involved, as exemplified by Vietnam. In contrast, Apple's vertically specialized value chains rely on a wide range of third-party suppliers, facilitating the growth of specialized suppliers like Foxconn. The final case of market disruption and emerging developing country brands emphasizes the importance of regional value chains in that the rise of new breeds of value chain actors and business strategies, such as *Shanzhai* phone producers and brands like Micromax in India and 'pinoy phone' makers in the Philippines, is deeply embedded with specialized suppliers like MediaTek and well-developed regional supplier bases in Asia.

This finding cast light on the role of firms and particularly MNEs in regional connection and interaction. Although regionalization is considered as a key element of regional integration, the role of firm actors and their strategies in the process has not be drawn a sufficient scholarly attention. While their roles may not always positive, our study affirms that more research is needed to understand the role of private, corporate actors in regional integration. Particularly, it highlights the role of extra-regional firms like Apple and their relationship with Asian firms. This suggests that regional integration is, to some degree, a joint project of internal and external actors.

Looking Forward

While this book provides a new perspective to mobile transformation and convergence and divergence in Asia, it also raises a number of questions for future research. One of the limitation of our study is that it mostly focuses on the economic dimension of mobile Asia and regional interaction and connection, with little attention to political and social dimensions. For example, a more connected society and region through mobile technology can bring forth various political consequences. We partly address the topic in Appendix, with the case of Korea's transition to mobile-rich society and the changing landscape of public sphere in the 2000s. The chapter shows that mobile telecom is reshaping the way people engage in the public sphere and political activities. Yet, much needed is a fuller assessment of various effects of mobile technology, industry, and service on political processes, democratization, and diverse forms of civic engagement within and across Asian countries.

Second, our study mainly focused on growth and upgrading in the Asian mobile telecom industry. However, mobile transformation may also be a process of generating inequality. Young workers in Shenzhen, China have to endure long working hours and hazardous factory conditions only to cater to increasingly picky and fast changing market and buyer demands; yet, most of the gains are taken by a handful of global brands (Pun *et al.* 2016). When poorer countries are struggling for making basic mobile services available and affordable for their population, affluent countries are moving fast towards mobile broadband like LTE (long-term evolution) service, making lessening digital divide a moving target. Thus, whether, and how, mobile Asia and regional value chains affect differentiation and inequality is an important topic for future research.

Third, our quantitative analysis of international trade data presents several new findings on inter- and intra-regional dynamics in mobile phone trade. Yet, the analysis presented in this book does not show the difference in value of traded goods. For instance, China may export more high-end parts to countries like Korea and Japan, while it does much lower-valued ones to India and Vietnam. To understand the differences, we need to analyze the unit value of exports and imports. At the same time, we also need to integrate international trade analysis with the analysis of FDI statistics and firm-level investment activities to fully capture the relationship between international trade flows and FDI activities.

Finally, we presented varieties of GVC integration and industrial upgrading in the mobile phone industry in Asia. What is yet to be fully addressed, however, is the drivers and mechanisms of such cross-national differences. Why was Korea successful in nurturing a handful of highly capable global brands, whereas Taiwan and Japan failed to do so? How does a country's relative strength in one segment of value chains relate to its weakness in others? What has driven the internal divergence of development paths in China? To answer these questions, a more in-depth analysis is necessary with a focus on the institutional and organizational aspects of the country cases, as well as the strategic decision-making of key domestic and foreign firms, within and outside of the mobile phone sector.

Appendix

Democratic Challenges in Mobile Asia: Korean Case

Democracy and Mobile Use

Democracy is nowadays under challenge.[1] Although classic *coups d'etat*, executive coups by elected leaders and blatant election-day vote fraud have declined in frequency, democracy has been in a global recession for most of the last decade (Bermeo 2016; Diamond 2015). Freedom House finds that the decline of democracy has been coincided by the resurgence of authoritarianism in the Middle East and North America, Eurasia, sub-Saharan Africa, Europe, Americas, and Asia. Democratic reversals affected freedom of expression, civil society, and the rule of law due to state surveillance, restrictions on SNS communication, and curbs on personal autonomy (Puddington 2015). This is close to what Larry Diamond (2015) has labeled "democratic recession."

Korea's democratization has been known to be a rare success case in the postwar Third World context, since it has not been challenged by military coups or dictatorial anti-constitutionalism after the country's 1987 democratic transition. Based on the government system of a single five-year presidency, there have been five presidential elections since 1987. In 1987, Roh Tae-Woo won the presidential election in the wake of feuds among pro-democracy movement leaders, such as Kim Dae-Jung and Kim Young-Sam. In 1992, Kim Young-Sam, a candidate who allied with Roh Tae-Woo's ruling party, was elected as president after about thirty years' rule by three presidents with military backgrounds since the 1961 coup, while early two presidents in the country between the years of 1948 and 1961 had had civilian backgrounds. In 1997, the oppositional political party won the presidential election, making Kim Dae-Jung president. In 2002, Roh Moo-Hyun, who had been a labor-rights lawyer in the 1980s, was unexpectedly elected as president, and the younger generation of politicians (so-called "386 generation politicians") who were associated with Roh and experienced student activism in the 1980s entered the power elite circle collectively. In 2007, the conservative party ("Grand National Party") became the ruling party again in ten years since it had lost power in 1997, and Lee Myung-Bak, a candidate of GNP, became president in February 2008. Park Keun-Hae from the GNP but name-changed *Saenuri* Party won presidency. According to Huntington's standard of formally measuring democracy (Huntington 1991), this peaceful second-time ruling-party shift by free and regular elections makes sufficient case for Korea to have entered democratic consolidation following Greece, Spain and Portugal.

Korea used to be characterized by a strong state and a weak civil society, with the underdeveloped latter repressed by the overdeveloped former. It is since late 1980s that civil society has begun to grow on a full scale. Social movement organizations, however, are not sufficiently developed to challenge the state. The state is still a dominant actor in organizing economy and society from top down. Yet its horizontal accountability on the basis of separation of powers among the executive, the legislative and the judiciary branches, and its vertical accountability over the people by public policy formation are not sufficiently established.

It is against this backdrop that Korea has succeeded in consolidating democracy even after completing transition to democracy a decade ago. For democracy to consolidate, a robust civil society is required. Capitalism is possible in the absence of civil society, but democracy is not possible without civil society (Fish 1994, 41). The existence of civil society is prerequisite not for the transition to democracy, but for the consolidation of democracy (Schmitter 1995).

There are three ways to conceive of civil society. First, social movement organizations make individual citizens into active subjects. A network of social movement organizations, such as NGOs, NPOs, VOs, and POs, intermediates conflicting interests among citizens. Second, social capital facilitates coordination and cooperation for mutual benefits for citizens. Composed of norms and trust, social capital fosters communication and interactions that allow dilemmas of collective action to be resolved. Third, public sphere provides social dialogue necessary for the shared values and interests among citizens. It is essential for shaping public opinion that presses increasing state accountability.

To activate civil society, Korea needs to strengthen interest politics among citizens. Unless social movement organizations do not aggregate various interests among diverse social classes and groups, civil society is not capable of channeling them into the state in formulating public policy. It is thus a good sign that businessmen, workers, farmers, urban poor, teachers, pharmacists, doctors, public servants all have formed civil associations for promoting their respective interests. Yet civil associations have not been successful in developing institutional channels for mediating differences among them. Interest politics are still unarticulated, hyperbolic and unruly (Im 2000, 23).

It is in this context that one can emphasize the role of discourse in the public sphere for institutionalizing civil society. No doubt, a greater use of ICT-mediated communication has been instrumental in energizing public sphere in Korea. Social movement organizations can rely on the SNS in representing different opinions among citizens through public discourse on the basis of social trust. As a matter of fact, it has been widely recognized in recent years that the SNS provides a useful means of diffusing ideas and tactics less constrained by time and space. The SNS turns out to be effective in communicating with one another among citizens.

A good example can be provided by the cyber-diffusion of contention that Citizens Consortium of various social movement organizations staged for a fair election of better candidates during the general election in April 2000. They set up a site for general public that happened to ignite citizens' concern for rejecting tainted candidates and electing reform-minded candidates. With its advantages of public accessibility and immediate effects, the Internet presented the potential of cyber campaign in mobilizing public opinion.

Technology and media affect how people express and exchange political ideas and engage in political action. For decades, ICT has significantly reshaped political participation and the public sphere, as already exemplified by voter mobilization using social networking sites in the 2001 Korean presidential election and citizen online journalism in Iranian election protests in 2009. Now as mobile communication has become an indispensable part of our daily life, the question raised is how mobile communication affects our political life. Undoubtedly, mobile use changes the way people engage in public debate and political action and affect the structure of the public sphere.

We try to answer the question by examining the experience of Korea as a good case of the mobile-rich society in Asia. It provides a unique opportunity to investigate the interaction between mobile communication and political development. Over the last decade or so, Korea has undergone a dual transition of digitalization and democratization. On the one hand, the country has been transformed into one of the most mobile-rich societies in the world. Mobile phones are no longer a luxury but a must-have. High-speed mobile broadband services, adding to the country's much touted fixed broadband network, are available not only in metropolitan areas but in countryside. At the same time, political transition was no less dynamic than mobile transformation. After decades of military dictatorship and authoritarianism, the public sphere was regained and energized by rising political participation, emerging civil and social movements, and growing emphasis on individual freedom and free speech.

Actually, the dual technology and political development was deeply intertwined with each other. As illustrated by the major political events of the last decade, notably a series of candlelight protests, Ferry *Saewol* sinking and spread of MERS-CoV, mobile communication has played no small role in changing the dynamic of the public sphere in Korea. Building upon the recent studies that document and analyze these events in a great detail (e.g., Choi 2008; Lee and Bae 2008; Lee and Jung 2009; Song 2007), we particularly highlight that the explosion of mobile use and its political use was deeply embedded in the political, economic, and social structure of the society. A "government-industry ICT complex" played a critical part in the introduction and diffusion of mobile communication. At the same time, its political use and impact on the public sphere largely depended on the way the burgeoning civil society responded to the technological opportunities emerged from the new mode of communication. By examining the political use of mobile communication in different temporal junctures and contextualizing it within broader political-economic changes, we stress that the trajectory of a national the public sphere is uniquely shaped by the interaction of techno-media development and political-economic dynamics.

The Impact of ICT on Political Participation: A Theoretical Background

Initial reactions to the effect of ICT on political participation and the public sphere largely diverged into two contrasting views: optimism and pessimism (Albrecht 2006; Anduiza *et al.* 2009). The optimistic view emphasized the potential of ICT-mediated communication in disseminating political information and ideas faster yet less costly and thus a high hope for a participatory democracy rejuvenated by cyberactivism, or a modern equivalent to the ancient Greek Agora (Rheingold 2003). In contrast, skeptics argued that the Internet would bring forth the decline of civic engagement and the decay of the public sphere by detaching individuals from intimate interactions in their local communities that used to be the centerpiece of the social fabrics that democracy relies on to flourish (Putnam 2000). The likely outcomes are individualized and atomized citizens and the political activism based on a shallow coalition among the like-minded (see Carty 2010; Sunstein 2007).

Recent studies, however, try to move beyond a dichotomy of optimism and pessimism, shedding light on a more complicate picture of the way ICT affects our political life (see Anduiza *et al.* 2009 for a review). First, more attention is paid to the interaction of online and offline spaces in political participation and action (Wellman 2010). It is suggested that online political activities are not separated from but closely related to real-world experience. For example, the Internet is likely to provide those who are already politically active in offline with a greater opportunity to augment their offline participation than those who are not. Despite a good deal of possibility that the Internet generates a new avenue of political participation for the disenfranchised in traditional media outlets (Anduiza *et al.* 2009), it is suggested that the Internet is more likely to enforce offline political action rather than replacing it. Thus, online political activity is to a large degree "an extension of offline activity" (Wellman *et al.* 2001, 448).

Second, moving beyond a dichotomous portrayal of cyberspace between well-connected communities and isolated and atomized individuals, recent studies suggest the presence of "networked individualism" (Boase *et al.* 2006) and the transformation of the public sphere. While people are getting more individualized and able to free themselves from place-bound, in-person interactions as they more rely on personal tools of telecommunication, it is suggested, they are not simply isolated and atomized but rather connected to a broader social network that otherwise would or could not have been tapped, nurturing a new type of socialness grounded on distant connectivity (Fortunati 2002). With this reconfigured social network, a place-bound public sphere becomes no longer a stable and single dominant place for public discourses as it was and coexists with information- and network-based public spheres increasingly organized through the globalized media system (Castells 2008).

This raises the question about the internal structure of the public sphere, that is, whether a greater use of ICT-mediated communication makes the public sphere more fragmented and fluid in the sense that new political discursive spaces constantly emerge across different forms of media only to quickly disappear or get abandoned at some point (Carty 2010; Sunstein 2007). On the one hand, the decentralization of the public sphere can lead to the increase of diversity and the inclusion of peripheral voices in political process, as advocated by a plural model of the public sphere (Benson 2009). However, at the same time, it also can bring about the "balkanization" of the public sphere, where cyberspace keeps being divided into separate, like-minded, ideological enclaves (Chang 2008).

Finally, there is a growing attention to cross-national, cross-cultural difference in the way new media influence the political deliberative process (Bimber 2003). The use of the Internet and mobile phones are highly dependent on the specific social context they are brought into (Katz 2008). Whether or not these media are used for a specific purpose and how they are used varies by society rather than being determined by technology. For example, the effect of ICT-medicated communication on political participation can be affected by the existing structure of political participation.

The use of new media could be greater in a society where the existing channels for participation are less open or more controlled by a few elites (Bimber 2003). Likewise, whether the rise of online communities would lead to an inclusive or divisive public sphere may hinge on the existing social contexts that affect the structure of the public sphere in a given society.

In investigating such social contexts, we call attention to the specific history and structure of a national public sphere. Criticizing the normative rather than empirical embrace of Habermas's public sphere concept (1989) that was grounded in the historical experience of modern Western Europe (Benson 2009; Rajagopal 2006), many scholars recently have paid attention to the historical singularity of the public sphere and its evolution in a national context. Starr (2004), for example, finds that unlike in Western Europe, the public sphere in the US was created at the turn of the 20th century by the state as part of a nation-building project. This generated the specificity of American democracy, in which the public sphere relies on media institutions, not individual members as it did in Europe. Researchers further cast light on the specificity of each country's public sphere by comparing different countries, for instance, abortion debates in Germany and the US (Ferree *et al.* 2002), and the construction of the "sexual harassment" notion in the US and France (Saguy 2003).

The empirical approach of this kind brings our attention closer to the internal configuration and boundary of the public sphere (Calhoun 1997). The public sphere could be elitist, deliberative, or pluralist in terms of how the media function (Benson 2009). It can be internally integrated and inclusive, or fragmented and divisive as in the emergence of "split public sphere" as a result of politicized

Hindu religious nationalism through a newly commercialized Indian television system (Rajagopal 2001). It may be under a strong control of the state, or driven by commercial interests, or both of the social forces (McChesney and Nichols 2002). Meanwhile, the growth of ICT-mediated communication makes the boundary of the public sphere more problematic than ever before. Unlike its traditional association with a national policy debate, the public sphere is now extending, on the one hand, to what Castells (2008) calls the "global public sphere." But, on the other hand, the fragmentation of the public sphere into issue-based, fluid, and flexible cyber-enclaves (Bimber 1998) makes even the national boundary inadequately large.

The literature surveyed above, while not exclusive on mobile communication, suggests that the use of mobile communication and its effect on the public sphere can be shaped by the historically specific context that it is brought into in a given society, not determined by its technological attribute alone. Whether or not and how mobile communication is deployed for a specific political purpose is contingent upon the way it is appropriated by various social forces in different historical junctures. Thus, the political consequence of mobile use should be examined through analyzing the historical confluence of political development and the evolution of the media system in a given society.

The Political-economic Origin of a Mobile-Rich Society

Korea is one of the most mobile-rich countries in the world.

As of 2008, the country had more than 46 million mobile cellular subscribers and 93.8 subscribers per 100 people. As third-generation (3G) mobile broadband subscribers reached a 20 million milestone on June 2009, a high-speed data service became available to approximately 44% of the total mobile subscribers. Wi-Fi hotspots are sprouting in major urban areas, and a local version of WiMAX service offers the high-speed streaming of multimedia content even in a fast-moving vehicle. A recent international comparison places Korea among high performers in mobile broadband (Berkman Center of Internet & Society 2010). All these mobile networks are linked to the country's much touted fixed broadband network, and mobile subscribers are served by globally competitive local mobile phone manufacturers. In 2008, Korea was placed on the third in the world's ICT Development Index (IDI) ranking, the first among Asia-Pacific countries (ITU 2010).

Korea's mobile transition, as with its post-war social transition (Chang 1999), is impressive because of its compressed nature. It took place in a very short period of time and concurrently on multiple technological fronts. Figures 1 compares Korea with the Organisation for Economic Co-operation and Development (OECD) countries and the world as a whole in terms of the diffusion of three major ICT services: mobile cellular, fixed broadband, and the Internet. It shows that for five years from 1998 to 2002 Korea made a dramatic progress in making all three advanced ICT services widespread across the population.[2] As of 2008, Korea was only slightly behind the OECD average in mobile cellular penetration though its penetration rate was still very high, and in the other two categories Korea's figures by far exceeded the OECD average, let alone the world as a whole.

(a) Mobile cellular subscribers, 1990-2014

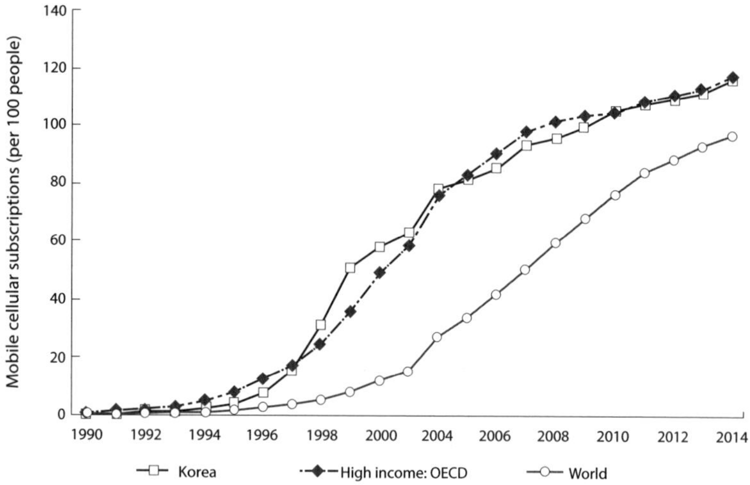

(b) Fixed broadband subscribers, 1998-2014

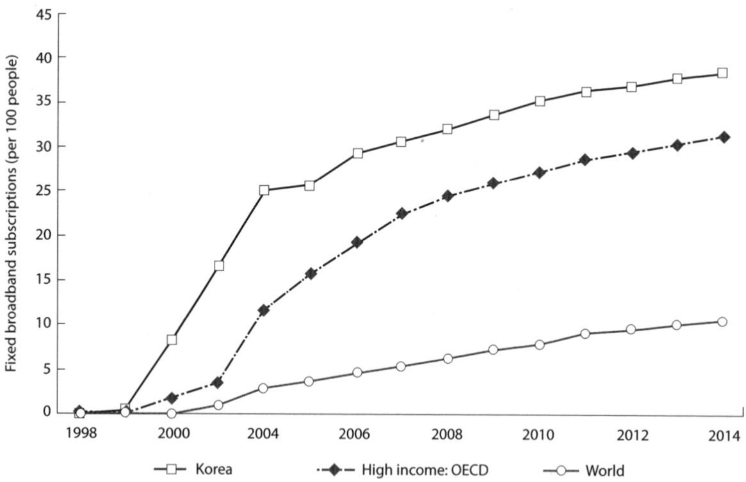

(c) Internet users, 1990-2014

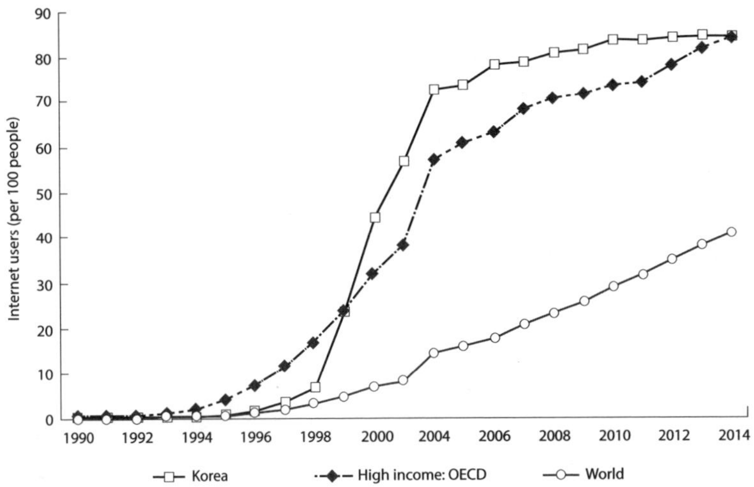

Figure 1. Diffusion of telecommunication services: Korea in comparison

Sources: Compiled from the World Development Indicators (WDI), World Bank.

Figure 2 presents a timeline of major ICT services in Korea. The country was the first in the world to commercialize a digital cellular service based on CDMA technology. Since then the country's mobile cellular infrastructure has upgraded into cutting-edge technologies to accommodate fast growing subscribers and advanced mobile service: Wideband-Code Division Multiple Access (2002) and High-Speed Downlink Packet Access (2007). In parallel, the first public Wi-Fi access service using 802.11a/b/g standards was launched in major cities in 2002, enabling a wireless Internet access within a hotspot via personal handheld devices. Digital Multimedia Broadcasting (DMB), a locally promoted mobile broadcasting service, was launched in 2005. Then WiBro, the Korean equivalent of WiMAX, was introduced in 2006 to offer a high-speed internet access (18.4 Mbps for downloading and 4

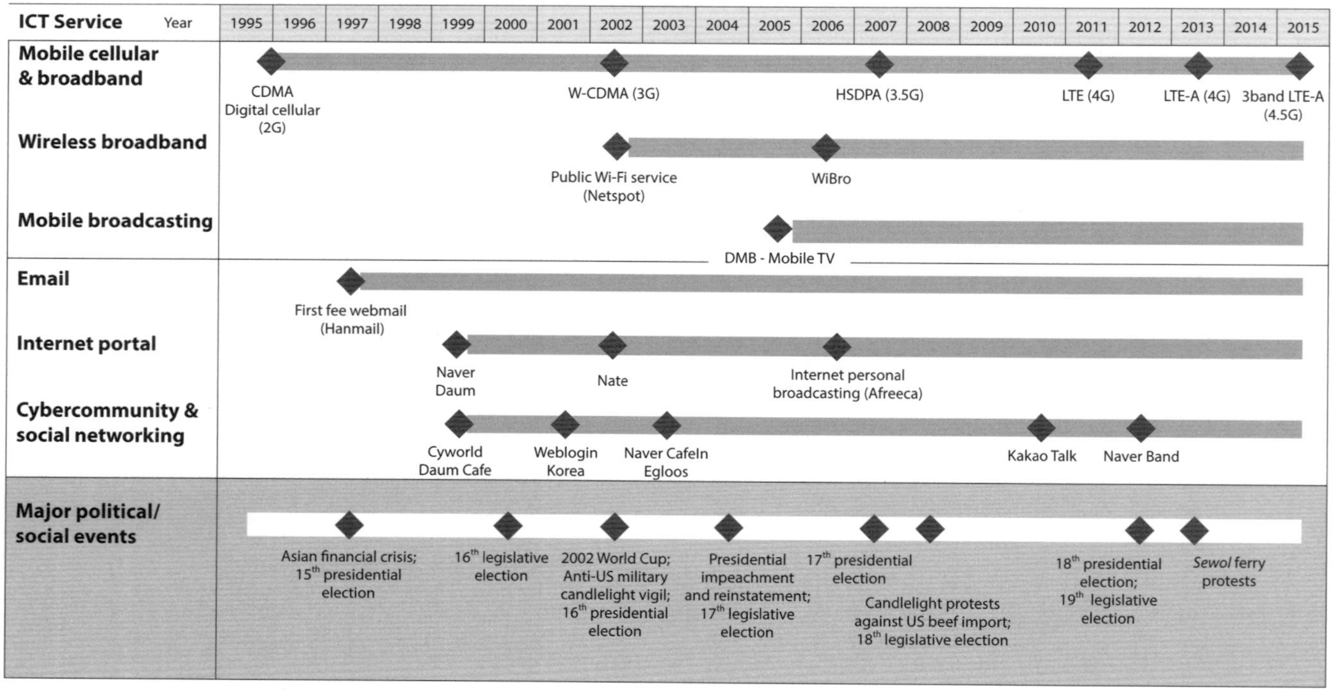

Figure 2. The timeline of ICT services and major political/social events in Korea, 1995-2015

Source: Compiled from various sources.

Mbps for uploading) to the device moving at a speed up to 120km/h. This sprawling web of mobile/wireless networks has turned the country's major metropolitan areas into mobile "hotspots" where Internet access is near-ubiquitous, from a café, in the car, and on the streets.

The wide diffusion of broadband service has greatly facilitated the rapid growth of Internet service as more Koreans are able to stay online around the clock via fixed and mobile network. Korea's rapid deployment of fixed broadband is well known and frequently acclaimed as one of the success stories in the country's ICT policy. Since the first broadband service was introduced in 1999, it quickly became popular (see Figure 1(b)), and as a result of aggressive and competitive network deployment by telecom companies now many Korean homes are connected online via a 100 Mbps optical link. Various Internet services have mushroomed over the fixed-mobile broadband infrastructure. The first free commercial webmail service, *Hanmail* (*Daum*), was launched in 1997. In 1999, *Naver* was established to become the country's leading Internet portal, and so was *Cyworld*, a pioneering social networking site. Internet users, dubbed "netizens," flocked into burgeoning online communities (locally known as "café") to satisfy their social and informational needs in a newly found public space and increasingly private space, such as weblog.[3]

The average Korean's daily use of the Internet more than doubled in 2002-2005 from 2.5 hours to six hours 57 minutes. They spent 30% of their daily active time in using the Internet, up from 20% in 2002 (Hwang and Yoo 2007). Mobile use also increased from 107 minutes to 143 minutes per month from 2001 to 2007, although mobile phone use in Korea is not particularly inexpensive compared to other OECD countries.[4] This growing ICT use has expanded the telecommunication market such that telecommunication revenue reached five% of the country's GDP in 2007, the highest among OECD countries. The proportion of mobile service rose to 45% of the total telecommunication revenue in 2007, up from 30% a decade ago (OECD 2009).

This rapid diffusion of advanced mobile technology and service, we argue, are deeply embedded in the political-economic structure of Korean society. The compressed mobile transition is largely the outcome of the "government-industry complex" that has driven ICT development for decades. The country has been heavily relying on the economic development strategy based on the high-tech ICT industry. Promoting the industry as the driver of its export growth has been a top priority for the Korean government since the 1970s when the country began to climb up the value chain from low-tech sectors like apparel. Over the decades, Korea's ICT exports have expanded from television and white goods to semiconductors, mobile phone, and high-end display products.

In this development model, the diffusion of new electronic products in the domestic market is in one way or another linked to the goal of promoting local manufacturing and export growth. For instance, pressure from local TV manufacturers lied behind the government's decision to start color television broadcasting in the early 1980s. Also while the government had been aware of growing public discontent to the shortage of telephone lines throughout the 1970s, modernizing the country's public telephone network gained traction only after it became clear that the project would help local manufacturers compete in export markets. A similar motivation was behind the government's move to commercialize then largely untested CDMA in the early 1990s (Lee 2003a) and the country's latest pursuit for indigenous technological standards, including DMB and WiBro.

This close relation of the state and the industry in ICT development has clearly proven to be successful in boosting the country's exports. High-tech exports accounted for a third of its manufactured exports in 2007, up from 16% in 1988, according to World Bank statistics. In 2009, the world's second and third largest mobile phone manufacturers – Samsung and LG – represented three out of ten mobile phones sold in the world (Gartner 2010b). And this success partly relies on the domestic market that provides local firms with a protected consumer market and technological test-bed for new products. At home the two global phone makers enjoyed comfortable market positions, combined accounting for about 78% of the total domestic sale in 2009. Market concentration looks barely different in telecom service. Two leading conglomerates ("*chaebol*") — SK Group and LG Group — and a privatized incumbent — KT Group — dominate fixed and mobile service markets either directly or through subsidiaries (see Table 1).

The government-industry complex has shaped the mobile transition in several ways. First, its supply-driven approach saturated the domestic market with advanced service and gadgets. The government made no delay in issuing new spectrum and service licenses even when the commercial viability of the service was questioned. Competition between cash-abundant conglomerates to pre-empt the market made a new ICT service quickly available while keeping smaller players at bay. Local ICT firms, in turn, took advantage of the presence of advanced network infrastructure and tech-savvy consumers in the domestic market, utilizing them as a

Table 1. Major Korean telecom companies and market share as of March 2016 (unit: %)

	KT Group	SK Group	LG Group	Total share
Fixed telephone*	KT (80.5)	SK Broadband (16.4)	LG U+ (3.1)	100.0
Fixed broadband access	KT (41.5)	SK Broadband SK Telecom (resale)(25.2)	LG U+ (17.4)	84.2
Mobile telephone**	SK Telecom (43.3)	KT (25.0)	LG U+ (20.0)	88.3
Wireless broadband (WiBro)	KT (88.5)	SK Telecom (11.5)	-	100.0

Notes: * Local, intercommunication system, ISDN subscribers, ** Market share of MVNO: 10%.
Source: IT Statistics of Korea (http://www.itstat.go.kr).

launch pad for innovation and export.

Second, it generated a society-wide pressure for learning and mastering the most up-to-date IT skills. The pressure of not falling behind comes down to virtually everyone in the society regardless of their age, gender, and education. The local equivalent of the computer illiterate [*k'ŏmmaeng*] has become a common word. Its derivative form — the network illiterate [*netmaeng*] — appeared as the Internet became a necessity, not a luxury. A recent news report of the "iPhone tutor," part-timers who teach how to use an iPhone (Lee 2010, May 12), only confirms such pressure in play and the continuation of a catching-up mentality behind the ICT drive as expressed by the campaign slogan popularized by a local newspaper in the mid-1990s, "*Late in Industrialization, but Let's Go Ahead in IT.*"

This catch-phrase, more importantly, indicates the extent to which ICT development has been intertwined with broader social changes in Korea, such as industrialization, globalization and democratization. While the celebration of democratization and decades of startling economic growth did not last long as economic crisis followed later in the decade, even the turmoil could not hamper the rise of a large group of middle-class consumers, the build-up of young, educated, and highly ICT-literate workforce, and a new generation of the people who are socially and culturally more liberal and individualistic. These changes were deeply linked to ICT development. The affluent middle class became key consumers for new ICT services. The workers formed a solid ground for the country's competitive ICT sector. And the new generation's lifestyle critically relied on advanced communication infrastructure, leading one to declare the "birth of neo-nomadism" in Korea (Yun 2007).[5]

It was amid these social changes that Korean civil society suddenly blossomed. It had been suppressed for decades of military dictatorship through a combination of political oppression, export mobilization, and, most importantly, media control. Following political liberalization and the retreat of the state from media censorship in the 1990s, however, the increased media window enabled by the Internet and broadband network led to the emergence of alternative, grassroots online journalism (Chang 2005; Hauben 2008; Song 2007). The first news media of this kind, *OhMyNews*, was established in 2000 and attracted a great deal of attention at home and abroad for its pioneering experiment of "citizen reporters" [*simin kija*], whereby the majority of its news articles were voluntarily contributed by ordinary citizens (Kang and Dyson 2007; Kim and Hamilton 2006). Its unexpected success soon drew similar attempts — initially by the progress-minded but followed by the conservative (Chang 2008) — and led to the rapid growth of independent online news media. It challenged the longstanding dominance of mainstream print and TV news media, which was also hit by the rapid rise of Internet portals as a major channel for news consumption (Lee and Lee 2009), and reshaped the structure of producing and exchanging public discourses.

The mobile-rich, ICT-abundant society on which Korea has built itself has its political and economic origin. The government-industry ICT complex critically shaped the country's mediascape through a supply-driven media policy and the concentrated industry structure dominated by a handful of chaebols. However, digital/mobile transition was deeply intertwined with the broader social changes the country experienced for the last decade or so. Democratization and social and cultural liberalization led to the revitalization of civil society and the public sphere, yet these changes significantly depended on the country's burgeoning ICT infrastructure, as detailed below.

Mobile Communication, Political Participation and the Public Sphere: Korea's Experiences

We zoom in mobile communication in this section by examining the recent political events in Korea whose unfolding was critically influenced by mobile use. Three events are discussed: the 2002 presidential election; a series of street protests throughout the last decade; and candlelight protests against importing US beef in 2008.

Short text messages and voter mobilization

On the eve of Korea's 16th presidential Election Day in 2002, a coalition partner of Mr. Roh Moo-Hyun, the presidential candidate of the ruling party coalition, announced the withdrawal of his support to him. This last-minute unexpected move surprised everyone from Roh's supporters to his rival favored by conservative mainstream media. When his election loss was on the brink, his devoted supporters (a.k.a. "Nosamo"), who had been known for their effective use of the Internet in political actions (Kang and Dyson 2007; Lim *et al.* 2004), deployed a massive final-hour campaign. Over the night, they sent out emails and short messages to his sympathetic supporters, as many as 800,000, mostly young in their twenties and thirties and white-collar professionals (Lim *et al.* 2004, 63) and urged to go to the polling stations to cast a vote and more importantly to pass the word along to their friends and family (Hong 2005).

Throughout the final hours of the election, *OhMyNews* became a situation room for reform-minded supporters. They monitored the hour-by-hour progress of the campaign and encouraged each other. The website of the then two-year-old online news site recorded staggering 6.23 million visitors and 19.1 million page views for eight hours from the withdrawal announcement leading to the opening of voting stations next morning, and mobile phone calls and texting reached an above-the-average level, according to calling data from the country's largest mobile operator (Han 2007, 67-68). Eventually, Roh won the presidential election yet only by a two% margin. It is believed that his election win would have not been possible without the Internet and SMS and, most of all, his supporters' shrewd use of the latest mobile technologies (Hong 2005).

The 2002 presidential election was one of the first political events in Korea that showed the utility of mobile communication in mobilizing massive actions in a short time. At the same time, the event highlighted the personal media aspect of mobile communication. Roh's supporters activated their personal contacts and used personal trust to mobilize a support, as indicated in the following:

> "I heard stories where Koreans would interrupt their ski trips and come into the city to vote because of panicked text messages from friends," says Jean Min, *OhMyNews* international director. "You might not trust what is coming out of the TV, but you take it seriously when the message comes from a friend." (excerpted from Hong 2005)

The ability of personal media to reach directly to the intended person not only reduced the time and cost in disseminating messages to a large group of people but also increased the creditability of the messages from the recipient's perspective.

The case also suggests that online campaign was particularly effective in taking a well-motivated, cohesive voting bloc to the polling stations. The use of new media particularly among the young generation was effective in boosting voter turnout among Roh's supporters, but it was less so for an overall increase of voter turnout. According to Han's analysis of exit poll results (2007), a strong turnout after 1 p.m. among the 20s and 30s helped Roh take the lead away from his rival and maintain it onwards. However, the overall turnout of this age group in the election followed a similar trend as that of older generations; it not only recorded the lowest among all age groups but also considerably dropped from the previous presidential election.[6] In this regard, the 2002 election case illustrates the effectiveness of mobile communication in activating a closely knitted personal network for political mobilization.

Mobile phones and political street gatherings

The ICT-oriented campaign strategy of Mr. Roh's supporter group, in fact, was indebted to the experience of online mobilization that Korean civil society had accumulated through a series of events. Earlier in 2002, voluntarily organized young football fans proposed a street cheering events to support the national soccer team in the FIFA World Cup Korea co-hosted with Japan. The events were extremely popular; according to an estimate, a total of 22 million people came out on to the streets of Seoul and other major cities in the country's seven football matches (Lowe-Lee 2010, May 12).

More importantly, it turned out to be an unexpected preview of what would follow in Korean civil society later when the experience of street cheering was revived for a political purpose. In November 2002, a netizen proposed a candlelight vigil for two Korean schoolgirls hit and killed by a US military armor vehicle in June 2002. His words spread quickly via Internet instant messenger. On the proposed date, November 30, approximately 10,000 citizens gathered at downtown Seoul to pray for the victims (Han 2007). A series of candlelight vigils lasted for a month to come. At one point more than 30,000 demonstrators gathered to protest against the acquittal of two US soldiers charged for the death. People not only came out for street protests but also many placed a white or black ribbon (▹◃,▸◂) on their instant messenger profiles to express their mourning, the practice now popular among Korean netizens.

Since 2002, candlelight gathering [*ch'otpul chiphoe*] has become the most visible part of Korean civil society. The World Cup street cheering offered people a hint of how to use the latest technologies to spread the word and make people gather in a short notice, functioning as "an intermediate phase of collective actions" (Han 2007, 61). Korean civil society, particularly ICT-savvy younger generations, translated the hint into political events. Accumulated experience and built confidence led to one after another candlelight protest over the last decade. It was not necessarily as big and nationwide as the ones against the presidential impeachment in 2004, as described in the following news report.

> Early in May 16-year-old Korean Lee Chun-Kil slyly text-messaged his friend during class. ... "Gwanghwamun station. 6:00." ... The next day in downtown Seoul, 400 students gathered to protest the severe pressures they must endure for the nation's highly competitive college-entrance exam. ... "I don't think the rally would have been big if we didn't have cell phones," says Im Soon-jae, one of the organizers. "We would not have been able to spread the information about this as quickly." (excerpted from Hong 2005)

Experience was quickly spread and emulated even by teens who had not considered politically active in public. Now they are easily spotted in candlelight protests.[7]

Mobile phones not only proved its effectiveness in massive mobilization but also changed the dynamics of massive gathering.[8] First of all, people can stay connected while in gathering. Even when thousands of people crowded the streets in downtown Seoul, they can easily be joined by their friends who come late to the rally. Furthermore, they can constantly communicate with and relay what's happening on the streets to the friends who are not in the rally. Mobile service gets more sophisticated from SMS to multimedia messages and mobile blogs, so does the protesters' use on the scene. As a handy digital camera, or *dika* as locally called, and camera-phones became popular in the early 2000s, the protesters took pictures of their and their friend's presence on the rally as well as what's happening on the street and easily post them on their blogs from where they are.

In fact, this is a stark contrast to a massive street demonstration in the, for which Korea was then known by international media. The street protest, or *kadu siwi,* was the political mainstay of the country's student activism against military dictatorship. Although it was illegal in most cases and thus participants had to run the risk of getting arrested, it was one of the few ways that protesters as a group could deliver their messages in public directly to citizens on the street in the period when anti-government messages were tightly censored under the state's media control. To avoid any disruption made by the police, the protest was secretly planned and tightly orchestrated. Protesters, mostly college students, were usually organized as a group in advance. They tried to maintain their line against the police that were attempting to isolate them from the rest of the public on the scene and scatter them out as soon as possible (Kim 2003; Park 2005). To do so, protesters, as well as the police, often resorted to physical confrontation and the use of weapons which on several occasions turned out to be deadly. Forced to constantly move, hide and regroup, protesters had virtually no tools and rooms to communicate with those who were not present on the rally, let alone little chance to immediately share their experience with others.

Much of the difference between the 1980s street protests and the candlelight protests of the last decade is attributed to democratization that interspersed the two periods. However, mobile phones and connectedness enabled by them certainly played a role. Lacking physical confrontation and street chasing, candlelight protesters now have a free space on the streets where they can share their stories with their friends who are not present over the phone and via the Internet. They do not need to worry about getting separated from their group not only because the police no longer physically crack down as much as it did decades ago, but also because even if they do, protesters can find a way to regroup as long as they stay connected via cellphone. When and where to gather is no longer secret as it was; people can join the protest as a group but also individually if they want.

It may have no point to ask what it would have happened if protesters had had mobile phones in the 1980s or imagine how candlelight protests would have been without mobile communication. And that suggests how closely political participation was intertwined with media development. The most recent large-scale candlelight protests, the ones against importing US beef in 2008, exhibits that the use of mobile communication has reached a new level of sophistication, further changing the dynamics of political participation in Korea.

Candlelight protests against importing US beef in 2008

In April 2008, a Korean TV network reported about concerns over the safety of US beef and questioned the government's trade negotiation that would lead to resuming US beef import banned for years on and off since the outbreak of mad cow disease. This media report drew a good deal of public attention, particularly among school teenagers and their parents who concerned that tainted beef might be used for school lunch. Active discussion followed in online communities, particularly in *Daum Agora*, one of the country's largest Internet discussion boards. It was all of the sudden that what had appeared to be an agricultural trade issue came into the center of school teenagers' discontent to the government that was then boiling up against the government's new education policy.

On May 2, around 10,000 people, mostly teenagers, showed up in the first candlelight protest against the import of US beef in downtown Seoul. This initial action soon generated snowballs and more protesters came out week by week as social activist groups joined and the public's disappointment in a newly elected government grew. By May 24, 16 new protest gatherings had been held. On June 10, a historic day of the country's democratization movement, massive political actions culminated with nationwide candlelight rallies. The organizers estimated that approximately 500,000 people took part only in Seoul. While mobilization slowed down after the government's pledge for a revised trade deal later, smaller protests continued until mid-August (Choi 2008; Song 2009).

To a large extent, the 2008 protest rallies have a good deal of similarities with the previous large-scale candlelight protests that have become a cultural as much as political phenomenon in Korean civil society. Cyberspace played a crucial role in drawing the public's attention to various social issues, such as the death of school girls by US military vehicle, the impeachment of the president, and in 2008 that was unpopular trade deals and public health concerns. In all these events, the Internet facilitated people to exchange information, debate ideas, organize protests, and mobilize people on to the streets.

The traffic trends of *Daum Agora*, the hotspot throughout the

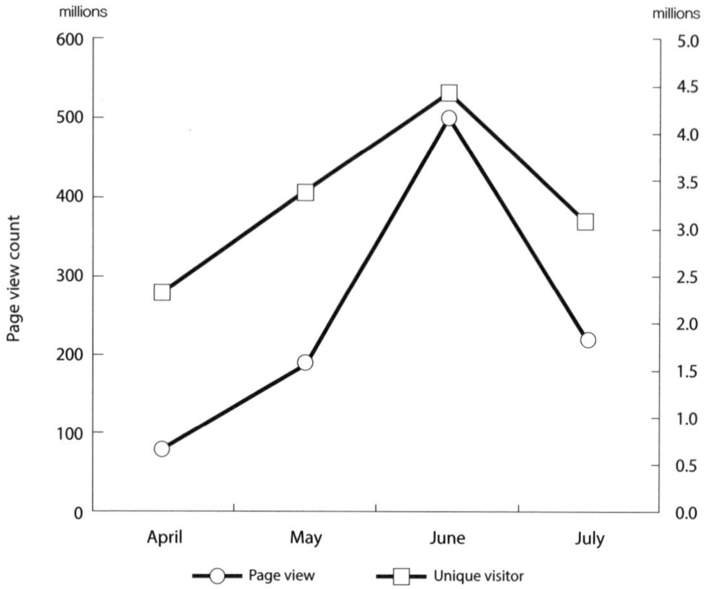

Figure 3. The page views and unique visitors of *Daum Agora*: First week of April to July, 2008

Source: Adapted from Song K. J. (2009, 64).

2008 protests, show how the public was drawn into cyberspace (see Figure 3). On the week when the first candlelight protest was held, the first week of May, the website attracted 187 million page views and 3.4 million unique visitors, much higher than the same week of the previous month. As protests heated up in the first week of June, the website set a record high with 499 million page views and 4.4 million weekly unique visitors. Traffics became leveled off as protests slowed down in July. The number of posts shows a similar pattern; it soared from 139 thousand posts in April to 1.1 million posts in June as US beef import and candlelight protests became hot-button topics. Most of the posts in this period related to those issues (Song 2009, 64-65). In a society where 24-hour broadband connections are available at work, at home, and on the streets, cyberspace is no doubt the best place to get the most information on the latest development around the clock, whether a fact, a hoax, or a rumor.

But a notable difference of the 2008 protests in terms of mobile use is that they showed how mobile-fixed convergence changed the way people experienced political participation. For months, many of the protest events were live streamed via the Internet. According to Afreeca, a user-generated video streaming service provider, a total of 17,222 live streams were posted on its website and watched by 7.8 million viewers during the period from May 25 to June 10. The day of the biggest gathering, June 10, recorded 1,357 live streams and about 700,000 viewers (Kim 2008, June 12). Those who could not attend but access online was able to follow development on the protest rally in real-time.

This type of Internet live-streaming of political events was first introduced in the 2007 presidential election by *OhMyNews*, and other online news media, political groups and individual video journalists soon followed suit. Generally, live actions are captured by video journalists on the rally scene and instantly transmitted via wireless broadband, usually WiBro, to the central server of a video streaming service like *Afreeca*. Then, the computer user can access the streaming service and watch the live scene of the protest over broadband at any place.

In a sense, this was made possible by a combination of what the Korean ICT industry has brought to the society over the last decade. Two new media technologies played a crucial role: WiBro and Internet live video-streaming. WiBro made a transmission from the scene much faster and more reliable than Wi-Fi, which was used before, getting rid of a key bottleneck in Internet live-streaming. And the streaming service of user-generated content (UGC), like *Afreeca,* has enabled many small online news media and activist groups to distribute their own live video feeds without having their own media server, which they can rarely afford (Lee and Bae 2008).[9] And this new technology and service, combined with the country's well-established fixed broadband network, provided a power tool for alternative visual media to reach the people sitting in front of the desk at work, at home and abroad.

This live-cast of protest rallies had implications on political participation and the public sphere. First, it allows citizen journalists and activists to bypass mainstream mass media in displaying their actions and delivering their message. This is a stark contrast to the street protests of two decades ago described above, where such efforts were blocked and isolated by the police on the streets and by the state in mass media. Now they can provide a full-time live broadcast of street actions directly to millions of viewers. Going further, some broadcasting groups offered their own commentary segments in between the live scenes from the rally (Lee and Bae 2008, 56). In this sense, the UGC infrastructure and personal and mobile broadband network has opened a new space for alternative visual media.

Second, a seamless linkage of mobile and fixed networks has blurred the boundary of participation and non-participation. Those who are in front of their computer are not a protest participant in the conventional sense, but they become a "virtual" participant by instantly posting comments on discussion boards about the scene they just watched on computer screen, or responding to phone calls from their friends and the blog posts written by rally participants, or relaying them information that they might not be able to obtain from the scene, such as an overall situation of the rally (Lee and Bae 2008, 69). Information and experience flow in both ways between "mobile" participants who are physically present in the rally and "fixed" participants virtually present online.

Overall, the 2008 candlelight protests illustrate how far Korean civil society has come over the last two decades in terms of the political use of mobile communication. Mobile-fixed convergence and broadband network have made information flow among citizens, whether on the streets or in front of their computer, instantaneous and increasingly visual, thereby narrowing the gap of information, experience, and emotion among them. And it was achieved without relying on traditional mainstream mass media but on burgeoning ICT services and mobile communication.

Conclusion

In this chapter, we have examined how mobile communication has changed the dynamic of political participation and the public sphere in Korea over the last decade.

First, our finding suggests that the effect of mobile communication on the public sphere was deeply embedded on the political and economic development of the society. A government-industry ICT complex played a crucial role in shaping the introduction and diffusion of mobile communication in Korea. Its supply-driven, export-oriented approach saturated the market with advanced services even when domestic demand was uncertain. And Korean civil society actively utilized the technological opportunities emerged from the ICT-driven development strategy. Aptly using new technologies and services, civic groups and alternative news media were able to deliver their messages directly to the public, bypassing the mainstream media. It also generated political participation both online and offline, restructuring political activism and the public sphere. Through the process, the revitalization of the public sphere has been increasingly tied to the country's ICT infrastructure driven by the state and the business.

This development may appear somewhat irony because building a vibrant civil society and public sphere has never been an agenda of the ICT development project, particularly to authoritarian regimes. In fact, the aggressive pursuit of ICT-based development by the Korean government and business corresponds to the finding that market-oriented authoritarian regimes are likely to embrace information technology out of the expectation of reaping economic benefit but not necessarily welcome its political consequences (Corrales and Westhoff 2006). Yet in one of the economic consequences, a mobile-rich, ICT-intensive society, critical voices within Korean civil society found and created a space to express their opinions, criticize government policies, and advance their political agenda. This suggests that the political consequence of ICT is more likely to depend upon the capability of a civil society to accommodate it in a way to promote a democratic and plural public sphere.

Second, this study has found that the way mobile communication affects the structure of political participation and the public sphere in Korea has evolved over time. Initially, it was mainly used and found effective in mobilizing political action in a short notice, while the constrained user interface of mobile devices limited its ability to facilitate a discursive participation. However, the constraint has been considerably removed by the convergence of fixed and mobile networks. As in the 2008 protests, constant interaction between online and offline space via fixed-mobile convergent networks further facilitated a new mode of participation grounded on virtual-informational presence.

All these developments generally helped promoting political participation and the plurality of the public sphere. Teens and women (particularly young and married) who were traditionally less engaged in politics has become connected and been a part of public discussion through mobile phones and online communities. So have Korean students and expatriates abroad, which opens a possibility of "diasporic public spheres" (Appadurai 1996). Yet, inequality in participation should not be underestimated. Not only evident socio-economic inequality in Internet use[10] but also participatory gap among those who have Internet access (Schlozman *et al.* 2010) may be more critical in a ICT-intensive society like Korea than any other, which further research should pay more attention to.

Third, Korea's experiences provide a more complicated picture to the question of whether the public sphere has become more fragmented and center-less in cyberspace. One interesting aspect of the 2008 protests is that non-political online communities were very active in debating and mobilizing actions. They are information-based groups whose activities are built around exchanging information about specific interests, such as fashion, sports, and celebrity gossip (Lee and Jung 2009). Despite their non-political orientation, they tend not to be completely exclusive on their specific topics. Members can try to initiate a discussion for various topics, including political ones, to invite other's response. In this way, political discussion piggybacks on the non-political exchange of information. And when a big issue comes out online, the center emerges and draws a great deal of attention, as *Daum Agora* did in 2008. Information flows between the center and the rest and across different communities. Hot topics constantly change, and so does the hotspot.

Overall, mobile communication has significantly changed the dynamics of the public sphere in Korea. The dramatic nature of the changes invites more questions than explored in this paper. First, a comparative analysis on the development of the public sphere in Asia needs to pay attention to the coevolution of political and media development. Similarities and differences among Asian countries in terms of political regime and democratic transition as well as the diffusion of mobile communication can highlight the dynamics of public sphere development at both national and regional level. Second, we need to know more about the entire ecology of media space — online and offline, mobile and fixed. People are versatile in mixing and matching different technologies and moving one online café to another to get and share information. Placing mobile communication within broader media ecology would help to get a fuller picture of the effect of ICT on the public sphere in the era of convergence.[11] Finally, the qualitative aspect of online political participation should be more explored. How much actual change in policy and politics was made by talks in cyberspace and by actions on the streets? Does this development change the public sphere in a more democratic way? Or is this just a "fast activism" (Wellman 2010) with little real consequence? We also need to be careful about the risk or trade-off that the growing reliance of civil society on ICT technology might have in terms of the quality of political action and public discourse. These are the important questions to be addressed by future research.

Notes

1. This chapter is an updated version of the paper first published in 2009. See Hyun-Chin Lim and Joonkoo Lee. "Mobile Communication, Political Participation and the Public Sphere: Korea's Experiences", *Media Asia Journal* 37(4): 244-256.

2. This compressed ICT deployment is more striking because it occurred in the wake of the worst economic crisis ever experienced by the country in its post-war history.

3. According to a recent Nielson report, Koreans spend the fifth most time in the world on social networking sites, over five hours a day in 2009 (*Economist* 2010, January 28).

4. Korea is above the average in both OECD's low-use and medium-use price baskets for mobile service, while in residential fixed-line the country's average price is below the average in all three — low-use, medium-use and high-use — baskets (OECD 2009, 270-277). For very high-speed fixed Internet access, Korea is ranked to the third lowest country among 30 OECD countries in prices (Berkman Center of Internet & Society 2010).

5. The picture has changed in recent years, of course. The middle class was hit hard by the neo-liberal economic reforms of the last decade, and inequality between the wealthy and the poor has deepened. More and more young generations find it hard to get a stable job even after years of education.

6. The 2002 presidential election voter turnout was lower than the previous presidential election, by 8.5% in the 20-24 age group, 14.7% in the 25-29 age group, 16.1% in the 30-34 age group; and 14.1% in the 35-39 age group. The average turnout of all ages, 70.8%, was 9.9% lower than in the previous election (National Election Commission, cited in Han 2007, 66).

7. Korean teens are avid users of mobile phone and texting. An international study finds that 90% of Korean children ages 8-18 own mobile phones and 99% use mobile messaging services, the highest among the six countries studied, including Japan, China, India, Mexico and Cyprus (GSM Association and NTT DoCoMo 2010).

8. This is partly based on one of the authors' personal observation of the 2004 Presidential impeachment protests and anti-US beef import protest in 2008.

9. *Afreeca* was established in 2006, the same year when WiBro was launched and *Time* magazine chose "You" as the Person of the Year, referring to individual content creators on the Internet (Grossman 2006). Piggybacking on the popularity of UGC in Korea and a "YouTube" phenomenon worldwide around that time, it started as a video streaming service in which individual users can upload their own videos and shows that others can watch in real-time. Yet the most of the content shared in the website is usually retransmitted TV shows.

10. According to the National Internet Development Agency of Korea, 90% of

the top income group (monthly income > 4 million Korean won) used the Internet, while only 26% of the bottom group (< 1 million Korean won) did in 2007.

11. For this point, the authors are indebted to vibrant discussions in the "Innovations in Mobile use" pre-conference, International Communication Association Conference, Singapore, June 21-22, 2010.

References

Abu-Lughod, Janet Lippman (1989), *Before European Hegemony: The World System A.D. 1250-1350,* New York: Oxford University Press.

Akamatsu, Kaname (1962), "A Historical Pattern of Economic Growth in Developing Countries", *The Developing Economies,* 1(s1), 3-25.

Aker, Jenny C. and Mbiti, Isaac M. (2010), "Mobile Phones and Economic Development in Africa", *Journal of Economic Perspectives,* 24(3), 207-232.

Albrecht, Steffen (2006), "Whose Voice Is Heard in Online Deliberation?: A Study of Participation and Representation in Political Debates on the Internet", *Information, Communication & Society,* 9(1), 62-82.

Ali-Yrkkö, Jyrki, Rouvinen, Petri, Seppälä, Timo and Ylä-Anttila, Pekka (2011), "Who Captures Value in Global Supply Chains? Case Nokia N95 Smartphone", *Journal of Industry, Competition and Trade,* 11(3), 263-278.

Amable, Bruno (2003), *The Diversity of Modern Capitalism,* Oxford; New York: Oxford University Press.

Amable, Bruno (2003), *The Diversity of Modern Capitalism,* Oxford: Oxford University Press.

Amsden, Alice H. (1989), *Asia's Next Giant: South Korea and Late Industrialization,* New York: Oxford University Press.

Anduiza, Eva, Cantijoch, Marta and Gallego, Aina (2009), "Political Participation and the Internet: A Field Essay", *Information, Communication & Society,* 12(6), 860-878.

Appadurai, Arjun (1996), *Modernity at Large: Cultural Dimensions of Globalization,* Minneapolis, Minn: University of Minnesota Press.

Appelbaum, Richard P. (2008), "Giant Transnational Contractors in East Asia: Emergent Trends in Global Supply Chains", *Competition*

& Change, 12(1), 69-87.

Appelbaum, Richard P. and Gereffi, Gary (1994), "Power and Profits in the Apparel Commodity Chain", in E. Bonacich, L. Cheng, N. Chinchilla, N. Hamilton, and P. Ong (eds.), *Global Production: The Apparel Industry in the Pacific Rim*, Philadelphia, PA: Temple University Press.

Appelbaum, Richard P., Parker, Rachel, Cao, Cong and Gereffi, Gary (2011), "China's (Not So Hidden) Developmental State: Becoming a Leading Nanotechnology Innovator in the Twenty-First Century", in F. L. Block and M. R. Keller (eds.), *State of Innovation: The U.S. Government's Role in Technology Development*, Boulder, CO: Paradigm Publishers.

Arndt, Sven W. and Kierzkowski, Henryk (eds.) (2001), *Fragmentation: New Production Patterns in the World Economy*, Oxford: Oxford University Press.

Aulakh, Gulveen (2014), "Micromax, Lava, Intex Intend to Beef up through Local Manufacturing". *The Economic Times*, June 24, available at: http://economictimes.indiatimes.com/articleshow/52894467.cms?utm_source=contentofinterest&utm_medium=text&utm_campaign=cppst.

Baek, Seung-Wook (2005), "Does China Follow "the East Asian Development Model"?" *Journal of Contemporary Asia*, 35(4), 485-498.

Bailey, David and De Propris, Lisa (2014), "Manufacturing Reshoring and Its Limits: The UK Automotive Case", *Cambridge Journal of Regions, Economy and Society*, 7(3), 379-395.

Bair, Jennifer (2005), "Global Capitalism and Commodity Chains: Looking Back, Going Forward", *Competition & Change*, 9(2), 153-180.

Bair, Jennifer (2009), "Global Commodity Chains: Genealogy and Review", in J. Bair (ed.), *Frontiers of Commodity Chain Research*, Stanford, CA: Stanford University Press.

Bair, Jennifer and Palpacuer, Florence (2015), "CSR Beyond the Corporation: Contested Governance in Global Value Chains", *Global Networks*, 15(s1), S1-S19.

Baldwin, John R. and Gu, Wulong (2004), "Trade Liberalization: Export-Market Participation, Productivity Growth, and Innovation", *Oxford Review of Economic Policy,* 20(3), 372-392.

Baldwin, Richard and Toshihiro, Okubo (2014), "Networked FDI: Sales and Sourcing Patterns of Japanese Foreign Affiliates", *World Economy,* 37(8), 1051-1080.

Barraclough, Geoffrey (1955), "The End of European History", *History in a Changing World,* Oxford: Blackwell.

Basole, Rahul (2009), "Visualization of Interfirm Relations in a Converging Mobile Ecosystem", *Journal of Information Technology,* 24(2), 144-160.

Bazan, Luiza and Navas-Alemán, Lizbeth (2004), "The Underground Revolution in the Sinos Valley: A Comparison of Upgrading in Global and National Value Chains", in H. Schmitz (ed.), *Local Enterprises in the Global Economy: Issues of Governance and Upgrading,* UK: Elgar, Cheltenham.

Benson, Rodney (2009), "Shaping the Public Sphere: Habermas and Beyond", *The American Sociologist,* 40(3), 175-197.

Beramendi, Pablo, Häusermann, Silja, Kitschelt, Herbert and Kriesi, Hanspeter (eds.) (2015), *The Politics of Advanced Capitalism,* Cambridge: Cambridge University Press.

Berkman Center of Internet & Society (2010), "Next Generation Connectivity: A Review of Broadband Internet Transitions and Policy from around the World", available at: http://cyber.law.harvard.edu/pubrelease/broadband/ [Accessed 15 April 2010].

Bermeo, Nancy (2016), "On Democratic Backsliding", *Journal of Democracy,* 27(1), 5-19.

Bernhardt, Thomas (2013), "Developing Countries in the Global Apparel Value Chain: A Tale of Upgrading and Downgrading Experiences", Capturing the Gains Working Paper 2013/22, available at: http://www.capturingthegains.org/publications/workingpapers/wp_201322.htm.

Biggart, Nicole Woolsey and Guillen, Mauro F. (1999), "Developing Difference: Social Organization and the Rise of the Auto Industries of South Korea, Taiwan, Spain, and Argentina", *American Socio-*

logical Review, 64(5), 722-747.

Bimber, Bruce (1998), "The Internet and Political Transformation: Populism, Community, and Accelerated Pluralism", *Polity,* 31(1), 133-160.

Bimber, Bruce (2003), *Information and American Democracy: Technology in the Evolution of Political Power,* Cambridge, UK: Cambridge University Press.

Boase, Jeffrey, Horrigan, John B. , Wellman, Barry and Rainie, Lee (2006), "The Strength of Internet Ties", *Pew Internet and American Life Project,* available at: http://www.pewinternet.org/pdfs/PIP_internet_ties.pdf [Accessed 15 April 2010].

Boli, John and Thomas, George M. (1999), *Constructing World Culture: International Nongovernmental Organizations since 1875,* Stanford, Calif: Stanford University Press.

Bonaglia, Federico, Goldstein, Andrea and Mathews, John A. (2007), "Accelerated Internationalization by Emerging Markets' Multinationals: The Case of the White Goods Sector", *Journal of World Business,* 42(4), 369-383.

Borrus, Michael G., Ernst, Dieter and Haggard, Stephan (eds.) (2000), *International Production Networks in Asia: Rivalry or Riches?* London: Routledge.

Brandt, Loren, and Eric Thun. (2011), "Going mobile in China: Shifting value chains and upgrading in the mobile telecom sector", *International Journal of Technological Learning, Innovation and Development* 4(1-3), 148-180.

Bremmer, Ian (2010), *The End of the Free Market: Who Wins the War between States and Corporations?* New York: Portfolio.

Calhoun, Craig J. (ed.) (1997), *Habermas and the Public Sphere,* Cambridge, Mass.: MIT Press.

Carroll, Bob, Bloomfield, Kevin and Maher, Meaghan (2014), "The Changing Headquarters Landscape for Fortune Global 500 Companies", available at: http://www.ey.com/Publication/vwLUAssets/EY-the-changing-headquarters-landscape-for-fortune-global-500-companies/$FILE/EY-the-changing-headquarters-landscape-for-fortune-global-500-companies.pdf.

Carty, Victoria (2010), "New Information Communication Technologies and Grassroots Mobilization", *Information, Communication & Society,* 13(2), 155-173.

Castells, Manuel (2008), "The New Public Sphere: Global Civil Society, Communication Networks, and Global Governance", *The ANNALS of the American Academy of Political and Social Science,* 616(1), 78-93.

Cattaneo, Olivier, Gereffi, Gary and Staritz, Cornelia (eds.) (2010a), *Global Value Chains in a Postcrisis World: A Development Perspective,* Washington, DC: World Bank.

Cattaneo, Olivier, Gereffi, Gary and Staritz, Cornelia (2010b), "Global Value Chains in a Postcrisis World: Resilience, Consolidation, and Shifting End Markets", in O. Cattaneo, G. Gereffi, and C. Staritz (eds.), *Global Value Chains in a Postcrisis World: A Development Perspective,* World Bank, Washington, DC, pp. 3-20.

Chan, Jenny (2013), "A Suicide Survivor: The Life of a Chinese Worker", *New Technology, Work and Employment,* 28(2), 84-99.

Chan, Jenny, Pun, Ngai and Selden, Mark (2013), "The Politics of Global Production: Apple, Foxconn and China's New Working Class", *New Technology, Work and Employment,* 28(2), 100-115.

Chang, Ha-Joon (1994), *The Political Economy of Industrial Policy,* New York: St. Martin's Press.

Chang, Ha-Joon (2006), *The East Asian Development Experience: The Miracle, the Crisis and the Future,* Penang, Malaysia; London: Zed Books and Third World Network.

Chang, Kyung-Sup (1999), "Compressed Modernity and Its Discontents: South Korean Society in Transtion", *Economy and Society,* 28(1), 30-55.

Chang, Woo-Young (2005), "Online Civic Participation, and Political Empowerment: Online Media and Public Opinion Formation in Korea", *Media, Culture & Society,* 27(6), 925-935.

Chang, Woo-Young (2008), "The Cyber Balkanization and Structural Transformation of the Public Sphere in Korea", *Journal of Contemporary Eastern Asia,* 7(2), 29-48.

Cheng, Ting-Fang and Chien, Chia-Hung (2016), "Taiwanese Tech

Sector Dragged into Depression by Apple", *Nikkei Asian Review,* 12 May, available at: http://asia.nikkei.com/Business/AC/Taiwanese-tech-sector-dragged-into-depression-by-Apple.

Chibber, Vivek (2002), "Bureaucratic Rationality and the Developmental State", *American Journal of Sociology,* 107(4), 951-989.

Chibber, Vivek (2003), *Locked in Place: State-Building and Late Industrialization in India,* Princeton: Princeton University Press.

Cho, Jin-young (2015), "50% of Samsung Mobile Phones Made in Vietnam", *Business Korea,* 28 January, available at: http://www.businesskorea.co.kr/english/news/industry/8785-samsung-made-vietnam-50-samsung-mobile-phones-made-vietnam.

Choi, Young Jae (2008), On-Line Public Sphere and Deliberative Democracy: Civility and Tolerance in the Anti-U.S. Beef Internet Protests in Korea, *The End of Journalism International Conference,* Luton, UK: University of Bedfordshire.

Chosun Ilbo (2004), "Firms Investing Aggressively in R&D Abroad", *Chosun Ilbo,* 18 January, available at: http://english.chosun.com/site/data/html_dir/2004/01/18/2004011861013.html.

Chosun Ilbo (2012), "Korean Firms Hire More Staff Overseas", 10 September, available at: http://english.chosun.com/site/data/html_dir/2012/09/10/2012091000421.html.

Chua, Beng Huat and Iwabuchi, Koichi (eds.) (2008), *East Asian Pop Culture: Analysing the Korean Wave,* Hong Kong: Hong Kong University Press.

CihinaFile (2013), "Who Supplies Apple? (It's Not Just China)", available at: https://www.chinafile.com/multimedia/infographics/who-supplies-apple-its-not-just-china-interactive-map.

Coe, Neil M. (2014), "Missing Links: Logistics, Governance and Upgrading in a Shifting Global Economy", *Review of International Political Economy,* 21(1), 224-256.

Coe, Neil M. and Hess, Martin (2013), "Global Production Networks, Labour and Development", *Geoforum,* 44, 4-9.

Coe, Neil M. and Yeung, Henry Wai-Chung (2015), *Global Production Networks: Theorizing Economic Development in an Interconnected*

World, Oxford: Oxford University Press.

Corrales, Javier and Westhoff, Frank (2006), "Information Technology Adoption and Political Regimes", *International Studies Quarterly,* 50(4), 911-933.

Cumings, Bruce (1984), "The Origins and Development of the Northeast Asian Political Economy: Industrial Sectors, Product Cycles, and Political Consequences", *International Organization,* 38(1), 1-40.

Cumings, Bruce (1999), "Webs with No Spiders, Spiders with No Webs: The Genealogy of the Developmental State", in M. Woo-Cumings (ed.), *The Developmental State,* Ithaca: Cornell University Press.

Datamonitor (2009), "Global Mobile Phones: Industry Profile."

De Marchi, Valentina, Di Maria, Eleonora and Ponte, Stefano (2014), "Multinational Firms and the Management of Global Networks: Insights from Global Value Chain Studies", *Advances in International Management,* 27, 463-486.

Dediu, Horace (2012), "The Phone Makret in 2012: A Tale of Two Disruptions": Asymco, available at: http://www.asymco.com/2012/05/03/the-phone-market-in-2012-a-tale-of-two-disruptions/.

Dedrick, Jason, Kraemer, Kenneth L. and Linden, Greg (2010), "Who Profits from Innovation in Global Value Chains? A Study of the iPod and Notebook PCs", *Industrial and Corporate Change,* 19(1), 81-116.

Dedrick, Jason, Kraemer, Kenneth L. and Linden, Greg (2011), "The Distribution of Value in the Mobile Phone Supply Chain", *Telecommunications Policy,* 35(6), 505-521.

Diamond, Larry (2015), "Facing up to the Democratic Recession", *Journal of Democracy,* 26(1), 141-155.

Dicken, P., Kelly, P. F., Olds, K. and Wai-Chung Yeung, H. (2001), "Chains and Networks, Territories and Scales: Towards a Relational Framework for Analysing the Global Economy", *Global Networks: A Journal of Transnational Affairs,* 1(2), 89-112.

Dicken, Peter (2011), *Global Shift: Mapping the Changing Contours of the World Economy,* New York: Guilford Press.

Djelic, Marie-Laure and Ainamo, Antti (1999), "The Coevolution of New Organizational Forms in the Fashion Industry: A Historical and Comparative Study of France, Italy, and the United States", *Organization Science,* 10(5), 622-637.

Donner, Jonathan (2008), "Research Approaches to Mobile Use in the Developing World: A Review of the Literature", *The Information Society,* 24(3), 140-159.

Duhigg, Charles and Bradsher, Keith (2012), "How the U.S. Lost out on iPhone Work", *The New York Times,* 21 January, available at: http://www.nytimes.com/2012/01/22/business/apple-america-and-a-squeezed-middle-class.html.

Dunning, John H. (1992), *Multinational Enterprises and the Global Economy,* Wokingham, England; Reading, Mass: Addison-Wesley.

Economist, The (2010, January 28), "Special Report on Social Networking: A World of Connections", *The Economist,* available at: http://www.economist.com/node/15351002.

Edgington, D. W. and Hayter, R. (2000), "Foreign Direct Investment and the Flying Geese Model: Japanese Electronics Firms in Asia-Pacific", *Environment and Planning A,* 32(2), 281-304.

EDN Staff. 2007. "2007 Top 100 Contract Manufacturers." EDN Network. Accessed 14 August, 2015. http://www.edn.com/electronics-news/4315992/2007-top-100-contract-manufacturers.

Einhorn, Bruce (2010), "Apple's Smartphone Rivalry with Htc Heats Up", *Bloomberg BusinessWeek,* 3 March, available at: http://www.businessweek.com/globalbiz/content/mar2010/gb2010033_648504.htm.

Ernst, Dieter (2000), "Evolutionary Aspects: The Asian Production Networks of Japanese Electronics Firms", in M. G. Borrus, D. Ernst, and S. Haggard (eds.), *International Production Networks in Asia: Rivalry or Riches?* London: Routledge, pp. 80-109.

Escaith, Hubert (2011), "Understanding International Trade Statistics", *International Trade Statistics 2011,* Geneva: World Trade Organization, pp. 4-5.

Euromonitor International (2011), "Mobile Phones in China",

Euromonitor International.

Euromonitor International (2012a), "Mobile Phones in China", Euromonitor International.

Euromonitor International (2012b), "Mobile Phones in Japan", Euromonitor International.

Euromonitor International (2013), "Mobile Phones in South Korea," Euromonitor International.

Euromonitor International (2015a), "Micromax Informatics Ltd in Consumer Electronics (World)", Euromonitor International.

Euromonitor International (2015b), "Mobile Phones in China", Euromonitor International.

Euromonitor International (2015c), "Mobile Phones in India", Euromonitor International.

Evans, Peter B. (1995), *Embedded Autonomy: States and Industrial Transformation,* Princeton: Princeton University Press.

Evans, Peter B. (1997), "The Eclipse of the State? Reflections on Stateness in an Era of Globalization", *World Politics,* 50(1), 62-87.

Fan, P. (2011), "Innovation, Globalization, and Catch-up of Latecomers: Cases of Chinese Telecom Firms", *Environment and Planning A,* 43(4), 830-849.

FCRI (2009), "Future Market Outlook of Key Devices for Next Generation Mobile Phone 2009", Fuji Chimera Research Institute, Tokyo.

Feenstra, Robert C. and Hamilton, Gary G. (2006), *Emergent Economies, Divergent Paths Economic Organization and International Trade in South Korea and Taiwan,* New York: Cambridge University Press.

Ferree, Myra Marx, Gamson, William Anthony, Gerhards, Jurgen and Rucht, Dieter (2002), *Shaping Abortion Discourse: Democracy and the Public Sphere in Germany and the United States,* Cambridge UK: Cambridge University Press.

Fields, Karl (1997), "Strong States and Business Organization in Korea and Taiwan", in S. Maxfield & R. Schneider (eds.), *Business and the State in Developing Countries,* Ithaca: Cornell University Press, pp. 122-151.

FIH Mobile (2014), "Global Presence", available at: http://www.fihmb.com/global/GlobalPresence.aspx (accessed 1 May, 2014.)

FIH Mobile (2016), "2015 Annual Report," FIH Mobile.

Fingleton, Eamonn (2012), "Unraveling the Cellphone Industry's Biggest Mystery", *Forbes*, 24 August, available at: http://www.forbes.com/sites/eamonnfingleton/2012/08/24/unraveling-the-cellphone-industrys-biggest-mystery/.

Firstpost (2016), "Budget 2016: With Duty on Components Raised, Mobile Phones and Tablets to Cost More", *Firstpost*, 29 February, available at: http://www.firstpost.com/business/budget-2016-with-duty-on-components-raised-mobile-phones-and-tablets-to-cost-more-2649100.html.

Fish, M. Steven (1994), "Russia's Fourth Transition", *Journal of Democracy*, 5(3), 31-42.

Fligstein, Neil (2001), *The Architecture of Markets: An Economic Sociology of Twenty-First-Century Capitalist Societies*, Princeton: Princeton University Press.

Fligstein, Neil (2008), *Euroclash: The EU, European Identity, and the Future of Europe*, Oxford; New York: Oxford University Press.

Folk, Richard (1993), "The Making of Global Citizenship", in J. Brecher, J. B. Childs and J. Cutler (eds.), *Global Visions: Beyond the New World Order*, Boston: South End Press.

Fortunati, Leopoldina (2002), "The Mobile Phone: Towards New Categories and Social Relations", *Information, Communication & Society*, 5(4), 513-528.

Fourcade-Gourinchas, Marion and Babb, Sarah L. (2002), "The Rebirth of the Liberal Creed: Paths to Neoliberalism in Four Countries", *American Journal of Sociology*, 108(3), 533-579.

Frank, Andre Gunder (1998), *Reorient: Global Economy in the Asian Age*, Berkeley: University of California Press.

Friedland, William H. (1994), "The Global Fresh Fruit and Vegetable System: An Industrial Organization Analysis", in P. McMichael (ed.), *The Global Restructuring of Agro-Food Systems*, Ithaca: Cornell University Press, pp. 173-189.

Fröbel, Folker, Heinrichs, Jurgen and Kreye, Otto (1980), *The New*

International Division of Labor: Structural Unemployment in Industrialised Countries and Industrialization in Developing Countries, Cambridge: Cambridge University Press.

Funk, Jeffrey L. (2009), "The Emerging Value Network in the Mobile Phone Industry: The Case of Japan and Its Implications for the Rest of the World", *Telecommunications Policy*, 33(1-2), 4-18.

Gao, Bai (2011), "The Informal Economy in the Era of Information Revolution and Globalization: The Shanzhai Cell Phone Industry in China", *Chinese Journal of Sociology*, 31(2), 1-41.

Gartner (2008), "Gartner Says Worldwide Mobile Phone Sales Increased 16 percent in 2007", available at https://www.gartner.com/newsroom/id/612207.

Gartner (2010a), "Gartner Says Worldwide Mobile Phone Sales Grew 35% in Third Quarter 2010; Smartphone Sales Increased 96%", available at: http://www.gartner.com/it/page.jsp?id= 1466313.

Gartner (2010b), "Worldwide Mobile Terminal Sales to End Users in 2009", available at: http://www.gartner.com/it/page.jsp?id=1306513 [Accessed 20 April 2010].

Gartner (2012), "Gartner Says Worldwide Smartphone Sales Soared in Fourth Quarter of 2011 with 47% Growth", available at: http://www.gartner.com/it/page.jsp?id=1924314.

Gartner (2013), "Gartner Says Smartphone Sales Grew 46.5% in Second Quarter of 2013 and Exceeded Feature Phone Sales for First Time", available at: http://www.gartner.com/newsroom/id/2573415.

Gartner (2014a), "Chinese Vendors Will Drive Growth of White-Box Smartphones and Tablets through 2015", available at: http://www.gartner.com/newsroom/id/2848717.

Gartner (2014b), "Gartner Says Annual Smartphone Sales Surpassed Sales of Feature Phones for the First Time in 2013", available at: http://www.gartner.com/newsroom/id/2665715.

Gartner (2015), "Gartner Says Smartphone Sales Surpassed One Billion Units in 2014", available at: http://www.gartner.com/newsroom/id/2996817.

Gartner (2016a), "Gartner Says Worldwide Smartphone Sales Grew

3.9% in First Quarter of 2016", available at: http://www.gartner.com/newsroom/id/3323017.

Gartner (2016b), "Gartner Says Worldwide Smartphone Sales Grew 9.7% in Fourth Quarter of 2015", available at: http://www.gartner.com/newsroom/id/3215217.

Gartner (2016c), "Gartner Says Worldwide Smartphone Sales Grew 9.7 Percent in Fourth Quarter of 2015", February 18, http://www.gartner.com/newsroom/id/3215217.

Gartner (2017), "Gartner Says Worldwide Sales of Smartphones Grew 7 Percent in the Fourth Quarter of 2016", February 15, https://www.gartner.com/newsroom/id/3609817.

Gartner (2018), "Gartner Says Worldwide Sales of Smartphones Recorded First Ever Decline during the Fourth Quarter of 2017", 22 February, https://www.gartner.com/newsroom/id/3859963.

Gereffi, Gary (1994), "The Organization of Buyer-Driven Global Commodity Chains: How US Retailers Shape Overseas Production Networks", in G. Gereffi and M. Korzeniewicz (eds.), *Commodity Chains and Global Capitalism,* Westport, Conn.: Greenwood Press, pp. 95-122.

Gereffi, Gary (1996), "Commodity Chains and Regional Divisions of Labor in East Asia", *Journal of Asian Business,* 12(1), 75-112.

Gereffi, Gary (1999), "International Trade and Industrial Upgrading in the Apparel Commodity Chains", *Journal of International Economics,* 48(1), 37-70.

Gereffi, Gary (2005), "The Global Economy: Organization, Governance, and Development", in N. J. Smelser and R. Swedberg (eds.), *The Handbook of Economic Sociology* (2nd Edition), Princeton: Princeton University Press, pp. 160-182.

Gereffi, Gary (2009), "Development Models and Industrial Upgrading in China and Mexico", *European Sociological Review,* 25(1), 37-51.

Gereffi, Gary (2014), "Global Value Chains in a Post-Washington Consensus World", *Review of International Political Economy,* 21(1), 9-37.

Gereffi, Gary and Fernandez-Stark, Karina (2011), "Global Value Chain Analysis: A Primer", Center on Globalization, Governance

& Competitiveness, Durham, NC, available at: http://www.cggc.duke.edu/pdfs/2011-05-31_GVC_analysis_a_primer.pdf.

Gereffi, Gary, Garcia-Johnson, Ronie and Sasser, Erika (2001a), "The Ngo-Industrial Complex", *Foreign Policy,* 125, 56-65.

Gereffi, Gary, Humphrey, John, Kaplinsky, Raphael and Sturgeon, Timothy J. (2001b), "Introduction: Globalisation, Value Chains and Development", *IDS Bulletin,* 32(3).

Gereffi, Gary, Humphrey, John and Sturgeon, Timothy (2005), "The Governance of Global Value Chains", *Review of International Political Economy,* 12(1), 78-104.

Gereffi, Gary and Korzeniewicz, Miguel (1990), "Commodity Chains and Footwear Exports in the Semiperiphery", in W. G. Martin (ed.), *Semiperipheral States in the World-Economy,* New York: Greenwood Press, pp. 45-68.

Gereffi, Gary and Lee, Joonkoo (2012), "Why the World Suddenly Cares about Global Supply Chains", *Journal of Supply Chain Management,* 48(3), 24-32.

Gereffi, Gary and Lee, Joonkoo (2016), "Economic and Social Upgrading in Global Value Chains and Industrial Clusters: Why Governance Matters", *Journal of Business Ethics,* 133(1), 25-38.

Giuliani, Elisa, Gorgoni, Sara, Günther, Christina and Rabellotti, Roberta (2014), "Emerging Versus Advanced Country MNEs Investing in Europe: A Typology of Subsidiary Global–Local Connections", *International Business Review,* 23(4), 680-691.

Greene, Jay and Verbergt, Matthias (2016), "Microsoft Takes Another Step out of the Cellphone Business, as Nokia Plots a Return", *The Wall Street Journal,* 18 May, available at: http://www.wsj.com/articles/nokia-to-return-to-cellphones-via-licensing-pact-1463567015.

Grossman, Lev (2006), "Time's Person of the Year: You", *Time,* 13 December, available at: http://www.time.com/time/magazine/article/0,9171,1569514,00.html.

Grundberg, Sven and Gryta, Thomas (2014), "Smartphone Makers Aim at Emerging Markets with Low-End Devices", *Wall Street Journal,* 26 February, available at: http://online.wsj.com/news/

articles/SB10001424052702304834704579405081452450174.

GSM Association and NTT DoCoMo (2010), Children's Use of Mobile Phones and Personal Relationships — an International Comparison 2010.

Guillen, Mauro F. (2001), "Is Globalization Civilizing, Destructive or Feeble? A Critique of Five Key Debates in the Social Science Literature", *Annual Review of Sociology*, 27(1), 235-260.

Guillén, Mauro F. (2001), *The Limits of Convergence: Globalization and Organizational Change in Argentina, South Korea, and Spain*, Princeton: Princeton University Press.

Habermas, Jürgen (1989), *The Structural Transformation of the Public Sphere: An Inquiry into a Category of Bourgeois Society*, Cambridge, Mass.: MIT Press.

Hall, Peter A. and Soskice, David W. (eds.) (2001), *Varieties of Capitalism: The Institutional Foundations of Comparative Advantage*, Oxford; New York: Oxford University Press.

Hall, Peter and D. Soskice (eds.) (2001), *Varieties of Capitalism: The Institutional Foundations of Comparative Advantage*, Oxford: Oxford University Press.

Hamilton-Hart, Natasha (2005), "The Regionalization of Southeast Asian Business: Transnational Networks in National Contexts", in T. J. Pempel (ed.), *Remapping East Asia: The Construction of a Region*, Ithaca: Cornell University Press, pp. 170-191.

Hamilton, Gary G., Senauer, Benjamin and Petrovic, Misha (eds.), (2011), *The Market Makers: How Retailers Are Reshaping the Global Economy*, Oxford; New York: Oxford University Press.

Hamilton, Gary G. and Biggart, Nicole Woolsey (1988), "Market, Culture, and Authority: A Comparative Analysis of Management and Organization in the Far East", *American Journal of Sociology*, 94, S52-S94.

Hamilton, Gary G. and Gereffi, Gary (2009), "Global Commodity Chains, Market Makers, and the Rise of Demand-Responsive Economies", in J. Bair (ed.), *Frontiers of Commodity Chain Research*. Stanford University Press, Stanford, Calif, pp. 136-161.

Han, Jongwoo (2007), "From Indifference to Making the Difference:

New Networked Information Technologies (Nnits) and Patterns of Political Participation among Korea's Younger Generations", *Journal of Information Technology & Politics*, 4(1), 57-76.

Hauben, Ronda (2008), "Online Grassroots Journalism and Participatory Democracy in South Korea", in R. D. Frank (ed.), *Korea Yearbook. Volume 1. Politics, Economy and Society 2007*, Leiden; Boston: Brill.

Held, David, McGrew, Anthony, Goldblatt, David and Perraton, Jonathan (1999), *Global Transformations: Politics, Economics and Culture*, Stanford, Calif: Stanford University Press.

Helsingin Sanomat (2005), "Perlos Expanding in China", 17 May, available at: http://www.hs.fi/english/article/Perlos+expanding+in+China/1101979526819.

Henderson, Jeffrey, Dicken, Peter, Hess, Martin, Coe, Neil and Yeung, Henry Wai-Chung (2002), "Global Production Networks and the Analysis of Economic Development", *Review of International Political Economy*, 9(3), 436-464.

Hess, Martin and Coe, Neil M. (2006), "Making Connections: Global Production Networks, Standards, and Embeddedness in the Mobile-Telecommunications Industry", *Environment and Planning A*, 38(7), 1205-1228.

Hesse, Markus and Rodrigue, Jean-Paul (2006), "Global Production Networks and the Role of Logistics and Transportation", *Growth and Change*, 37(4), 499-509.

Hobday, Mike (1998), "Latecomer Catch-up Strategies in Electronics: Samsung of Korea and Acer of Taiwan", *Asia Pacific Business Review*, 4(2-3), 48-83.

Hong, Cathy (2005), "New Political Tool: Text Messaging", *USA Today*, 30 June, available at: http://www.usatoday.com/tech/news/2005-06-30-politics-text-tool_x.htm.

Hopkins, Terence K. and Wallerstein, Immanuel (1986), "Commodity Chains in the World-Economy Prior to 1800", *Review*, 10(1), 157-170.

Hopkins, Terence K. and Wallerstein, Immanuel (1994), "Commodity Chains: Construct and Research", in G. Gereffi and M.

Korzeniewicz (eds.), *Commodity Chains and Global Capitalism*, Greenwood Press, Westport, Conn., pp. 17-20.

Horner, Rory (2016), "A New Economic Geography of Trade and Development? Governing South–South Trade, Value Chains and Production Networks", *Territory, Politics, Governance*, 4(4), 400-420.

Hsieh, Michelle F. (2011), "Similar Opportunities, Different Responses: Explaining the Divergent Patterns of Development between Taiwan and South Korea", *International Sociology*, 26(3), 364-391.

Humphrey, John (2007), "The Supermarket Revolution in Developing Countries: Tidal Wave or Tough Competitive Struggle?" *Journal of Economic Geography*, 7(4), 433-450.

Humphrey, John and Schmitz, Hubert (2001), "Governance in Global Value Chains", *IDS Bulletin*, 32(3), 19-29.

Humphrey, John and Schmitz, Hubert (2002), "How Does Insertion in Global Value Chains Affect Upgrading in Industrial Clusters?", *Regional Studies*, 36(9), 1017-1027.

Hung, Quoc (2013), "Samsung Kicks Off US$3.2 Bil. Project in Thai Nguyen", *The Saigon Times*, 27 March, available at: http://english.thesaigontimes.vn/28456/Samsung-kicks-off-US$32-bil-project-in-Thai-Nguyen.html.

Huntington, Samuel P. (1991), *The Third Wave: Democratization in the Late Twentieth Century*, Norman: University of Oklahoma Press.

Hwang, Jooseong and Yoo, Jiyeon (2007), "A Study on Changing Trends and Causes of Internet Usage in Everyday Life: Comparison between 2002 and 2005", *Chŏngbohwa chŏngch'aek = Informatization Policy*, 14(1), 10-43 [in Korean].

Im, Hyug Baeg (2000), "South Korean Democratic Consolidation in Comparative Perspective", in L. J. Diamond and B.-K. Kim (eds.), *Consolidating Democracy in South Korea*, Boulder, Colo: Lynne Rienner.

ITU (2010), *Measuring the Information Society 2010*, International Telecommunication Union, Geneva, Switzerland.

Johnson, Chalmers A. (1982), *MITI and the Japanese Miracle: The*

Growth of Industrial Policy, 1925-1975, Stanford, Calif: Stanford University Press.

Johnson, Chalmers A. (1999), "The Developmental State: Odyssey of a Concept", in M. Woo-Cumings (ed.), *The Developmental State,* Ithaca: Cornell University Press.

Kaletsky, Anatole (2010), *Capitalism 4.0: The Birth of a New Economy in the Aftermath of Crisis,* New York: PublicAffairs.

Kallerberg, Arthur L. (1966), "The Logic of Comparison: A Methodological Note on the Comparative Study of Political Systems", *World Politics* 19(1): 69-82.

Kang, Daniel Jisuk and Dyson, Laurel Evelyn (2007), "Internet Politics in South Korea: The Case of Rohsamo and Ohmynews", 18th Australasian Conference on Information Systems, Toowoomba.

Kao, Hung-hsiang and Lee, Jen-fang (2010), "The Application of Shanzhai Innovation Model in China: The Examples of Mobile Phone, Notebook Computer, and Automobile", The Summer Conference "Opening Up Innovation: Strategy, Organization and Technology", Imperial College London Business School.

Kaplinsky, Raphael (2000), "Globalisation and Unequalisation: What Can Be Learned from Value Chain Analysis?" *Journal of Development Studies,* 37(2), 117-146.

Kaplinsky, Raphael and Farooki, Masuma (2010), "Global Value Chains, the Crisis, and the Shift of Markets from North to South", in O. Cattaneo, G. Gereffi and C. Staritz (eds.), *Global Value Chains in a Postcrisis World: A Development Perspective,* Washington, DC: World Bank, pp. 125-153.

Kaplinsky, Raphael, Terheggen, Anne and Tijaja, Julia (2011), "China as a Final Market: The Gabon Timber and Thai Cassava Value Chains", *World Development,* 39(7), 1177-1190.

Karippacheril, Tina George, Nikayin, Fatemeh, de Reuver, Mark and Bouwman, Harry (2013), "Serving the Poor: Multisided Mobile Service Platforms, Openness, Competition, Collaboration and the Struggle for Leadership", *Telecommunications Policy,* 37(1), 24-34.

Katz, James Everett (ed.) (2008), *Handbook of Mobile Communication Studies,* Cambridge, Mass.: MIT Press.

Katzenstein, Peter J. (2006), "East Asia — Beyond Japan", in P. J. Katzenstein and T. Shiraishi (eds.), *Beyond Japan: The Dynamics of East Asian Regionalism,* Ithaca: Cornell University Press, pp. 1-33.

Katzenstein, Peter J. and Shiraishi, Takashi (eds.) (2006), *Beyond Japan: The Dynamics of East Asian Regionalism,* Ithaca: Cornell University Press.

Keane, Michael, Fung, Anthony and Moran, Albert (2007), *New Television, Globalization, and the East Asian Cultural Imagination,* Hong Kong: Hong Kong University Press.

Keck, Margaret E. and Sikkink, Kathryn (1998), *Activists Beyond Borders: Advocacy Networks in International Politics,* Ithaca: Cornell University Press.

Keller, Kevin (2010), "iPhone 4 Carries Bill of Materials of $187.51, According to iSuppli", iSuppli Press Release, available at: http://www.isuppli.com/Teardowns/News/Pages/iPhone-4-Carries-Bill-of-Materials-of-187-51-According-to-iSuppli.aspx.

Kim, Baek-yŏng (2003), "Kaduchŏngch'iŭi Kongganhak: 1980-Yondae Sŏulsinae Daehaksaeng Kadusiwie Taehan Kongganjŏk Punsŏk = A Spatial Analysis of Street Politics: A Spatial Analysis of Colleage Student Street Protests in Seoul in the 1980s", in Hanguk Sanŏpsahoe Yŏn'guso (ed.), *Sahoeirongwa Sahoepyŏnhyŏk,* Sŏul-si, Hanul, pp. 358-378 [in Korean].

Kim, Eun-Gyoo and Hamilton, James W. (2006), "Capitulation to Capital? *Ohmynews* as Alternative Media", *Media, Culture & Society,* 28(4), 541-560.

Kim, Eun Mee (1997), *Big Business, Strong State: Collusion and Conflict in South Korean Development, 1960-1990,* Albany: State University of New York Press.

Kim, Kyong-Dong (2017a), *Korean Modernization and Uneven Development: Alternative Sociological Accounts*, Singapore: Palgrave.

Kim, Kyong-Dong (2017b), *Confucianism and Modernization in East Asia,* Singapore: Palgrave.

Kim, Kyong-Dong (2017c), *Alternative Discourse on Modernization and Development: East Asian Perspectives,* Singapore: Palgrave.

Kim, Hyun-seok (2012), "Samsung Electronics Restructuring

Oveaseas Mobile Phone Production Facilities, Closing Shenzhen Plants and Increasing Capacity in Vietnam and India", *Hankyung Daily*, 20 March, available at: http://www.hankyung.com/news/app/newsview.php?aid=2012032075781.

Kim, Soon-Ki (2008, June 12), "More Than 7 Million Viewers Watched Candlelight Protest Live Streamings on Afreeca", *Electronic Times*, available at: http://www.etnews.co.kr/news/detail.html?id=200806110161 [in Korean].

Kinkel, Steffen (2012), "Trends in Production Relocation and Backshoring Activities: Changing Patterns in the Course of the Global Economic Crisis", *International Journal of Operations & Production Management*, 32(6), 696-720.

Kotaro, Hosokawa (2016), "Falling Apple Sales Hit Japanese Device Makers", *Nikkei Asian Review*, 13 May, available at: http://asia.nikkei.com/Business/Companies/Falling-Apple-sales-hit-Japanese-device-makers?n_cid=NARAN012.

KOTRA (2006), "Report on Taiwan's Information Technology Industry: Mobile Phones," Korea Trade-Investment Promotion Agency, Seoul [in Korean].

Kraemer, Kenneth L., Linden, Greg and Dedrick, Jason (2011), "Capturing Value in Global Networks: Apple's iPad and iPhone", Personal Computing Industry Center, University of California, Irvine, available at: http://pcic.merage.uci.edu/papers/2011/Value_iPad_iPhone.pdf.

Kristensen, Peer H. and Morgan, Glenn (2014), "Theoretical Contexts and Conceptual Frames for the Study of Twenty-First Century Capitalisms", G. Morgan and R. Whitley (eds.), *Capitalisms and Capitalism in the 21st Century*, Oxford: Oxford University Press.

Krugman, Paul (1994), "The Myth of Asia's Miracle", *Foreign Affairs*, 73(6), 62-78.

Krugman, Paul (1995), "Growing World Trade: Causes and Consequences", *Brookings Papers on Economic Activity*, 1995(1), 327-377.

Kushida, Kenji (2011), "Leading without Followers: How Politics and Market Dynamics Trapped Innovations in Japan's Domestic

"Galapagos" Telecommunications Sector", *Journal of Industry, Competition and Trade,* 11(3), 279-307.

Kushida, Kenji E. (2008), "Wireless Bound and Unbound: The Politics Shaping Cellular Markets in Japan and South Korea", *Journal of Information Technology & Politics,* 5(2), 231-254.

Laha, Somjita (2014), "Informality in E-Waste Processing: An Analysis of the Indian Experience", *Competition and Change,* 18(4), 309-326.

Lane, Christel (2008), "National Capitalisms and Global Production Networks: An Analysis of Their Interaction in Two Global Industries", *Socio-Economic Review,* 6(2), 227-260.

Law, Pui-lam and Peng, Yinni (2008), "Mobile Networks: Migrant Workers in Southern China", in J. E. Katz (ed.), *Handbook of Mobile Communication Studies,* Cambridge, Mass.: MIT Press, pp. 55-64.

Lee, Chang-Ho and Bae, Ae-Jin (2008), "An Analysis of Various Types of Social Movement through the New Media: Focusing on the 2008 Candle Rally", *Han'guk ŏllon chŏngbo hakbo = Korean Journal of Communication and Information,* 44, 44-75 [in Korean].

Lee, Chang-Ho and Jung, Eui-Chul (2009), "The Possibilities and Limitations of Internet Cafe Bulletin Board as a Public Sphere: Focusing on 'Zzubang Club' and 'Bizarrerie or Truth'", ŏllon kwahak yŏn›gu = *Journal of Communication Science,* 9(3), 388-424 [in Korean].

Lee, Chang-Ho and Lee, Ho-Young (2009), "The Pattern of Portal News Use among Portal Users and Their Recognition of Portal as a Press", *Han'guk ŏllon chŏngbo hakbo = Korean Journal of Communication and Information,* 46, 177-211 [in Korean].

Lee, Hang Young and Lee, Joonkoo (2012), "China's Post-WTO Export Growth and the Restructuring of Asian Production Network: A Global Value Chain Approach", *Han'guk Sahoe [Korean Society],* 23(1), 223-250.

Lee, Hyun-Ho (2015), "5 out of 10 Sec's Mobile Phones 'Made in Vietnam'", *Seoul Economy,* 27 January, available at: http://www.sentv.co.kr/news/view/467518.

Lee, Jang-Hyŏk (2010, May 12), "iPhone Tutor Wanted in the Midst of iPhone Fever", *ZDNet Korea*, available at: http://www.zdnet.co.kr/ArticleView.asp?artice_id=20100512110227 [in Korean].

Lee, Ji-Ren and Chen, Jen-Shyang (2000), "Dynamic Synergy Creation with Multiple Business Activities: Toward a Competence-Based Growth Model for Contract Manufacturers", *Advances in Applied Business Strategy,* 6A, 209-228.

Lee, Joonkoo (2003), "The Formation and Transformation of the Korean Telecommunication Regime, 1979-1995", *Chŏngbowa sahoe = Information and Society,* 5, 57-101 [in Korean].

Lee, Joonkoo (2010), "Global Commodity Chains and Global Value Chains", in R.A. Denemark (ed.), *The International Studies Encyclopedia,* Oxford: Wiley-Blackwell, pp. 2987-3006.

Lee, Joonkoo (2016), "Global Value Chains and the Changing Pattern of North-South Trade: Apparel, Electronics and Automotive Sectors in 2005-2014", *Journal of International Trade & Commerce,* 12(6), 1-21.

Lee, Joonkoo and Gereffi, Gary (2013), "The Co-Evolution of Concentration in Mobile Phone Global Value Chains and Its Impact on Social Upgrading in Developing Countries", Capturing the Gains Working Paper 2013/25, University of Manchester, available at: http://www.capturingthegains.org/publications/workingpapers/wp_201325.htm.

Lee, Joonkoo and Gereffi, Gary (2015), "Global Value Chains, Rising Power Firms and Economic and Social Upgrading", *critical perspectives on international business,* 11(3/4), 319-339.

Lee, Joonkoo, Kim, Jong-Cheol and Lim, Jinho (2016), "Globalization and Divergent Paths of Industrial Development: Mobile Phone Manufacturing in China, Japan, South Korea and Taiwan", *Journal of Contemporary Asia,* 46(2), 222-246.

Lee, Joonkoo, Lee, Sang-Hoon and Park, Gwan-Ho (forthcoming), "Revisiting the Miracle: South Korea's Industrial Upgrading from a Global Value Chain Perspective", in D. Nathan, M. Tewari and S. Sarkar (eds.), *Development with Global Value Chains: Upgrading and Innovation in Asia,* Cambridge: Cambridge University Press, Chapter 13.

Lee, Keun and Jung, Moosup (2015), "Overseas Factories, Domestic Employment, and Technological Hollowing Out: A Case Study of Samsung's Mobile Phone Business", *Review of World Economics,* 151(3), 461-475.

Lee, Kwang-kun (2013), "Jabonjuui Segyegyeongjewa Ilgukjeok Chejeui Gujohwa: Haenwija Jihyangjeok Segyecheje Bunsoek" [the Structuration of the Capitalist World-Economy and a National Regime: An Actor-Oriented World-Systems Approach]", *Hanguksahoehak* [*Korean Sociological Review*], 47(2).

Lee, Yong Wook and Kwak, Sun Young (2009), "Neo-Liberal Korea and Still Developmentalist Japan: Myth or Reality?" *Global Economic Review,* 38(3), 277-295.

Lim, Haeran (2010), "The Transformation of the Developmental State and Economic Reform in Korea", *Journal of Contemporary Asia,* 40(2), 188-210.

Lim, Hyun-Chin, Kim, Yong-Ho, Suh, Yi-Jong, Lee, Hang-Woo and Chung, Young-Chul (2004), *A Study on the Influences of Internet Communities on Politics, Economy, and Civil Society,* A Final Report to Minister of Information and Communication, April 30 [In Korean].

Lim, Hyun-Chin and Lee, Joonkoo (2010), "Mobile Communication, Political Participation and the Public Sphere: South Korea's Experiences", *Media Asia,* 37(4), 244-256.

Lim, Hyun-Chin, Nederveen Pieterse, Jan and Hwang, Suk-Man (forthcoming), "Capitalism in Asia: Introduction", in H.-C. Lim, J. Nederveen Pieterse and S.-M. Hwang (eds.), *Capitalism in Asia: Diversity and Commonality.*

Lim, Hyun-Chin, Schäfer, Wolf and Hwang, Suk-Man (eds.) (2010), *New Asias: Global Futures of World Regions,* Seoul: Seoul National University Press.

Linden, Greg, Kraemer, Kenneth L. and Dedrick, Jason (2009), "Who Captures Value in a Global Innovation Network?: The Case of Apple's iPod", *Communications of the ACM,* 52(3), 140-144.

Low, Patrick (2013), "The Role of Services", in D. K. Elms and P. Low (eds.), *Global Value Chains in a Changing World,* Geneva:

World Trade Organization, Fung Global Institute and Temasek Foundation Centre for Trade & Negotiations, pp. 61-81.

Lowe-Lee, Florence (2010, May 12), "Korea: From Rags to Riches (19) — Red Devils Created Global Culture of Street Cheering", *Korea Times*, available at: http://www.koreatimes.co.kr/www/news/biz/2010/05/291_65771.html

Luk, Lorraine (2014), "Foxconn Profit Rises on iPhone Demand", *Wall Street Journal*, 13 November, available at: http://www.wsj.com/articles/foxconn-profit-rises-on-iphone-demand-1415877728.

Lüthje, Boy (2002), "Electronics Contract Manufacturing: Global Production and the International Division of Labor in the Age of the Internet", *Industry and Innovation*, 9(3), 227-247.

Marin, Dalia (2006), "A New International Division of Labor in Europe: Outsourcing and Offshoring to Eastern Europe", *Journal of the European Economic Association*, 4(2-3), 612-622.

MarketLine (2014), "Marketline Industry Profile: Global Mobile Phones", Manchester, UK: Progressive Media Group.

Martin, William G. (ed.) (1990), *Semiperipheral States in the World-Economy*, New York: Greenwood Press.

Marukawa, Tomoo (2009), "Why Japanese Multinationals Failed in the Chinese Mobile Phone Market: A Comparative Study of New Product Development in Japan and China", *Asia Pacific Business Review*, 15(3), 411-431.

McChesney, Robert Waterman and Nichols, John (2002), *Our Media, Not Theirs: The Democratic Struggle against Corporate Media*, New York: Seven Stories.

McLain, Sean (2016), "India's Micromax Plans to Sell Smartphones in China, Raise Cash", *The Wall Street Journal*, 3 June, available at: http://www.wsj.com/articles/indias-micromax-plans-to-sell-smartphones-in-china-go-public-1464845743.

McMichael, Philip (1990), "Incorporating Comparison within a World-Historical Perspective: An Alternative Comparative Method", *American Sociological Review*, 55(3), 385-397.

McMichael, Philip (2012), *Development and Social Change: A Global Perspective*, Los Angeles, Calif: Sage.

McNeill, William Hardy (1963), *The Rise of the West: A History of the Human Community,* Chicago: University of Chicago Press.

Milberg, William S. and Winkler, Deborah (2013), *Outsourcing Economics: Global Value Chains in Capitalist Development,* Cambridge: Cambridge University Press.

Ministry of Knowledge Economy (2012), "IT Products Export & Import Statistics", Ministry of Knowledge Economy, Seoul [in Korean].

Mittelman, James H. (2000), *The Globalization Syndrome: Transformation and Resistance,* Princeton: Princeton University Press.

Morgan, Glenn and Whitley, Richard (eds.) (2012), *Capitalisms and Capitalism in the Twenty-First Century,* Oxford; New York: Oxford University Press.

Morishima, Michio (1982), *Why Has Japan 'Succeeded'?: Western Technology and the Japanese Ethos,* Cambridge; New York: Cambridge University Press.

Morris, Mike, Staritz, Cornelia and Barnes, Justin (2011), "Value Chain Dynamics, Local Embeddedness, and Upgrading in the Chothing Sectors of Lesotho and Swaziland", *International Journal of Technological Learning, Innovation and Development,* 4(1-3), 96-119.

Mudambi, Ram (2008), "Location, Control and Innovation in Knowledge-Intensive Industries", *Journal of Economic Geography,* 8(5), 699-725.

Murray, Philomena and Rees, Nicholas (2010), "European and Asian Regionalism: Form and Function", *International Politics,* 47(3), 269-275.

Nam, Kyung-Min (2009), "Spatial Integration of Corporate R&D and Mass Production Activities in High-Tech Manufacturing: A Case Study of Samsung Electronics", *Kukt'oyŏn'gu* [*The Korea Spatial Planning Review*], 62, 125-145.

Narayana, M. R. (2011), "Telecommunications Services and Economic Growth: Evidence from India", *Telecommunications Policy,* 35(2), 115-127.

Navas-Alemán, Lizbeth (2011), "The Impact of Operating in Multiple

Value Chains for Upgrading: The Case of the Brazilian Furniture and Footwear Industries", *World Development*, 39(8), 1386-1397.

Nederveen Pieterse, Jan (2010), "Twenty-First Century Globalization-Propositions and Perspectives", in H.-C. Lim, W. Schäfer and S.-M. Hwang (eds.), *New Asias: Global Futures of World Regions*, Seoul: Seoul National University Press.

Nederveen Pieterse, Jan (2012), "Twenty-First Century Globalization: A New Development Era", *Forum for Development Studies*, 39(3), 367-385.

Nederveen Pieterse, Jan (2015), "Capitalism in East and West: A Comparative Perspective", Paper presented at the International Conference on Capitalism and Capitalisms in Asia: Origin, Commonality, and Diversity, Seoul National University, Seoul, Korea, October 22-23.

Neilson, Jeff and Pritchard, Bill (2009), *Value Chain Struggles: Institutions and Governance in the Plantation Districts of South India*, Chichester, West Sussex; Malden, Mass.: Wiley-Blackwell.

Neilson, Jeffrey, Pritchard, Bill and Yeung, Henry Wai-chung (2014), "Global Value Chains and Global Production Networks in the Changing International Political Economy: An Introduction", *Review of International Political Economy*, 21(1), 1-8.

Newman, Susan A. (2009), "Financialization and Changes in the Social Relations Along Commodity Chains: The Case of Coffee", *Review of Radical Political Economics*, 41(4), 539-559.

NIPA (2011), "The Rise of EMS/ODM Industry and Its Implications", National IT Industry Promotion Agency, Seoul [in Korean].

Nolan, Peter (2012), *Is China Buying the World?* Cambridge: Polity Press.

O'Brien, Kevin J. (2005), "Asian Rival Takes over Siemens Cellphones", *The New York Times*, 8 June, available at: http://www.nytimes.com/2005/06/07/technology/07iht-siemens.html?_r=0.

O'Rourke, Dara (2006), "Multi-Stakeholder Regulation: Privatizing or Socializing Global Labor Standards?" *World Development*, 34(5), 899-918.

OECD (2009), OECD Communications Outlook 2009, Paris: OECD

Publishing.

OECD (2011), "Global Value Chains: Preliminary Evidence and Policy Issues", Organisation for Economic Co-operation and Development, DSTI/IND(2011)3, Paris, available at: http://www.oecd.org/dataoecd/18/43/47945400.pdf.

OECD (2013), "Interconnected Economies: Benefiting from Global Value Chains", Paris: OECD Publishing, Paris, available at: http://dx.doi.org/10.1787/9789264189560-en.

OECD, WTO and World Bank (2014), "Global Value Chains: Challenges, Opportunities, and Implications for Policy", Report prepared for submission to the G20 Trade Ministers Meeting, Sydney, Australia, 19 July.

Ono, Shigeru and Tang, Puay (2010), "The Role of Mobile Handsets in Advanced Network Service Evolution: Evidence from Japan", *Telecommunications Policy,* 34(8), 444-460.

Park, Mi (2005), "Organizing Dissent against Authoritarianism: The South Korean Student Movement in the 1980s", *Korea Journal,* 45(3), 261-289.

Park, Tae-Young (2013), "How a Latecomer Succeeded in a Complex Product System Industry: Three Case Studies in the Korean Telecommunication Systems", *Industrial and Corporate Change,* 22(2), 363-396.

Park, Yong Soo (2011), "Revisiting the South Korean Developmental State after the 1997 Financial Crisis", *Australian Journal of International Affairs,* 65(5), 590-606.

Pempel, T. J. (1999), "The Developmental Regime in a Changing World Order", in M. Woo-Cumings (ed.), *The Developmental State,* Ithaca: Cornell University Press.

Pempel, T. J. (2005), *Remapping East Asia: The Construction of a Region,* Ithaca: Cornell University Press.

Petras, James (2006), "Past, Present and Future of China: From Semi-Colony to World Power?", *Journal of Contemporary Asia,* 36(4), 423-441.

Pietrobelli, Carlo and Saliola, Federica (2008), "Power Relationships Along the Value Chain: Multinational Firms, Global Buyers and

Performance of Local Suppliers", *Cambridge Journal of Economics,* 32(6), 947-962.

Piore, Michael J. and Sabel, Charles F. (1984), *The Second Industrial Divide,* New York: Basic Books.

Ponte, Stefano and Sturgeon, Timothy (2014), "Explaining Governance in Global Value Chains: A Modular Theory-Building Effort", *Review of International Political Economy,* 21(1), 195-223.

Prange, Christiane (ed.) (2016), *Market Entry in China: Case Studies on Strategy, Marketing, and Branding,* Switzerland: Springer Science and Business Media.

Przeworski, Adam and Henry Teune (1970), *The Logic of Comparative Social Inquiry: Comparative Studies in Behavioral Science,* New York: Wiley-Interscience.

Puddington, Arch (2015), "A Return to the Iron Fist", *Journal of Democracy,* 26(2), 122-138.

Pun, Ngai, Shen, Yuan, Guo, Yuhua, Lu, Huilin, Chan, Jenny and Selden, Mark (2016), "Apple, Foxconn, and Chinese Workers' Struggles from a Global Labor Perspective", *Inter-Asia Cultural Studies,* 17(2), 166-185.

Putnam, Robert D. (2000), *Bowling Alone: The Collapse and Revival of American Community,* New York: Simon & Schuster.

Raikes, Philip, Jensen, Michael Friis and Ponte, Stefano (2000), "Global Commodity Chain Analysis and the French Filière Approach: Comparison and Critique", *Economy & Society,* 29(3), 390-417.

Rajagopal, Arvind (2001), *Politics after Television Religious Nationalism and the Reshaping of the Indian Public,* Cambridge: Cambridge University Press.

Rajagopal, Arvind (2006), "An American Theory of the Public Sphere", *Sociological Forum,* 21(1), 147-157.

Ramamurti, Ravi and Singh, Jitendra V. (2009), *Emerging Multinationals in Emerging Markets,* Cambridge: Cambridge University Press.

Rao, Rajiv (2016), "India's Micromax Gets Knocked Down by the Chinese", *ZDNet,* available at: http://www.zdnet.com/article/indias-micromax-gets-knocked-down-by-the-chinese/.

Rasiah, Rajah, Miao, Zhang and Xin Xin, Kong (2012), "Can China's

Miraculous Economic Growth Continue?" *Journal of Contemporary Asia,* 43(2), 295-313.

Rassweiler, Andrew (2014), "iPhone 6 Plus: $100 Costlier for Consumers to Buy—Just $15.50 More Expensive for Apple to Make", IHS Markit, available at: https://technology.ihs.com/511475/iphone-6-plus-100-costlier-for-consumers-to-buyjust-1550-more-expensive-for-apple-to-make.

Rheingold, Howard (2003), *Smart Mobs: The Next Social Revolution, ,* Cambridge, Mass.: Perseus Pub.

Rooney, Ben (2012), "China at Heart of Nokia's Troubles", *The Wall Street Journal,* 19 April, available at: http://blogs.wsj.com/tech-europe/2012/04/19/china-at-heart-of-nokias-troubles/.

Sabat, Hemant Kumar (2002), "The Evolving Mobile Wireless Value Chain and Market Structure", *Telecommunications Policy,* 26 (9-10), 505-535.

SACOM (2010), "Workers as Machines: Military Management in Foxconn", Students & Scholars Against Corporate Misbehavior, Hong Kong, available at: http://sacom.hk/workers-as-machines-military-management-in-foxconn/.

Saguy, Abigail Cope (2003), *What Is Sexual Harassment? From Capitol Hill to the Sorbonne,* Berkeley, Calif: University of California Press.

Samsung Electronics (2015), "Samsung Sustainability Report 2015", Samsung Electronics, available at: http://www.samsung.com/us/aboutsamsung/sustainability/sustainabilityreports/download/2015/SAMSUNG_SUSTAINABILITY_REPORT_2015_ENG.pdf.

Satariano, Adam and Burrows, Peter (2011), "Apple's Supply-Chain Secret? Hoard Lasers", *Bloomberg Businessweek,* 3 November, available at: http://www.businessweek.com/magazine/apples-supplychain-secret-hoard-lasers-11032011.html.

Sato, Yukihito (1997), "Diverging Development Paths of the Electronics Industry in Korea and Taiwan", *The Developing Economies,* 35(4), 401-421.

Schäfer, Wolf and Lim, Hyun-Chin (2010), "The New Asias and the Rise of Global Regions", in H.-C. Lim, W. Schäfer and S.-M.

Hwang (eds.), *New Asias: Global Futures of World Regions,* Seoul: Seoul National University Press.

Schlozman, Kay Lehman, Verba, Sidney and Brady, Henry E. (2010), "Weapon of the Strong? Participatory Inequality and the Internet", *Perspectives on Politics,* 8(2), 487-509.

Schmitter, Philippe C (1995), "Transitology: The Science of the Art of Democratization?", in J.S. Tulchin and B. Romero (eds.), *The Consolidation of Democracy in Latin America,* Boulder, Colo: Lynne Rienner Publishers.

Schmitz, Hubert (2004), *Local Enterprises in the Global Economy: Issues of Governance and Upgrading,* Cheltenham: Edward Elgar.

Schmitz, Hubert and Knorringa, Peter (2000), "Learning from Global Buyers", *Journal of Development Studies,* 37(2), 177-205.

Shin, Jang-Sup and Chang, Ha-Joon (2003), *Restructuring Korea Inc.,* London; New York: Routledge Curzon.

Sinkovics, Noemi, Sinkovics, Rudolf R. and Yamin, Mo (2014), "The Role of Social Value Creation in Business Model Formulation at the Bottom of the Pyramid – Implications for MNEs?" *International Business Review,* 23(4), 692-707.

Slaughter, Matthew J. (2013), "American Companies and Global Supply Networks: Driving U.S. Economic Growth and Jobs by Connecting with the World", Business Roundtable, the United States Council for International Business and the United States Council Foundation, available at: http://www.uscib.org/docs/2013_american_companies_and_global_supply_networks.pdf.

Smelser, Neil J. (1976), *Comparative Methods in the Social Sciences,* Englewood Cliffs, NJ: Prentice-Hall.

Song, Kyong Jae (2009), "Civil Movement in the Network Age: Focusing on 2008 Candle Demonstration", *Hyŏndae chŏngch'i yŏn'gu = Contemporary Politics Research,* 2(1), 55-83 [in Korean].

Song, Yonghoi (2007), "Internet News Media and Issue Development: A Case Study on the Roles of Independent Online News Services as Agenda-Builders for Anti-US Protests in South Korea", *New Media & Society,* 9(1), 71-92.

Starr, Paul (2004), *The Creation of the Media: Political Origins of Modern*

Communications, New York: Basic Books.

Steinbock, Dan (2005), *The Mobile Revolution: The Making of Mobile Services Worldwide*, London; Sterling, VA: Kogan Page.

Storz, Cornelia, Amable, Bruno, Casper, Steven and Lechevalier, Sebastien (2013), "Bringing Asia into the Comparative Capitalism Perspective", *Socio-Economic Review*, 11(2), 217-232.

Stubbs, Richard (2011), "The East Asian Developmental State and the Great Recession: Evolving Contesting Coalitions", *Contemporary Politics*, 17(2), 151-166.

Sturgeon, Timothy J. (2002), "Modular Production Networks: A New American Model of Industrial Organization", *Industrial and Corporate Change*, 11(3), 451-496.

Sturgeon, Timothy J. and Gereffi, Gary (2009), "Measuring Success in the Global Economy: International Trade, Industrial Upgrading, and Business Function Outsourcing in Global Value Chains", *Transnational Corporations*, 18(2), 1-36.

Sturgeon, Timothy J. and Kawakami, Momoko (2011), "Global Value Chains in the Electronics Industry: Characteristics, Crisis, and Upgrading Opportunities for Firms from Developing Countries", *International Journal of Technological Learning, Innovation and Development*, 4(1-3), 120-147.

Sturgeon, Timothy J. and Lee, Ji-Ren (2005), "Industry Co-Evolution: A Comparison of Taiwan and North American Electronics Contract Manufacturers", in S. Berger and R. K. Lester (eds.), *Global Taiwan: Building Competitive Strengths in a New International Economy*, Armonk, New York: M.E. Sharpe, pp. 33-75.

Sturgeon, Timothy J. and Memedovic, Olga (2011), "Mapping Global Value Chains: Intermediate Goods Trade and Structural Change in the World Economy", UNIDO Development and Strategic Research Branch Working Paper 05/2010, United Nations Industrial Development Organization, Vienna, available at: http://www.unido.org//fileadmin/user_media/Publications/Research_and_statistics/Branch_publications/Research_and_Policy/Files/Working_Papers/2010/WP%2005%20Mapping%20Glocal%20Value%20Chains.pdf.

Sunstein, Cass R. (2007), *Republic.Com 2.0,* Princeton: Princeton University Press.

Tachiki, Dennis (2005), "Between Foreign Direct Investment and Regionalism: The Role of Japanese Production Networks", in T. J. Pempel (ed.), *Remapping East Asia: The Construction of a Region,* Ithaca: Cornell University Press, pp. 149-169.

Taplin, Ian M. (2014), "Who Is to Blame? A Re-Examination of Fast Fashion after the 2013 Factory Disaster in Bangladesh", *critical perspectives on international business,* 10(1/2), 72-83.

The Economist (2015), "The Future of Factory Asia: A Tightening Grip", *The Economist,* 14 March, available at: http://www.economist.com/news/briefing/21646180-rising-chinese-wages-will-only-strengthen-asias-hold-manufacturing-tightening-grip.

Thorbecke, Willem and Salike, Nimesh (2011), "Understanding Foreign Direct Investment in East Asia", ADBI Working Paper No. 290, Asian Development Bank Institute, Tokyo, available at: http://www.adb.org/sites/default/files/publication/156145/adbi-wp290.pdf.

Thorpe, Nick (2011), "Romania's 'Nokia City' Hopes Dashed", *BBC News,* 22 December, available at: http://www.bbc.co.uk/news/world-europe-16290078.

Tilly, Charles (1984), *Big Structures, Large Processes, Huge Comparisons,* New York: Russell Sage Foundation.

Timmer, Marcel P., Erumban, Abdul Azeez, Los, Bart, Stehrer, Robert and de Vries, Gaaitzen J. (2014), "Slicing up Global Value Chains", *Journal of Economic Perspectives,* 28(2), 99-118.

Troianovski, Anton (2012), "Htc's Phones Losing Their Luster", *Wall Street Journal,* 6 April, available at: http://online.wsj.com/news/articles/SB10001424052702303302504577327160946995708.

Tu, Weiming (1984), *Confucian Ethics Today: The Singapore Challenge,* Curriculum Development Institute of Singapore, Singapore.

Tuoi Tre News (2013), "Samsung Vietnam Uses Korean Suppliers as Local Firms Below Standard", 24 July, available at: http://tuoitrenews.vn/business/11689/samsung-vietnam-uses-korean-suppliers-as-local-firms-below-standard.

UNCTAD (2013), "Global Value Chains and Development: Investment and Value Added Trade in the Global Economy", United Nations Conference on Trade and Development, Geneva, available at: http://unctad.org/en/publicationslibrary/diae2013d1_en.pdf.

Vascellaro, Jessica E. and Ramstad, Evan (2012), "The Two-Horse Smartphone Race", *Wall Street Journal,* April 24, available at: http://www.wsj.com/articles/SB10001424052702303978104577362140799316460.

Wade, Robert (1990), *Governing the Market: Economic Theory and the Role of Government in East Asian Industrialization,* Princeton: Princeton University Press.

Weiss, Linda (1998), *The Myth of the Powerless State,* Ithaca: Cornell University Press.

Weiss, Linda (2003), "Guiding Globalization in East Asia: New Roles for Old Developmental States", in L. Weiss (ed.), *States in the Global Economy: Bringing Domestic Institutions Back In,* New York: Cambridge University Press, pp. 245-270.

Weiss, Linda (2005), "Global Governance, National Strategies: How Industrialized States Make Room to Move under the WTO", *Review of International Political Economy,* 12(5), 723-749.

Wellman, Barry (2010), "The Contentious Internet — An Introduction to the Special CITASA Section on Contentious Politics On and Off Line", *Information, Communication & Society,* 13(2), 151-154.

Wellman, Barry, Haase, Anabel Quan, Witte, James and Hampton, Keith (2001), "Does the Internet Increase, Decrease, or Supplement Social Capital?: Social Networks, Participation, and Community Commitment", *American Behavioral Scientist,* 45(3), 436-455.

Westra, Richard (2012), "The Japanese Economy in the Crossfire", *Journal of Contemporary Asia,* 42(4), 697-706.

Whittaker, D., Zhu, Tianbiao, Sturgeon, Timothy, Tsai, Mon and Okita, Toshie (2010), "Compressed Development", *Studies in Comparative International Development,* 45(4), 439-467.

Whitley, Richard and Glenn Morgan (2014), "Capitalisms and Capitalism n the Twenty-First Century", G. Morgan and R.

Whitley (eds.), *Capitalisms and Capitalism in the 21st Century,* Oxford: Oxford University Press.

Wilde, Joseph and de Hann, Esther (2006), The High Cost of Calling: Critical Issues in the Mobile Phone Industry, SOMO - Centre for Research on Multinational Corporations, Amsterdam, the Netherlands.

Williamson, Oliver (1975), *Markets and Hierarchies: Analysis and Antitrust Implications,* New York: Free Press.

Williamson, Oliver (1985), *The Economic Institutions of Capitalism: Firms, Markets, Relational Contracting,* New York: Free Press.

Woo-Cumings, Meredith (1991), *Race to the Swift: State and Finance in Korean Industrialization,* New York: Columbia University Press.

Woo-Cumings, Meredith (ed.) (1999), *The Developmental State,* Ithaca: Cornell University Press.

Woo, Meredith Jung-En (ed.) (2007), *Neoliberalism and Institutional Reform in East Asia,* New York: Palgrave Macmillan.

World Bank (1993), *The East Asian Miracle: Economic Growth and Public Policy,* New York: Oxford University Press.

World Bank (2009), Information and Communications for Development 2009: Extending Reach and Increasing Impact, Washington, DC: World Bank.

WTO and IDE-JETRO (2011), "Trade Patterns and Global Value Chains in East Asia: From Trade in Goods to Trade in Tasks", World Trade Organization and Institute of Developing Economies, Geneva and Tokyo, available at: http://www.wto.org/english/res_e/publications_e/stat_tradepat_globvalchains_e.htm.

Xia, Jun (2012), "Competition and Regulation in China's 3g/4g Mobile Communications Industry—Institutions, Governance, and Telecom Soes", *Telecommunications Policy,* 36(7), 503-521.

Xing, Yuqing and Detert, Neal (2010), "How the iPhone Widens the United States Trade Deficit with the People's Republic of China", ADBI Working Paper Series, Asian Development Bank Institute, available at: http://www.adbi.org/files/2010.12.14.wp257.iphone.widens.us.trade.deficit.prc.pdf.

Yamin, Mo and Sinkovics, Rudolf R. (2009), "Infrastructure or Foreign

Direct Investment?: An Examination of the Implications of MNE Strategy for Economic Development", *Journal of World Business,* 44(2), 144-157.

Yeung, Henry Wai-chung, Liu, Weidong and Dicken, Peter (2006), "Transnational Corporations and Network Effects of a Local Manufacturing Cluster in Mobile Telecommunications Equipment in China", *World Development,* 34(3), 520-540.

Young, Anne (2002), "Nec to Start Supply of I-Mode Handsets to Kpn", *NEC Press Release,* 25 February, available at: http://www.nec.co.jp/press/en/0202/2501.html.

Yun, Young-Min (2007), "Birth of Neo-Nomadism in Korea", *Development and Society,* 36(2), 153-175.

Zainudeen, Ayesha (2006), "Telecom Use on a Shoestring: The Case of Bangladesh", *WDR Dialogue Theme 3rd cycle Discussion Paper WDR0601,* available at: http://ssrn.com/abstract= 1553608.

Zhixiang, Yu (2008), "Mountain Village Handsets Storm Market", *China Economic Net,* 19 July, available at: http://en.ce.cn/Industries/Telecoms/200807/19/t20080719_16212016.shtml#.

Zhu, Sheng and Shi, Yongjiang (2010), "*Shanzhai* Manufacturing–an Alternative Innovation Phenomenon in China: Its Value Chain and Implications for Chinese Science and Technology Policies", *Journal of Science and Technology Policy in China,* 1(1), 29-49.

Zhu, Shengjun and Pickles, John (2014), "Bring in, Go up, Go West, Go Out: Upgrading, Regionalisation and Delocalisation in China's Apparel Production Networks", *Journal of Contemporary Asia,* 44(1), 36-63.

Index

Joonkoo Lee

Joonkoo Lee is Assistant Professor of Organization Studies in the School of Business at Hanyang University, Seoul. Before joining Hanyang in 2012, he was a postdoctoral research scholar in the Social Science Research Institute at Duke University, and a sector coordinator for the Capturing the Gains research program. In 2014-2015, he was a visiting research fellow at Asia Center at Seoul National University. His research interests include globalization and development, global value chains, organizational studies, political economy in Asia, and cultural and creative industries. His work has appeared in *Proceedings of the National Academy of Sciences of the United States of America, Journal of Business Ethics, Journal of Contemporary Asia,* and *Journal of Supply Chain Management.* He received his Ph.D. in Sociology from Duke University, and his M.A. and B.A. from Seoul National University.

Hyun-Chin Lim

Hyun-Chin Lim is Professor Emeritus of Sociology and Founding Director of Asia Center at Seoul National University. He is an elected member of the National Academy of Sciences, Republic of Korea. Currently, he is chairing the Committee on Civil Society Development, Office of the Prime Minister. He received his B.A. and M.A. in Sociology from Seoul National University, and his Ph.D. in Sociology from Harvard University. He was previously the dean of Faculty of Liberal Education, the dean of the College of Social Sciences, and the founding director of Asia Center, all at Seoul National University. He worked as a member of the Executive Council, Society for the Advancement of Socio-Economics. He also served as the president of professional associations including Korean Association of NGO Studies, Korean Sociological Association, International Development and Cooperation Association, Korean Association for Political Society, and Korean Social Science Research Council. His publications include more than 55 books and over 250 scholarly articles on dependency, development, democracy, and civil society in East Asia and Latin America.